American
Civil Rights
Almanac

American Civil Rights Almanac

Volume 2:
Hispanic Americans
Native Americans
Selected Immigrant Groups
Selected Nonethnic Groups

Phillis Engelbert

Betz Des Chenes, Editor

AN IMPRINT OF THE GALE GROUP

DETROIT · SAN FRANCISCO · LONDON
BOSTON · WOODBRIDGE, CT

Phillis Engelbert

Staff

Elizabeth Des Chenes, *U·X·L Senior Editor*
Carol DeKane Nagel, *U·X·L Managing Editor*
Thomas L. Romig, *U·X·L Publisher*

Keasha Jack-Lyles, *Permissions Associate (Pictures)*

Rita Wimberley, *Senior Buyer*
Evi Seoud, *Assistant Production Manager*
Dorothy Maki, *Manufacturing Manager*

Pamela A. E. Galbreath, *Senior Art Director*
Cynthia Baldwin, *Product Design Manager*

Graphix Group, *Typesetting*

Library of Congress Cataloging-in-Publication Data
Engelbert, Phillis.
    American civil rights: almanac/Phillis Engelbert.
        p.cm.
    Includes bibliographical references.
Contents: v.1. Civil rights of African Americans; Civil Rights of
    Asian Americans—v.2. Civil rights of Hispanic Americans;
    Civil rights of Native Americans; civil rights of nonethnic
    groups; civil rights of selected immigrant groups.
ISBN 0-7876-3172-8 (set).—ISBN 0-7876-3171-X (v.1.).—ISBN 0-
    7876-3174-4 (v.2).
    1. Civil rights—United States—Juvenile literature. 2. Civil rights—
    United States—History—Juvenile literature. [Civil rights].
    I. Title.
JC599. U5E54 1999
323. 1'73'09—DC21

Printed in the United States of America
10 9 8 7 6 5 4 3

Contents

Volume 1

A lunch counter sit-in.
Reproduced by permission of AP/Wide World Photos.

Martin Luther King Jr.
Reproduced by permission of the Library of Congress.

A Japanese American family awaits internment.
Reproduced by permission of the National Archives and Records Association.

Vincent Chin. *Reproduced by permission of UPI/Corbis-Bettmann.*

Volume 2

César Chávez. *Reproduced by permission of The Library of Congress.*

Native Americans protest relocation. *Reproduced by permission of Corbis-Bettmann.*

An immigrant neighborhood. *Reproduced by permission of the Library of Congress.*

Advisory Board

Special thanks are due for the invaluable comments and suggestions provided by U•X•L's American Civil Rights Reference Library advisors:

- Eduardo Bonilla-Silva, Professor of Sociology, Texas A&M University, College Station, Texas

- Frances Hasso, Assistant Professor of Sociology, Antioch College, Yellow Springs, Ohio

- Annalissa Herbert, Graduate student, American Culture program, University of Michigan, Ann Arbor, Michigan

- Patrick R. LeBeau, Assistant Professor of American Thought and Language, Michigan State University, East Lansing, Michigan

- Premilla Nadasen, Assistant Professor of African American History, Queens College, New York City

- Kamal M. Nawash, Esq., Director of Legal Services, American-Arab Anti-Discrimination Committee, Washington, D.C.

- Diane Surati, Teacher, Crossett Brook Middle School, Waterbury, Vermont
- Jan Toth-Chernin, Media Specialist, Greenhills School, Ann Arbor, Michigan

Reader's Guide

American Civil Rights: Almanac presents a comprehensive overview of the history and current status of the civil rights of various racial, ethnic, and nonethnic groups in the United States. The two volumes examine the discriminatory laws and practices to which groups of people were and in some cases still are subjected, the social movements that worked and continue to work to bring about change, and the legislation that has been enacted to protect existing civil rights. People who advanced—and in some cases, hindered—the development of civil rights, as well as significant events and ideas that helped to shape the movement, are also discussed.

Format

American Civil Rights: Almanac is divided into six chapters. Volume 1 contains Civil Rights of African Americans and Civil Rights of Asian Americans; Volume 2 contains Civil Rights of Hispanic Americans, Civil Rights of Native Americans, Civil Rights of Selected Immigrant Groups, and Civil Rights of Selected Nonethnic Groups (including women, lesbians and gay men, and people with disabilities). Sidebar boxes sprinkled throughout the two volumes examine related events, issues, legislation, and people, while more than 125 photographs and illustrations help illuminate the text. Each volume contains an introduction, a timeline of major civil rights events, a glossary, a list of research and activity ideas, an organization bibliography, and a cumulative index.

Dedication

These books are dedicated to all the heroic women and men, of all races, who have championed civil rights throughout U.S. history and to the young people who will work to expand civil rights in the next millennium.

Special Thanks

Special thanks goes to Elizabeth Des Chenes, senior developmental editor at U•X•L, for her support and guidance; to copyeditor Nancy Dziedzic for her careful attention to detail; to all members of the advisory board for reading long manuscripts and offering thoughtful suggestions; to James W. Sullivan for providing access to his extensive private library; to Alfonso H. Lozano for answering questions about Mexican history and translating Spanish terms; to the reference librarians at the Ann Arbor Public Library for assistance in locating obscure resources; to William F. Shea for his unique insights; and to Ryan Patrick Shea for his inspiration.

Comments and suggestions

We welcome your comments on this work as well as your suggestions for topics to be featured in future editions of *American Civil Rights: Almanac*. Please write: Editors, *American Civil Rights: Almanac,* U•X•L, 27500 Drake Rd., Farmington Hills, MI 48331–3535; call toll-free: 1–800–877–4253; fax: 248–414–5043; or send e-mail via www.galegroup.com.

Introduction

Civil rights are a broad range of guarantees of equal treatment and freedom from discrimination for all United States citizens. The term "civil rights" originally described the citizenship rights granted to African Americans after the abolition (elimination) of slavery in 1865. Citizenship rights (which were not fully granted to women and Native Americans until the twentieth century) are all rights to which United States citizens are entitled, such as the right to vote, the right to receive an education, and the right to equal protection under the laws.

The term civil rights took on new meaning in the 1950s and 1960s when African Americans, primarily in the South, demanded enforcement of the citizenship rights they were granted a century earlier. An aggressive campaign on the part of civil rights activists and lawyers resulted in passage of three civil rights acts guaranteeing racial minorities a wide range of protections in the areas of employment, housing, education, voting, accommodations, and the administration of civil and criminal laws. The civil rights acts of the 1960s were designed to fulfill the empty promises of post-Civil War

(1861–1865) legislation. Today civil rights laws protect not only African Americans but many other groups that have been traditionally discriminated against, such as Hispanic Americans, Asian Americans, American Indians, people of various ethnic and religious groups, women, people with disabilities, and lesbians and gay men.

Throughout much of America's history there has been a wide gap between the idea of civil rights and the reality of racial injustice. In 1776 Thomas Jefferson (1743–1826) wrote in the Declaration of Independence that "all men are created equal." Those words, however, rang hollow against the backdrop of slavery. It wasn't until ninety years after the Declaration of Independence that slavery was abolished and blacks gained legal rights as American citizens. It took another ninety years for civil rights legislation to be enforced.

The history of African Americans and other minority groups in the United States speaks more to the exclusion of civil rights than to the protection of civil rights. For example, for much of the country's history, the very humanity of blacks has been denied. In 1787 the Constitution of the United States counted slaves—for the purposes of taxation and representation in Congress (which is based on population)—as three-fifths of a person. In 1857 the United States Supreme Court ruled in *Dred Scott v. Sanford* that blacks, whether free or slaves, "had no rights which the white man was bound to respect." Even after slaves were freed in 1865, the ideology of white supremacy—the notion that whites are superior to all other races—survived. It was not until desegregation in the 1960s, when laws calling for the separation of the races were eliminated, that the white-dominated power structure affirmed in word, if not in deed, the humanity of African Americans.

Native Americans have also been denied their civil rights throughout much of United States history. They have been removed from their land and forbidden to practice their religion, have faced assaults on their culture, have had their children sent to boarding schools, and have been massacred in large numbers. It was only in the 1970s that Native Americans began to gain rights in the areas of education, religious freedom, cultural preservation, children's welfare, and self-government.

Civil rights in America are a continual work-in-progress. For the most part, this progress is in the direction of the expansion of rights; rights, however, can also be taken away. Two examples of the loss of civil rights include the internment of Japanese Americans during World War II (1939–1945) and the current rollback of affirmative action (policies designed to correct historic patterns of racial discrimination in the last quarter of the twentieth century). Examples of recent gains in civil rights include protections granted to lesbians and gay men by various local and state governments and to people with disabilities by the federal government's 1990 Americans with Disabailities Act. And while economic rights—including the right to a minimum standard of living—are not presently guaranteed, they represents an area into which civil rights may expand in the future.

While modern civil rights legislation has brought American society a step closer to the ideal of "liberty and justice for all," it has not taken American citizens the full measure. Uneven enforcement of civil rights legislation combined with racist policies, practices, and attitudes serve to keep racial minorities and other groups disenfranchised economically, politically, socially, and legally. In its 1998 report, the international human rights organization Human Rights Watch admonished the United States for racial inequality. And as the 1990s drew to a close, there was still a conspicuous absence of federal legislation granting equality, in all aspects of life, to women, lesbians, and gay men.

Civil rights are a reflection of societal attitudes; they are not simply created by lawmakers and judges. Civil rights are only adopted when large numbers of people demand them. The history of civil rights in America and the stories of the thousands of brave women and men who fought, and continue to fight, for them are told in these volumes.

Timeline of Events in the American Civil Rights Movement

1778–1871 The U.S. government and Native American nations sign more than 400 treaties. By the early 1900s, as a result of the treaties and subsequent agreements, Native Americans had lost 98 percent of their pre–1778 land base.

1789 The U.S. Constitution takes effect. For purposes of taxation and representation in the House of Representatives, the document states that slaves are to be counted as three-fifths of a white person and Native Americans are not to be counted at all.

1830 Congress passes the Indian Removal Act, requiring the forced removal of American Indians living east of

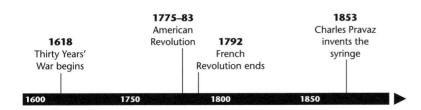

1618
Thirty Years'
War begins

1775–83
American
Revolution

1792
French
Revolution ends

1853
Charles Pravaz
invents the
syringe

1600   1750   1800   1850

Suffragists rally for the right to vote. *Reproduced by permission of AP/Wide World Photos.*

Susan B. Anthony. *Reproduced by permission of the Library of Congress.*

the Mississippi River to a tract of land called "Indian Territory" (present-day Oklahoma).

1848   The first women's rights convention is held in Seneca Falls, New York. Women's suffrage (the right to vote) and the abolition of slavery are items on the convention agenda.

1857   The Supreme Court rules in *Dred Scott v. Sanford* that slaves are not American citizens and therefore cannot bring suit in a court of law; the Court also holds that blacks (free or slave) "had no rights which the white man was bound to respect."

1865   Slavery is abolished with the passage of the Thirteenth Amendment.

1882   The Chinese Exclusion Act forbids Chinese workers from entering the United States for a period of ten years (with exceptions made for a small number of students, teachers, and merchants) and reiterates that Chinese people already in the United States are ineligible to become U.S. citizens.

May 2, 1886 Striking workers at Chicago's McCormick Harvesting Machine Company hold a rally in Haymarket Square. Seven police officers are killed by a dynamite bomb, a crime for which eight union leaders are later convicted despite a lack of evidence. Four of the people convicted—three of whom are German American—are hanged.

1887   The General Allotment Act (also called the Dawes General Allotment Act) mandates the division of reservation lands into 160-acre parcels to be owned by Indian families or individuals. Upon receiving his or her allotment, a Native American would be made a U.S. citizen.

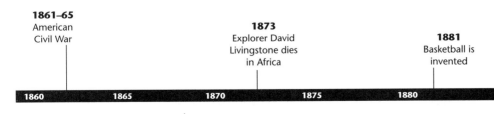

1861–65
American
Civil War

1873
Explorer David
Livingstone dies
in Africa

1881
Basketball is
invented

1860   1865   1870   1875   1880

1890   U.S. forces massacre between 150 and 370 Native Americans at Wounded Knee in South Dakota.

1896   In *Plessy v. Ferguson,* the Supreme Court upholds a Louisiana law ordering separate railroad cars for black and white passengers. The larger implication of this ruling is judicial endorsement of Jim Crow laws.

1898   The Spanish-American War ends, and Spain gives up control of Puerto Rico, Cuba, and the Philippines to the United States.

1909   The National Association for the Advancement of Colored People (NAACP), a civil rights organization that continues to fight for racial equality and the end of racial prejudice, is founded.

1920   The Nineteenth Amendment is passed, granting women the right to vote.

1924   The Snyder Act is passed, granting U.S. citizenship to all Native Americans.

1934   The Indian Reorganization Act is passed, spelling the end of allotment, returning "surplus" reservation lands to the tribes, recognizing tribal governments, and recommending that Native American nations adopt their own constitutions.

February 19, 1942   President Franklin D. Roosevelt signs Executive Order 9066, authorizing the internment of 120,000 Japanese Americans in camps from 1942 through 1945.

March 20, 1946   The last of the internment camps for Japanese Americans, Tule Lake in California, is closed.

Two Native American boys in their boarding school uniforms. *Reproduced by permission of the National Archives and Records Administration.*

W. E. B. Du Bois. *Reproduced by permission of the Fisk University Library.*

1891
Britain's's Labour
Party is founded

1914–18
World War I

1929
Great Depression
begins

1935
Vitamin B is
synthesized

| 1890 | 1900 | 1910 | 1920 | 1930 | 1940 |

Medgar Evers. *Reproduced by permission of AP/Wide World Photos.*

May 17, 1954 In *Brown v. Board of Education of Topeka, Kansas,* the Supreme Court declares school segregation unconstitutional.

December 5, 1955–December 20, 1956 Black residents of Montgomery, Alabama stage a boycott of city buses, resulting in the racial integration of city bus service. Civil rights pioneer Rosa Parks is arrested during the boycott for refusing to move to the back of a bus.

January 10 and 11, 1957 The Southern Christian Leadership Conference (SCLC) is founded in Atlanta, Georgia.

April 16–18, 1960 The Student Nonviolent Coordinating Committee (SNCC; sometimes pronounced "snick") is founded in Raleigh, North Carolina.

1961 Civil rights activists conduct Freedom Rides throughout the South, testing the enforcement of Supreme Court rulings outlawing segregated seating on interstate (crossing state lines) buses and trains.

June 12, 1963 Activist Medgar Evers is assassinated in Jackson, Mississippi.

August 23, 1963 More than 250,000 people participate in the March on Washington for Jobs and Freedom. Martin Luther King Jr. delivers his famous "I Have a Dream" speech.

September 15, 1963 A bomb explodes in Birmingham's Sixteenth Street Baptist Church, killing four young girls.

November 22, 1963 President John F. Kennedy is assassinated in Dallas, Texas.

June–August 1964 One thousand college student volunteers descend on Mississippi for Freedom Summer. The stu-

1945 World War II ends

1951 UNIVAC computer is introduced

1958 Atomic test ban proposed

1962 John Glenn orbits the Earth

| 1945 | 1948 | 1951 | 1954 | 1957 | 1960 | 1963 |

dents register voters, run freedom schools, and organize the Mississippi Freedom Democratic Party.

July 2, 1964 President Lyndon B. Johnson signs the Civil Rights Act, which outlaws a variety of types of discrimination based on race, color, religion, or national origin.

August 24, 1964 The bodies of civil rights activists James Chaney, Andrew Goodman, and Michael Schwerner are pulled from an earthen dam near Philadelphia, Mississippi.

1965 The Crusade for Justice is founded in Denver, Colorado.

1965 The National Farm Workers Association, which changes its named to the United Farm Workers (UFW) in April 1966, is founded in Delano, California.

February 21, 1965 Malcolm X is assassinated in Harlem, New York.

March 7, 1965 On this day, later called "Bloody Sunday," state troopers in Selma, Alabama, viciously beat civil rights demonstrators trying to cross the Edmund Pettus Bridge en route to Montgomery, Alabama.

August 6, 1965 President Lyndon B. Johnson signs the Voting Rights Act, thereby outlawing all practices used to deny blacks the right to vote and empowering federal registrars to register black voters.

August 11–21, 1965 Rioting in the Watts ghetto of Los Angeles claims thirty-four lives and leaves forty-five square miles in ruins. This was one of many urban riots in black ghettoes between 1964 and 1968 that erupted in response to poverty, housing segregation, overcrowding, joblessness, racism, and police brutality.

Slain civil rights worker Andrew Goodman. *Reproduced by permission of AP/Wide World Photos.*

Marchers are stopped by the state police in Selma, Alabama. *Reproduced by permission of Archive Photos.*

1965
World population
reaches 3.3 billion

1967
Arab-Israeli War
begins

1968
My Lai massacre
in Vietnam

1964   1965   1966   1967   1968

A gay pride parade in New York City. *Photograph by Evy Mages. Reproduced by permission of Reuters/Archive Photos.*

October 1966 The Black Panther Party is founded in Oakland, California.

April 4, 1968 Martin Luther King Jr. is assassinated in Memphis, Tennessee.

April 10, 1968 President Lyndon B. Johnson signs the Fair Housing Act, thereby outlawing racial discrimination by private individuals or businesses in housing and real estate transactions.

June 5, 1968 Robert F. Kennedy is assassinated in Los Angeles, California.

July 1968 The American Indian Movement (AIM) is founded in Minneapolis, Minnesota.

June 27, 1969 The Stonewall Rebellion—a massive demonstration by gay men and lesbian in New York City—is instigated by a police raid of a gay bar in Greenwich Village. The rebellion is considered the start of the gay liberation movement.

September 1–September 4, 1972 The La Raza Unida political party holds its national convention in El Paso, Texas.

November 2–November 8, 1972 Members of AIM occupy the Bureau of Indian Affairs building in Washington, D.C., and demand the restoration of tribes' treaty-making status, the return of stolen Indian lands, and the revocation of state government authority over Indian affairs.

February 27–May 8, 1973 Members of AIM and other reservation residents occupy the village of Wounded Knee on the Pine Ridge Reservation in South Dakota, in protest of the corrupt tribal government of chairman Dick Wilson.

AIM protesters at Wounded Knee. *Reproduced by permission of Corbis-Bettmann.*

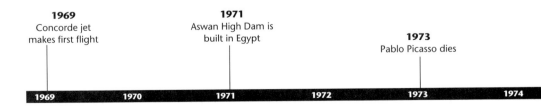

1969 Concorde jet makes first flight

1971 Aswan High Dam is built in Egypt

1973 Pablo Picasso dies

| 1969 | 1970 | 1971 | 1972 | 1973 | 1974 |

1975   Congress passes the Indian Self-Determination and Education Assistance Act, transferring control over the administration of all government assistance and education programs from the U.S. government to Indian tribes.

1978   In *Regents of the University of California v. Bakke,* the Supreme Court outlaws the use of racial quotas in affirmative action programs while affirming the legitimacy of the affirmative action programs overall.

October 11, 1985 Alex Odeh, Southern California regional director of the American-Arab Anti-Discrimination Committee, is killed by a pipe bomb in Santa Ana, California.

1988   With the Civil Liberties Act of 1988, Congress authorizes the payment of $20,000 to each Japanese American survivor of the World War II internment camps and issues an apology to all former detainees.

1990   Congress passes the Americans with Disabilities Act, thereby prohibiting discrimination against people with disabilities in the areas of employment, government-run programs and services, public accommodations, and telecommunications.

April 29–May 3, 1992 Riots erupt in south-central Los Angeles in the wake of not-guilty verdicts for the police officers whose vicious beating of black motorist Rodney King was captured on videotape. The rioting claims fifty-two lives and causes over $1 billion in damage.

1996   The Passage of Proposition 209 in California ends that state's policy of affirmative action in government agencies.

Elaine Kim. *Reproduced by permission of Manso-Manso.*

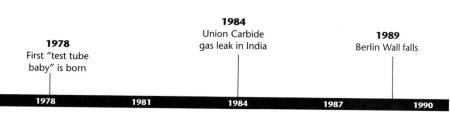

1978
First "test tube baby" is born

1984
Union Carbide gas leak in India

1989
Berlin Wall falls

1975   1978   1981   1984   1987   1990

Timeline of Events in the American Civil Rights Movement

Students in San Francisco protest Proposition 187.
Reproduced by permission of Reuters/Lou Dematteis/Archive Photos.

November 3, 1998 In separate statewide referenda, voters in Alaska and Hawaii reject legalizing same-sex marriage in their states. These votes came two years after Congress passed the Defense of Marriage Act, which defined marriage as the union of one man and one woman.

February 1999 White supremacist John William (Bill) King is convicted of murder for the dragging death of a forty-nine-year-old African American man named James Byrd Jr.

April 20, 1999 Rosa Parks—one of the most famous figures in the civil rights movement—is awarded the Congressional Gold Medal.

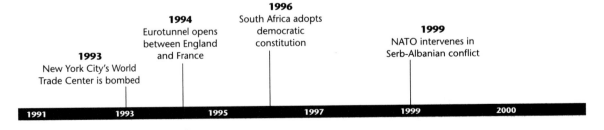

1993
New York City's World Trade Center is bombed

1994
Eurotunnel opens between England and France

1996
South Africa adopts democratic constitution

1999
NATO intervenes in Serb-Albanian conflict

| 1991 | 1993 | 1995 | 1997 | 1999 | 2000 |

Words to Know

A

Abolitionism: The belief that slavery should be immediately terminated; the social movement to eliminate slavery.

Abolitionist: A person who works for the immediate termination of slavery.

Abortion: The expulsion or removal of an embryo or fetus from the womb.

Affirmative action: A set of federal government policies, primarily in education and employment, that give preferential treatment to racial minorities and women (groups that have historically been victims of discrimination).

Agribusiness: Farming processes—for example, the storage and distribution of produce—operated on a large, industrial scale.

Alianza Federal de Mercedes: This organization (whose name is Spanish for Federated Alliance of Land Grants) was formed in 1963 by a group of Mexican

Americans in New Mexico. The Alianza sought to reclaim lands that had been taken from Mexican American farmers since the end of the U.S.-Mexico War (1846–1848).

Allotment: The U.S. government policy, implemented in the late 1800s and early 1900s, of dividing up reservation lands and parceling them out to individual Native Americans.

American Indian Movement (AIM): The best-known and most militant Native American-rights organization of the 1960s and 1970s.

Americans with Disabilities Act (ADA): Federal legislation, passed in 1990, that prohibits discrimination against people with disabilities in the areas of employment, government-run programs and services, public accommodations (such as hotels, restaurants, and movie theaters), and telecommunications.

Anglo: Term used by Hispanic Americans to describe a person of European descent.

Anti-coolie clubs: Organizations in California in the 1850s and 1860s that sought to drive Chinese laborers from the workforce and to expel Chinese immigrants from the communities in which the clubs were located.

Asiatic Exclusion League: An organization founded in California in 1905 that used violent tactics and legal maneuvering to remove Japanese and Korean laborers from the workplace.

Assimilation: The process of becoming like, or being absorbed into, the dominant culture.

B

Black Cabinet: A group of influential African Americans that served as informal advisors to President Franklin D. Roosevelt (1882–1945; served as president from 1933 to 1945).

Black Codes: Laws developed after the Civil War (1861–1865) that denied black Americans the right to vote, the right to own property, and the right to pursue employment or otherwise advance their economic status.

Black nationalism: Movement to create political, economic, and social self-sufficiency among black people.

Black Panther Party (BPP): Organization founded in Oakland, California, in 1966 by black activists seeking to stop police abuse and provide social services (including a free breakfast program and a free health clinic). BPP members carried arms in public and came into frequent conflict with the police.

Black power: Social movement and rallying cry of radical black activists in the mid-1960s through mid-1970s. To many African Americans, the slogan stood for racial pride and the belief that blacks held the power to create a better society for themselves.

Blockbusting: Literally meaning "busting apart a block," blockbusting was a practice used by Realtors to maintain housing segregation. Realtors would move a single black family onto an all-white block and pressure whites to sell their homes at low prices. Realtors would then sell those homes to middle-class blacks at much higher prices.

Bloody Sunday: March 7, 1965—the day on which state troopers in Selma, Alabama, viciously beat civil rights demonstrators trying to cross the Edmund Pettus Bridge on their way to Montgomery, Alabama.

Boycott: The refusal to purchase a product or use a service; a boycott gives an oppressed group economic leverage in their struggle for social change.

Bracero Program: U.S. government program from 1942–1964 to bring Mexican workers to the U.S. to work in factories, and on farms and railroads ("bracero" is Spanish for "manual laborer").

Brown Berets: Activist group of young Chicanos in the late 1960s who carried arms to protect themselves and their community from police brutality.

Brown v. Board of Education of Topeka, Kansas: Supreme Court decision in 1954 that declared school segregation unconstitutional.

C

Chicano: Term used by politically active Mexican Americans to describe themselves; it symbolized their pride in their cultural heritage.

Civil disobedience: Nonviolent action in which participants refuse to obey certain laws, with the purpose of challenging the fairness of those laws.

Civil Rights Act of 1964: The most expansive civil rights policy in American history, this act outlawed a variety of types of discrimination based on race, color, religion, or national origin.

Communism: A political and social system based on sharing goods equally in the community and owning property collectively.

Congress on Racial Equality (CORE): Civil rights organization formed in 1942 that promoted nonviolent direct action.

Counter-Intelligence Program (COINTELPRO): A Federal Bureau of Investigation (FBI) program whose official purpose was to combat domestic terrorism. In actuality, COINTELPRO was used to weaken the anti-Vietnam War and civil rights movements, the Black Panther Party, AIM, and other militant organizations of people of color.

Crusade for Justice: Chicano-rights and social-service organization, founded in 1965 in Denver, Colorado, that worked to end police brutality and discrimination in the public schools.

D

Desegregation: The elimination of laws and social customs that call for the separation of races.

Disability: A restriction or lack of ability to perform an activity considered part of the range of normal human behaviors.

E

Enfranchisement: The granting of the right to vote.

Executive Order 9066: Decree issued by President Franklin D. Roosevelt in 1942 that led to the internment of 120,000 Japanese Americans in camps during World War II. The first internment camp opened in 1942, and the last camp closed in 1946.

F

Fair Housing Act: This legislation—Title VIII of the Civil Rights Act of 1968—forbid racial discrimination by private individuals or businesses in housing and real estate transactions.

Fascism: A political philosophy that places nation and race above the individual. Fascist governments are run by a single, dictatorial leader and are characterized by extreme social and economic restrictions.

Fish-in: A form of civil disobedience in which Indian activists fished in violation of state laws, in order to assert their treaty rights. This tactic was frequently used in the 1960s and 1970s in Washington and Oregon.

Freedom Rides: Journeys made throughout the South by integrated groups of people to test the enforcement of a pair of Supreme Court rulings striking down the constitutionality of segregated seating on interstate (crossing state lines) buses and trains.

Freedom Summer: Mississippi civil rights campaign in the summer of 1964, in which about 1,000 northern college-student volunteers registered voters and operated educational and social programs.

G

Glass ceiling: An invisible barrier in private and public agencies that keeps many women and racial minorities from holding top positions.

Grandfather clause: A policy that exempted white people from literacy tests to qualify to vote. The clause stated that all people entitled to vote in 1866, as well as their descendants, could vote without taking a literacy test. All descendants of 1866 voters were white, since blacks only gained the constitutional right to vote in 1870.

Great Depression: The worst economic crisis to hit the United States, the Depression began with the stock market crash in 1929 and lasted until 1939.

H

Handicap: A physical or mental condition that prevents or limits a person's ability to lead a normal life.

Hate Crimes Prevention Act (HCPA): Proposed federal legislation that would amend current federal law—which permits federal prosecution of a hate crime based on religion, national origin, or color—to include real or perceived sexual orientation, sex, and disability.

Heterosexuality: Sexual desire or behavior exhibited between persons of opposite sexes.

Highlander Folk School: A civil rights and social justice institute in founded in 1932 in Tennessee. Highlander was unique in the pre-civil rights South because it was a racially integrated facility.

Hispanic American: A person living in the United States who was born in, or whose descendants were born in, a Spanish-speaking country (synonymous with Hispanic or Hispano).

Homosexuality: Sexual desire or behavior exhibited between persons of the same sex.

I

Indian Civil Rights Act: Legislation passed by Congress in 1968 to guarantee the civil rights of American Indians living on reservations.

Indian Removal Act: Legislation signed in 1830 by President Andrew Jackson, mandating the relocation of American Indians living east of the Mississippi River to a tract of land called "Indian Territory" (present-day Oklahoma).

Indian Reorganization Act: Legislation passed in 1934 that put an end to allotment, returned "surplus" reservation lands to the tribes, recognized tribal governments, and recommended that Indian nations adopt their own constitutions.

Integration: The combination of facilities, previously separated by race, into single, multiracial systems.

Internment: The act of being confined against one's will.

Involuntary servitude: Any situation in which a person is made to perform services against her or his will.

J

Jim Crow laws: A network of legislation and customs that dictated the separation of the races on every level of society.

K

Ku Klux Klan: Anti-black terrorist group formed in the South in the aftermath of the Civil War (1861–1865) that has for decades intimidated and committed acts of violence against black Americans and members of other racial and ethnic minorities.

L

La Raza Unida: Mexican American political party (pronounced la RAHssa oonEEDa; the name means "The People United") founded in 1969 that embraced bilingual education, the regulation of public utilities, farm subsidies, and tax breaks for low-income people.

Latino: Person living in the United States who was born in, or whose descendants were born in, the geographic region of Latin America.

Literacy test: Selectively administered to black applicants, the test required would-be voters to read and/or interpret a section of the state Constitution to the satisfaction of the registrar.

Lynching: Execution-style murder of a person (usually an African American), often by hanging, by a white mob.

M

Manifest Destiny: The belief that the United States had a "God-given right" to all the territory between the Atlantic and Pacific oceans. This doctrine served to justify the United States' westward expansion during the 1800s.

Mexican American Legal Defense and Education Fund (MALDEF): Organization formed in 1968 to promote the civil rights of Mexican Americans through the legal system.

Mississippi Freedom Democratic Party (MFDP): Multi-racial political party created in Mississippi in 1964 that served as an alternative to the all-white Democratic Party.

"Model minority": The stereotypical belief that the majority of Asian Americans have blended into the dominant American culture and met with greater educational and economic success than any other racial or ethnic group. The "model minority" concept masks the needs of a large portion of the Asian American community (particularly recent immigrants) for social service programs; it also places enormous pressure on young Asian Americans to excel.

N

Nation of Islam (NOI): Organization of Black Muslims that advocates prayer, self-discipline, separatism, and economic self-help for African American communities.

National American Woman Suffrage Association (NAWSA): Organization, founded in 1890, that fought for the passage of a constitutional amendment guaranteeing women the right to vote.

National Association for the Advancement of Colored People (NAACP): Civil rights organization formed in 1909 that promotes racial equality and the end of racial prejudice.

Nativist: A person who opposes the presence of foreigners and works for foreigners' removal.

New Deal: Set of programs instituted by President Franklin Delano Roosevelt (1882–1945) in the mid-1930s aimed at ending the Great Depression (1929–1939).

Nonviolence: The rejection of all forms of violence, even in response to the use of violence by one's adversaries.

O

Organization of Afro-American Unity (OAAU): A black-nationalist group formed by Malcolm X (1925–1965), the OAAU advocated that African Americans practice self-defense, study African history and reclaim African culture, aspire to economic self-sufficiency, and become active in their communities.

P

Passive resistance: The quiet but firm refusal to comply with unjust laws, passive resistance involves putting one's body on the line, risking arrest, and attempting to win over one's foes with morally persuasive arguments.

Personal Justice Denied: Report published in 1983 by the congressionally appointed Commission on Wartime

Relocation and Internment of Civilians. The report explored the harm caused by the exclusion, evacuation, and internment of Japanese Americans during World War II.

Plenary powers: The authority of Congress to revoke treaties with Indian tribes, as defined by the Supreme Court in 1913. In the early 1900s, plenary powers served as a justification for government invasion into virtually every aspect of Native Americans' lives.

***Plessy v. Ferguson*:** An 1896 Supreme Court decision upholding the constitutionality of the Jim Crow laws. *Plessy* specifically upheld a Louisiana law mandating separate railroad cars for black and white passengers.

Poll tax: A tax that blacks were required to pay in order to vote. Once at the voting booth, voters had to provide proof of that they had paid the tax.

Poor People's March on Washington: Protest march to the nation's capital by poor people of all races, from all parts of the country, in May 1968. The march had been initiated by Martin Luther King Jr. before his death.

R

Radicalization: The process of moving toward drastic, fundamental change.

Reconstruction: The post-Civil War era in which emancipated slaves were granted civil rights and the Southern states reincorporated into the nation.

Red Power: American Indian rights movement of the 1960s and 1970s.

Redlining: Discriminatory practice used by banks and insurance companies that involved drawing red lines on city maps between black and white neighborhoods and only granting mortgages, or selling insurance to, prospective homeowners in the geographic zones on the "white" side of the red lines.

Relocation: U.S. government policy, beginning in 1949, by which American Indians were encouraged to move from reservations and into cities.

Reservation: Tract of land set aside by the U.S. government for use by an Indian tribe.

Roe v. Wade: Landmark 1973 Supreme Court case that resulted in the legalization of abortion throughout the United States.

S

Scabs: Workers hired to take the place of, and weaken the resolve of, striking workers.

Segregation: The separation of the races, as dictated by laws and social customs.

Segregationist: A person who promotes or enforces the separation of the races.

Separatism: The rejection of the dominant culture and institutions, in favor of a separate culture and institutions comprised of one's own minority group.

Sharecropper: Landless farmer who works a plot of land and in return gives the landowner a share of the crop.

Sit-in: Form of civil rights protest in which black students, sometimes joined by white students, requested service at segregated lunch counters and refused to leave when denied service.

Southern Christian Leadership Conference (SCLC): Organization of black ministers, formed in 1957, that coordinated civil rights activities in the South in the 1960s and continues to work for racial justice today.

Southern Manifesto: Denunciation of the Supreme Court's 1954 school desegregation ruling by 101 southern congressional representatives and senators.

Sovereignty: State of being independent and self-governed.

Spanish-American War: War, in 1898, between U.S. forces and Spanish forces in Puerto Rico. At the war's end

Spain ceded (gave up) to the U.S. its possessions of Puerto Rico, Cuba, and the Philippines.

Stereotype: Simple and inaccurate image of the members of a particular racial or ethnic group.

Student Nonviolent Coordinating Committee (SNCC; pronounced "snick"): Student civil rights organization that engaged in voter registration activities and nonviolent protests in the 1960s.

Suffrage: The right to vote in public elections.

Suffragist: A person who works for the right to vote in public elections.

Sweatshop: Factory in which workers are paid low wages and toil in unpleasant and often dangerous conditions.

T

Termination: U.S. government policy in the 1950s of terminating (ending) the standing relationships, governed by treaties, between the United States and Native American tribes.

Third World Strikes: A series of demonstrations by students of color in 1968 and 1969 at University of California, Berkeley, and San Francisco State College. The students demanded that courses on the history and accomplishments of non-Europeans in the United States be included in the curricula.

Trail of Broken Treaties: Protest by the American Indian Movement (AIM) at the Bureau of Indian Affairs (BIA) in Washington, D.C., in the fall of 1972. AIM demanded the restoration of tribes' treaty-making status, the return of stolen Indian lands, and the revocation of state government authority over Indian affairs. AIM demonstrators occupied the BIA building for six days.

Treaty: Agreement between two independent nations, usually defining the benefits to both parties that will result from one side ceding (giving up) its land.

Treaty of Fort Laramie: Treaty drawn up in April 1868 between the Sioux nation and the United States in which the U.S. government promised to return to the Sioux all lands in South Dakota west of the Missouri River, including Mount Rushmore and the rest of the Black Hills.

Treaty of Guadelupe Hidalgo: Treaty signed in 1848 that end the United States-Mexico War (1846–1848). The treaty transferred more than 530,000 miles of Mexican land to the United States. It also guaranteed U.S. citizenship to Mexicans living on that land, and promised the Mexicans the right to retain their property.

U

United Farm Workers (UFW): Union of farm workers, led by César Chávez, formed in Delano, California, in 1966.

United States-Mexico War: Armed conflict from 1846 to 1848 in which the United States captured much of the northern territory of Mexico (that land is today the southwestern region of United States).

V

Vietnam War: War lasting from 1954 to 1975 in which the United States sided with South Vietnam in the fight against communism in North Vietnam.

Vigilante: Member of a citizens' group that uses extra-legal means to intimidate a certain group of people, for example, foreigners or people of color.

Voting Rights Act: Legislation enacted in 1965 that outlawed all practices used to deny blacks the right to vote and empowered federal registrars to register black voters.

W

White Citizens' Council: Organization of white businessmen and professionals that worked to forestall the political and economic advancement of African Americans in the South from the 1950s through the 1970s.

White primary: Practice adopted by southern states in the late 1800s that excluded blacks from Democratic Party primaries. Since the Democratic Party held a virtual monopoly over political power in the South, the only meaningful votes were cast in the primaries. White primaries effectively denied blacks the right to vote.

White supremacist: A person who believes in the inherent supremacy of the white race above all other races.

Wounded Knee: Tiny village on the Pine Ridge Reservation in South Dakota. In 1890 Wounded Knee was the site of a massacre of between 150 and 370 Indians by U.S. forces; in 1973 the village was occupied by members of the American Indian Movement (AIM) and other reservation residents for ten weeks, in protest of the corrupt tribal government of chairman Dick Wilson.

Y

Yellow Power movement: The struggle for racial equality and social justice by Asian American activists in the late 1960s and 1970s.

Young Lords Party: Organization of young Puerto Ricans, formed in 1966, that engaged in armed self-defense of their communities and held protest actions (such as strikes, sit-ins, and boycotts) over living conditions in poor neighborhoods.

Research and Activity Ideas

The following list of research and activity ideas is intended to offer suggestions for complementing social studies and history curricula, to trigger additional ideas for enhancing learning, and to suggest cross-disciplinary projects for library and classroom use.

Affirmative Action Debate: Study the history of affirmative action and the current controversy surrounding its application. Then form two teams—one in favor of affirmative action and the other against it—and debate the issues.

Freedom Routes: You will need a large map of the United States, a box of pushpins, and two spools of thread of different colors. Using one spool of thread and pushpins, map out the various routes of the Underground Railroad. Using the other spool of thread and pushpins, trace the path of the Freedom Rides.

Civil Rights Tour: Pretend you are a travel agent and create a civil rights tour. For each city on your tour, write a description of events that transpired there during the civil rights era.

Nonviolence Workshop: Contact local churches or universities to find an expert on nonviolence. Invite that person to your school to hold a nonviolence workshop similar to those attended by civil rights activists in the 1960s.

Where Are They Now?: Using periodical searches and the Internet, track down one of the "Little Rock Nine," the nine African American students who integrated Little Rock's Central High School in 1957. Find out what your person did after high school, where he or she currently lives, and what he or she is doing now. If possible, conduct a phone interview with the person you select to research.

Support a Boycott: Visit the United Farm Workers' web site (http://www.ufw.org) to learn which products are currently on the UFW's boycott list and why. Spread the word about the boycotts in your school. Try to convince your parents and your school cafeteria not to purchase boycotted products.

What If They Had Lived?: Write an essay speculating on how the course of events over the last thirty years may have been different in the United States had Martin Luther King Jr., Malcolm X, and Robert Kennedy not been killed.

Same-Sex Marriage Debate: Study the history of the gay rights movement and gay rights legislation in the United States. Then form two teams—one in favor of same-sex marriage and the other against it—and debate the issues.

Accessibility Study: Borrow a wheelchair and travel through your city. Keep a list of the places of public accommodation (such as stores, banks, restaurants, places of worship, and movie theaters), sidewalks, street corners, buses, and subways that are inaccessible to you.

Tell Their Stories: Reenact the 1981 hearings of the Commission on Wartime Relocation and Internment of Civilians regarding the internment of Japanese Americans during World War II. Individuals in your class can play the roles of former detainees by reading their testimony from the book *Personal Justice Denied* (Washington, D.C.: Government Printing Office, 1983).

Native American Land Loss: On a large map of the United States, use a highlighter to mark the land inhabited by Native Americans in 1700. With a different colored highlighter, shade the present-day Native American land holdings. What percentage of Native American land has been lost over the last three centuries?

Rent a Video: There are many informative and entertaining videos on civil rights topics available at video rental stores and public libraries. The following is a short list—check one out next time you have a free evening: *Amistad* (Steven Spielberg, 1997); *Chicano! The History of the Mexican American Civil Rights Movement* (NLCC Educational Media, 1996); *Eyes on the Prize: America's Civil Rights Years* (Blackside Productions, 1986); *Eyes on the Prize II: America at the Racial Crossroads—1965–1985* (Blackside Productions, 1989); *Four Little Girls* (Spike Lee, 1997); *Fundi: The Story of Ella Baker* (Joanne Grant, 1981); *Ghosts of Mississippi* (Rob Reiner, 1996); *Incident at Oglala: The Leonard Peltier Story* (Michael Apted, 1992); *Malcolm X* (Spike Lee, 1992); *Mississippi Burning* (Alan Parker, 1988); and *Thunderheart* (Michael Apted, 1992).

Civil Rights of Hispanic Americans

Hispanic Americans or Hispanics, also called Latinos, are people living in the United States who were born in, or whose families were born in, Spanish-speaking countries. (The Spanish-speaking world consists of Spain, Mexico, and most of the countries of Central America, South America, and the island nations in the Caribbean Sea, such as Cuba, Puerto Rico, and the Dominican Republic.) In some areas of the United States, the term Latino is preferred over the term Hispanic. Latinos are defined as people living in the United States who came from, or whose families came from, the geographic region to the south of the United States known as Latin America (see box entitled "A Discussion of Labels").

The two largest groups of Hispanics in the United States today are from Mexico (64 percent) and Puerto Rico (10.5 percent). Large numbers of Hispanics also trace their roots to Cuba, the Dominican Republic, El Salvador, and Nicaragua. Nearly 14 percent of Latinos are from countries of Central and South America.

Hispanic Americans have migrated, and continue to migrate, to the United States for a variety of reasons. Some come seeking economic opportunities; others come to escape political repression or war in their homelands; and still others come to be reunited with family members. The earliest Mexican Americans did not actually come to the United States. Rather, the United States annexed or conquered lands that once belonged to Mexico, bringing the people who lived in those areas under United States control.

Hispanic communities in the United States

In 1995 the U.S. Census Bureau estimated the number of Hispanic Americans in the United States to be about 27 million. In fact, Hispanics are poised to replace African Americans as the nation's largest minority group by the year 2005 (perhaps as early as 2000, by some estimates). According to U.S. Census Bureau figures, by the year 2050 there will be 81 million Hispanics in the United States. Hispanics will account for 21 percent of the total population and will outnumber all other minority groups combined.

While Hispanics reside throughout the United States today, they are concentrated in certain parts of the country. A third of all Hispanics live in California, a fifth live in Texas, and a tenth live in New York state. The states with the next largest populations of Hispanics are Florida, Illinois, New Jersey, Arizona, New Mexico, and Colorado, in that order. There are more than five million Hispanics

in Los Angeles and more than three million Hispanics in New York City.

Separate peoples with common struggles

Hispanics are difficult to define as a group. While often described as having a brown skin color, in reality Hispanics have a variety of skin colors ranging from white to black. Generally considered to be Spanish speakers—depending on the length of time they have been in the United States—Hispanics may speak only Spanish, only English, both Spanish and English, or any of a number of other languages. Each nationality of Hispanics has a unique history and distinct social customs.

The single biggest factor uniting Hispanics as a group is a social and political one: Hispanics are defined by their cultural and linguistic differences from the white majority—as well as other ethnic groups—in the United States. Hispanic groups have in common the misfortune of having been, or continuing to be, victims of racism and discrimination. Most Hispanic groups have faced discrimination in the areas of immigration, language, employment, educational opportunities, health care, voting, law enforcement, and access to the political system. As a result, Hispanics have a difficult time advancing socially and economically in the United States.

A 1998 study by the Clinton Administration's Council of Economic

A Discussion of Labels

The two labels most frequently used to describe the entire population of Spanish-speaking people (or descendants of Spanish-speaking people) in the United States are "Hispanic" and "Latino."

"Hispanic," which is a synonym for "Spanish," is the official term used by the U.S. Census Bureau to describe Spanish-speaking groups. Some Spanish-speaking people reject the term "Hispanic," however, because it was imposed on them by the U.S. government and because it is not entirely accurate. Many of these people prefer the term "Latino," which defines the group in terms of geography. The category "Latino" is not limited to people of the Spanish-speaking world; it also includes members of non-Spanish-speaking Latin American nations such as Brazil, Haiti, and parts of Panama and Nicaragua.

In the United States people's preference for one label or another varies according to geographic region. For example, in the Southeast and in much of Texas, the preferred term is "Hispanic." New Yorkers are split between "Latino" and "Hispanic."

In Chicago, the term of choice is "Latino." In California, the preference for the term "Latino" is so strong that the *Los Angeles Times* newspaper has banned the word "Hispanic" from its pages.

Most groups of Latinos prefer a term that describes their national origins more specifically than either "Hispanic" or "Latino," such as Mexican, Puerto Rican, Nicaraguan, and Cuban. Within given nationalities, some groups further identify themselves by their geographic location in the United States. For instance, Puerto Ricans in New York City call themselves "Nuyoricans" (pronounced nu-yor-EE-cans); Mexicans living in Texas are "Tejanos" (pronounces tay-HAH-noes); and Mexicans living in New Mexico are "Nuevomexicanos" (pronounced new-ay-vo-meh-hee-CAH-noes).

Many Mexicans, particularly young or politically active people, call themselves "Chicano" ("Chicana" for females), a word some people believe comes from the Aztec term "Meshicano," or Mexico.

Advisors revealed that only 62 percent of Hispanics aged twenty-five to twenty-nine had finished high school (as opposed to 93 percent of whites). The study also noted that Hispanic families have a median annual family income of $26,179 (for whites the median income is $47,023). And only 43 percent of Hispanic families own their own home (compared to 71.7 percent of white families).

While Hispanic groups have sometimes banded together to assert their civil rights, it has been more common for each group—given its

Mexican American students at the Drachman School, circa 1913. For decades, Mexican Americans were subjected to legalized segregation in many areas, including education. *Reproduced by permission of the Arizona Historical Society Library.*

unique history and current position in society—to fight its own battles. The rest of this chapter is divided into three sections outlining the history of civil rights of three groups of Hispanic Americans: Mexican Americans, Puerto Ricans, and people from Cuba and the Dominican Republic.

Mexicans in the United States

Mexicans in the United States have suffered from a legacy of discrimination, both within and beyond the confines of the law. Like African Americans in the South, Mexican Americans in the Southwest were subjected to legalized segregation. Through the late 1940s, and in some locations as late as 1970, Mexican Americans were restricted to "Mexican-only" schools that were markedly inferior to "white-only" schools. Mexican Americans were also excluded from public facilities such as swimming pools, barber shops, restaurants, and even cemeteries. Movie theaters either excluded Mexican Americans or assigned them to segregated sections.

Mexican Americans have historically been restricted to the most exhausting and menial jobs, such as picking crops, building railroads, and mining. At an October 1947 National Conference for the Protection of the Foreign-Born, held in Cleveland, Ohio, Isabel Gonzalez testified about job discrimination to the Panel on Discrimination. Gonzalez remarked that "history had made economic exploitation by American interests the lot of the Mexican people both north and south of the border. Powerful interests, like the great Western Sugar Company, the greatest importer of Mexican labor, the railroads, the mining and lumbering industries, the cotton and fruit growers, and the cattle and sheep industries have succeeded in keeping the Mexican the most underpaid and most oppressed worker so that they will always have a surplus of cheap labor."

The U.S. takes over Mexican land

When Mexico gained its independence from Spain in 1821, Mexican territory was almost twice as large as it is today. Within twenty-five years, however, Mexico had lost the northern half of its land to the United States. The first Mexican land lost was Texas. The U.S. government (as well as the Mexican government, which profited from the sale of lands) had encouraged U.S. citizens to settle in Texas. As the number of white settlers in Texas grew, they became increasingly dissatisfied with the Mexican government. The settlers' complaints included a lack of protection against raids by the Comanche Indians, a cumbersome system of criminal justice and taxation, and a distance of 500 miles between most white settlements and the government headquarters in Saltillo, Coahuila. The slave-holding settlers were also at odds with the antislavery Mexican government.

In 1836, following a bloody rebellion, Texas became an independent nation. Over the following decade, some 90,000 new whites settled in Texas. In 1845, at the request of the Texan government, the United States annexed the land and made it the twenty-eighth state. The Mexican government, which had never recognized Texas as an independent nation, was outraged by this action.

"Manifest destiny"

The acquisition of Texas only increased the U.S. appetite for territorial expansion. President James K. Polk (1795–1849; served in office from 1845–1849), was determined to fulfill the doctrine of "manifest destiny" (the belief that the United States had a God-given right to all territory between the Atlantic and Pacific Oceans). To that end, in 1845 Polk offered the Mexican government up to $25 million for the purchase of New Mexico and California. When Mexico refused, Polk looked for a reason to invade Mexico and take the land by force.

In 1846 Polk ordered General Zachary Taylor (1784–1850; succeeded Polk as president in 1859) to move troops into southern Texas, where there was a dispute over the U.S.-Mexico border. The United States claimed that Texas extended south to the Rio Grande, while Mexico argued that Texas's southern border was farther north, at the Nueces River. Taylor's forces provoked skirmishes with Mexican forces near the Rio Grande. On May 11, 1846, Polk asked Congress for a declaration of war against Mexico. Over the next two years, U.S. forces defeated Mexican forces in a series of battles.

The Treaty of Guadelupe Hidalgo

The United States-Mexico War (which Mexican history books refer to as "The U.S. Invasion") ended in 1848 with the signing of the Treaty of Guadelupe Hidalgo. Under the treaty, Mexico ceded (gave up) 530,706 square miles of land to the United States in exchange for $15 million. This land was later carved into the states of California, New Mexico, Arizona, and parts of Colorado, Nevada, and Utah. The 80,000 Mexicans living on that land were declared United States citizens. The treaty promised respect for their personal rights and protection for their property rights.

In 1853 the U.S. government purchased the southern parts of New Mexico and Arizona from Mexico. This transaction was known as the Gadsden Purchase. The guarantees offered by the Treaty of Guadelupe Hidalgo were extended to Mexicans living on the newly purchased land.

Mexicans within U.S. borders face discrimination

For the thousands of Mexicans living on land suddenly made part of the United States, the promises of Treaty of Guadelupe were short-lived. As the white population on those lands increased, both the citizenship rights and the lands of Mexicans were in jeopardy. Mexicans faced discrimination, hostility, and violence on the part of their white neighbors and law enforcement authorities. In many regions (except where they formed a majority), Mexican Americans were not allowed to vote and could not serve in local or state governments.

Through a variety of tactics, white ranchers and developers took much of the Mexican Americans' land in the Southwest. One way this occurred was by requiring proof of ownership in the form of a deed. When

Early Mexican American Labor Strikes

Mexican immigrants in the United States have been historically (and in many cases still are) forced to endure a host of terrible working conditions. The work performed by early immigrants was physically exhausting and unsafe. Mexicans were expected to work long hours for little pay. On a number of occasions, Mexican workers banded together and demanded better conditions. In most cases employers were unwilling to bargain.

One of the first Mexican labor strikes occurred in 1903 in Metcalf, Arizona. Hundreds of copper miners walked off the job, demanding enforcement of the state's new eight-hour-workday law. The strike was punctuated by gunfights between miners and police. Eighteen strike leaders were jailed.

The Metcalf strike, although ultimately unsuccessful, inspired a wave of strikes by copper miners and coal miners throughout the Southwest. In almost every case, law enforcement officials brutalized the strikers and their families. Many mine owners opted to seal their mines shut rather than make concessions to workers. Many workers were evicted from their homes, deported, or killed. During a 1914 coal miners' strike in southern Colorado, miners were fired upon by security guards with machine guns, and their homes were set on fire. The death toll among miners reached sixty-six.

A series of successful, large-scale labor actions occurred in California between 1928 and 1930. An alliance of thousands of Mexican and Japanese workers forced concessions from cantaloupe and lettuce growers in the Imperial Valley in southern California. A third strike in 1933 resulted in improved working conditions for immigrants in the strawberry fields of El Monte (in Los Angeles County).

the Mexican landowners could not produce a deed, they had to forfeit (give up) farms that had been in their families for generations. In some cases the owner produced a deed that had been issued by the Spanish government (which controlled the land before Mexican independence) only to find that it was not honored by U.S. courts. Still more Mexican American land was lost through ploys by con artists or outright theft. Mexican American peasants who were stripped of their land had no choice but to work as hired hands on ranches or farms owned by whites; in fact, many of these displaced people ended up as workers on the land they once owned.

Early Mexican immigration to the United States

One of the first waves of Mexican immigration to the United States occurred during the California Gold Rush of 1849. The experienced Mexican miners brought their skills not only to California but also to the gold and silver mines of New Mexico and Arizona. When large numbers of whites arrived in California in 1850, the California state government enacted a Foreign Miner Tax. The tax was intended to dissuade Mexicans from participating in the Gold Rush. Mexican miners who continued working despite the tax were subjected to violence and intimidation by white miners.

Large-scale Mexican immigration began in the 1880s, after the construction of a railroad line through the southwestern United States and into the heart of Mexico. The railroad increased traffic and commerce in the southwestern United States, which created a demand for labor. The railroad also made it easier for Mexicans to travel to the United States. Between 1880 and 1900, 127,000 Mexicans came to work in the United States, swelling the ranks of the 200,000 Mexicans already living in the Southwest. Most of the Mexican immigrants found work picking cotton or sugar beets or in the construction of new railroad tracks. Many of the Mexicans became migrant workers (agricultural workers who move throughout the country harvesting crops as the seasons change).

The second wave of Mexican immigration came during the Mexican Revolution of 1911–1914. The revolution was begun by armed groups of Mexicans seeking to overthrow the dictator of thirty-five years, Porfirio Díaz

(1830–1915). Under Díaz's reign, a tiny proportion of Mexicans controlled a tremendous amount of wealth, while the majority of the population lived in poverty. Many Mexicans left the country during the war to escape the violence and political turmoil.

Large numbers of Mexicans continued emigrating to the United States in the 1910s. During World War I (1914–1918), there was an especially high demand for Mexican workers. Although the United States was not involved militarily for the first three years of the war, it did supply goods for warring European countries. When U.S. soldiers joined the battle in 1918, employers faced a labor shortage in the midst of an economic boom. Mexican workers were actively recruited to work in munitions factories, in oil fields, on farms, and in meat-packing plants and steel mills.

The Immigration Act of 1917 Many of the Mexicans who came to the United States to work during the war had to do so illegally. The Immigration Act of 1917 required that any immigrant to the United States be able to read and write as well as pay an $8 tax. Most Mexicans, having little money or education, could not meet these requirements. Even after the Immigration Act's restrictions were loosened for Mexicans in June 1917, the bureaucratic entanglements associated with lawful immigration caused most Mexican immigrants (assisted by U.S. agricultural growers and factory owners) to enter the country illegally.

In 1918, as World War I came to a close, U.S. government officials sought to rid the country of "illegal" Mexican immigrants and make room in the labor market for returning veterans. Undocumented workers were rounded up and driven across the border. This importation and subsequent deportation of Mexican workers was an early example of the United States' "revolving door" policy regarding Mexican immigration. Even today, the border opens to the north when Mexican workers are in demand and opens to the south when the labor market shrinks.

The "Mexico Lindo" years

"Mexico Lindo," Spanish for "Pretty Mexico," described the pride that Mexican immigrants of the 1920s took in their Mexican heritage. Most of the Mexicans who came to work in U.S. fields, mines, and cities during the economic boom of the 1920s settled in communities with other people from their home regions. Rather than trying to assimilate into American society and culture, however, they continued to observe their own traditions and celebrate their own holidays.

The members of the "Mexico Lindo" generation banded together to fight segregation, police brutality, abuse in the workplace, and other forms of discrimination to which they were subjected. In Texas, Mexican Americans formed El Congreso Mexicanista (The Mexican Congress) to fight unjust laws and violence against Mexicans. In 1925 the Asamblea Mexicana (Mexican Assembly) was founded in Houston to protect the rights of Mexican Americans in U.S. courts. Chapters of La Liga Protectora Mexicana (The Mexican Protective League) were established in numerous cities to prevent the executions of Mexican American prisoners.

The spirit of Mexico Lindo faded during the 1930s. Four hundred thousand Mexicans (many of whom were U.S. citizens) were deported from the United States during the Great Depression, when joblessness was rampant and Mexicans were seen as unwanted competition by white workers. (The Great Depression was the worst economic crisis to hit the United States. It began with the stock market crash in 1929 and lasted through the late 1930s.) The Mexicans who remained in the United States were the first generation of immigrants to consider themselves "Mexican American," embracing a mixture of Mexican and U.S. cultures.

The Bracero Program

During World War II (1939–1945), U.S. employers were in desperate need of Mexican workers. The war had sparked high levels of economic activity; at the same time, the loss of fourteen million soldiers sent to fight in Europe had created a serious labor shortage. As part of the Bracero Program ("bracero" is Spanish for "manual laborer"), Mexican workers were recruited to come to the United States to work in factories, farms, and railroads.

In 1942 the United States formalized the Bracero Program in a

The Zoot Suit Riots

During the World War II years (1939–1945), Hispanics suffered from a surge in racist attacks. The U.S. government's incarceration of 100,000 citizens of Japanese ancestry during the war fostered a general acceptance of racism. (In 1942 President Franklin Delano Roosevelt signed an executive order mandating that all people of Japanese ancestry in the western United States be placed in internment camps. The stated purpose of this action was to prevent Japanese immigrants from engaging in acts of sabotage against the United States or otherwise assisting Japan in its war effort. Japanese American internees were freed from the camps by a 1944 Supreme Court order. For more information on the internment of Japanese Americans, see chapter 2.)

In one well-publicized incident of anti-Hispanic racism, Los Angeles police framed nine Mexican American youngsters for the murder of a white man in 1942. The nine were imprisoned, only to be freed years later. The men's sentences were commuted by an appeals court, which cited a lack of evidence to uphold their convictions.

For several nights in June 1943, a wave of violence against Mexican Americans, known as the Zoot Suit Riots, took place in Oakland, California. U.S. sailors and marines on leave ventured into the ghettoes and beat up Hispanics and African Americans. They particularly targeted youths wearing "zoot suits": knee-length jackets with pants tapered at the ankle, which were fashionable among Hispanics at the time. When the troops found a young man wearing a zoot suit, they would strip off his clothing and beat him. The police were aware of the situation, but chose to ignore it. One night the police arrested more than forty youths who had been beaten, but none of their attackers.

Throughout the month of June, marauding bands of U.S. servicemen swept through minority neighborhoods of southern California, assaulting Hispanics, blacks, and Filipinos. At the time, the media and the U.S. military blamed the attacks on minority youths, calling them "zoot suit hoodlums." A state investigative panel later placed the blame for the attacks squarely on the servicemen.

treaty with Mexico that authorized the use of contract labor. (Contract labor, similar to indentured servitude in that workers are required to serve a particular employer for a given period of time, was outlawed in the United States—as it pertained to U.S. citizens—in 1886.) Fewer than 250,000 Mexican workers were brought in between the years 1942 and 1945. After the end of World War II in 1945, however, the Bracero Program was stepped up and brought in millions of agricultural workers.

While the Bracero treaty had provisions for the protection of workers' rights, those provisions were largely ignored. Workers were forced to endure dangerous working conditions and substandard housing (some workers were given no housing and slept in cars, fields, or caves). They received meager wages and ended up spending most or all of their pay on basic necessities, which they purchased at inflated prices in company stores (the workers had no transportation and thus had no choice but to shop at the company stores). Indeed, many of the workers ended up indebted to the owners. In later years the Bracero Program was characterized as "legalized slavery" by the U.S. Labor Department official who was in charge of the program from 1959 until its conclusion in 1964.

Operation Wetback Many of the Mexican workers brought in by the Bracero Program—especially those active in union efforts—were deported or jailed during Operation Wetback of 1954. A U.S. government program, Operation Wetback made scapegoats of Mexican workers during the economic downturn at the end of the Korean War (1950–1953). At that time there was a tightening of the labor market resulting from the decline of arms production, coupled with the return of U.S. soldiers who sought employment.

The word "wetback" had long been used (and is still used today) as a derogatory term for Mexicans and refers to people who enter the United States illegally by crossing the waters of the Rio Grande. Once again, at a time convenient to U.S. interests, the revolving door of immigration swung open to the south.

Fighting discrimination after World War II

Mexican American soldiers, many of whom had served with distinction in World War II, returned home to face discrimination. (One-third of the nearly 500,000 Mexican American soldiers who served in the war were killed or wounded.) The veterans felt they had paid their dues to the United States and it was time for the nation to start treating them as first-class citizens. They found unacceptable the system of segregation that kept Mexicans out of schools and public facilities. Nothing better exemplified the unjust treatment of Mexican Americans in the post-World War II era than the refusal of a funeral home in Three Rivers, Texas, to bury fallen Mexican American soldier Félix Longoria. (Longoria was later buried with full military honors at Arlington National Cemetery.)

The G.I. Forum World War II veterans of Mexican descent formed an organization in Texas called the G. I. Forum to fight discrimination against them. While the initial goal of the G.I. Forum was to inform Mexican American veterans of their rights under the G.I. Bill and improve their access to services at Veterans Administration hospitals, the organization soon developed into a broad-based, anti-dis-

The Fight for School Desegregation

In 1946 the League of United Latin American Citizens (LULAC) filed and won a school desegregation lawsuit called *Mendez v. Westminster School District*. The lawsuit involved four school districts in Orange County, California, where Mexican American students were placed in segregated schools. In 1948 LULAC filed a second successful school desegregation lawsuit called *Delgado v. Bastrop Independent School District*.

While these two rulings were legal victories for Mexican Americans, they did not bring about the complete desegregation of schools. The lawsuits were significant in that they helped pave the way for the landmark 1954 *Brown v. Board of Education of Topeka, Kansas,* Supreme Court decision which ended lawful segregation of African American students. The *Brown* ruling, however, did not apply to Hispanic students. It was not until 1970 that a federal court outlawed the segregation of Mexican American schools, finding that "Mexican Americans constitute an identifiable ethnic minority with a pattern of discrimination."

crimination organization opposing segregation and police brutality. Over the years, the G.I. Forum has conducted voter registration drives and filed lawsuits in cases of discrimination. The G.I. Forum remains an important antidiscrimination voice for Mexican

Americans today, with branches in more than twenty states.

The League of United Latin American Citizens Another organization active in defending the rights of Mexican Americans in the post-World War II era was the League of United Latin American Citizens (LULAC). Formed in 1929, LULAC strove to increase educational opportunities for Mexican Americans and fought discriminatory laws and practices. LULAC filed lawsuits over school desegregation and jury selection. In its successful jury selection case, LULAC pointed out that over a twenty-five-year period in Texas, not a single Mexican American had been selected to sit on a jury. LULAC remains the nation's largest Hispanic civil rights organization, with more than 100,000 members.

Farm workers fight for their rights

The 1960s were a time of profound change in the United States. While the African American civil rights struggle and the groundswell of opposition to the Vietnam War (1954–1975) were the two best-known social movements of the era, it was also a time of intense civil rights activity by Mexican Americans. In the fields and in the cities, Mexican Americans waged struggles for land, for the right to decent employment and education, for political power, and for an end to the war in Vietnam. The best-documented struggle for Mexican American rights, however, was the farm workers' fight for justice.

Workers lead difficult lives Between 1950 and 1960 more than 3,300,000 Mexican agricultural workers came to the United States. They were seeking a way out of the poverty and unemployment they endured in their home country. Through their many hours of back-breaking labor, Mexican farm workers helped build up and sustain the large commercial farms that are known today as "agribusiness."

In 1965 tens of thousands of Mexican American farm workers labored in the fertile vineyards of central California's San Joaquín Valley. The workers migrated up and down the 500-mile-long stretch of land, from one grape harvest to the next. In the course of their work, the migrant laborers were constantly exposed to dangerous pesticides. The only tool available to the farm workers at that time was the short hoe, a six-inch-long instrument (since declared illegal) that forces a person to constantly stoop over or kneel when working. The average life expectancy of a farm worker was forty-nine years; in comparison, the average life expectancy of a white U.S. citizen in 1965 was seventy years.

Farm workers were housed in one-room shacks with no heat or running water. It was typical on large farms to have only one toilet for every 400 workers. Most farm workers were illiterate, having a maximum of only two or three years of formal education. The children of migrant workers were frequently pulled out of school, either to move with their families or to contribute to the family's income by working in the fields.

Farm workers put in long days, yet few earned more than $2,000 per year. They lived a hand-to-mouth existence, and most found it impossible to accumulate any savings. The farm workers, individually, were powerless to change their situation. They were at the mercy of the growers, who used this fact to their advantage. The growers did not regard the workers with any respect or dignity; rather, they factored them into profit equations like other expenses, such as manure or fertilizer. In the words of one farm worker, the growers saw the workers as "ignorant, lazy, dirty, stupid, and poor."

The formation of the United Farm Workers

In 1962 a community organizer named César Chávez (1927–1993), who had himself been a farm worker for several years, and two other organizers named Dolores Huerta and Gilberto Padillo, moved to Delano and established the National Farm Workers Association (NFWA). The NFWA held dozens of secret meetings with small groups of farm workers (so they would not be discovered by growers), gathering information about working conditions and the laborers' aspirations for better lives. The NFWA—which later changed its name to the United Farm Workers (UFW)—had 1,700 members in 1965 when it first began to consider itself a labor union.

In 1962 César Chávez—together with Dolores Huerta and Gilberto Padillo—established the National Farm Workers Association. *Reproduced by permission of the Library of Congress.*

"Huelga!" While discontent had been brewing among the workers for decades, the question of whether or not to strike was thrust before the NFWA rather suddenly in September 1965. Six hundred Filipino workers in Delano had initiated their own strike. The growers had responded by firing the workers and evicting them from their homes. The Filipino workers turned to the NFWA for support. By remaining on the job, the Mexican workers would have essentially condoned the growers'

treatment of the Filipinos. By walking off the job, they would be asserting the rights of all farm workers. At the same time, striking meant risking their livelihood and deportation. The union was unprepared for such an action and had no strike fund to sustain workers through a period with no income.

Members of the NFWA, fearful of meeting in their homes where they could be found out by the growers, met in the woods or on riverbanks. They discussed the pros and cons of walking off the job. On September 16, 1965 (Mexican Independence Day), the NFWA voted to go on strike.

The following day, workers walked out of the vineyards surrounding Delano, California. They demanded a living wage, decent housing, and education for their children. They chanted "Huelga!" (pronounced who-EL-gah), the Spanish word for "strike." While the workers knew that the future was uncertain, none of them could have predicted the length or intensity of the struggle to come.

Growers respond with violence One week after the walkout, there were 3,000 farm workers on strike from dozens of farms in the San Joaquín Valley. The growers responded with violence. They ripped up picket signs and destroyed car windows with shotguns. Ranch foremen kicked and beat the picketers and tried to run them over with trucks. Police arrested numerous strikers but none of the foremen.

Growers brought in other workers (called "scabs" by union members

On September 16, 1965, the National Farm Workers Association voted to strike for better wages, livable housing, and better education for their children. *Reproduced by permission of Magnum Photos.*

and "replacement workers" by growers) to take the place of the strikers. They then obtained legal injunctions that prohibited workers from picketing on or near their property. The injunctions greatly restricted the pickets.

With their actions the growers forced the strikers to adopt a new strategy. The strikers decided on a grape boycott. Of the thirty growers being struck, two winemakers were targeted for the boycott: Schenley Corporation, owned by Seagram's, and DiGiorgio Corporation, which pro-

duced Treesweet and S&W products. The strikers took their picket signs out of the fields and onto the sidewalks of downtown Delano.

The grape boycott attracted many supporters from all across the nation, especially students, religious leaders, union members, and members of civil rights organizations. Many people came to Delano and joined the farm workers' picket lines or sent food and money. The grape boycott was a catalyst for other types of social activism. Strike leaders and supporters

Senator Robert Kennedy Supports Farm Workers

The plight of the farm workers was of great concern to Senator Robert F. Kennedy (1925–1968), brother of assassinated President John F. Kennedy (1917–1963) and an outspoken supporter of civil rights. In the spring of 1966, Kennedy, who served on the Senate Migratory Subcommittee, called for hearings to investigate the conditions of farm workers. The senators on the subcommittee came to Delano for televised hearings; in the process they cast a national spotlight on the strike and the grape boycott.

Kennedy questioned Sheriff Gaylen of Kern County (which includes Delano) about his treatment of farm workers. When the sheriff admitted he was arresting workers on suspicion that they might commit an illegal act, Kennedy informed him that his actions were in violation of the U. S. Constitution.

At the conclusion of the hearings, Kennedy held a press conference with César Chávez. "We have come clearly to the conclusion that an ignored part of our population has been the farm workers," stated Kennedy. "The farm workers have suffered over the last thirty years, and that has to be changed. It's not just a question of wages. It's a question of housing. It's a question of living conditions. It's a question of hope for the future."

Over the next two years, Kennedy frequently championed the farm workers' cause. When Chávez broke his twenty-five-day fast in March 1968, Kennedy was by his side. Robert Kennedy was a consistent supporter of Mexican American civil rights until he was killed by an assassin's bullet in June 1968.

talked about nonviolence and human rights, and called for the end of police brutality and racism in the schools. The farm workers' strike represented the early stages of a Mexican American civil rights movement.

The Delano to Sacramento March By February 1966 the strike had been going on for five months, and the growers were still refusing to come to the bargaining table. Perceiving the need for a change in tactics, the strikers decided to embark on a 250-mile-long march from Delano to the state capital of Sacramento. The march (or "pilgrimage," as it was called by many participants) was seen as a way to renew the commitment of striking workers, to make contact with farm workers outside of Delano, and to refocus national attention on the struggle.

The march began in Delano on March 18, 1966. At the front of the line was a flag bearing a picture of the Virgin of Guadelupe, the patron saint of Mexico. This religious imagery reflected the Catholic faith of most of the marchers. The second flag in the line bore a black eagle within a white circle on a red background (the logo of the farm workers' union). A line of guitarists came next, who would uplift the marchers' spirits with their songs. The marchers began each morning with a mass and concluded each evening with a rally. Their numbers swelled with each passing town.

Twenty-one days into the march, the procession stretched for miles, and word came that the Schenley Corporation was ready to meet the strikers' demands. The grower agreed to raise workers' pay from $1.10 per hour to $1.85 per hour, to provide paid holidays and vacations for full-time workers, and to install a hiring hall where union members could hire workers. The settlement with Schenley was the first farm labor contract in the history of the United States, with the exception of one agreement reached years earlier on a pineapple plantation in Hawaii.

After the settlement the NFWA agreed to join the American Federation of Labor-Congress of Industrial Organizations (AFL-CIO), the largest conglomerate of labor unions in the country. At the same time, the NFWA merged with the Filipino workers' union (the Agricultural Workers Organizing Committee) and changed its name to the United Farm Worker Organizing Committee (UFWOC), also called the United Farm Workers (UFW).

On Easter Sunday, April 11, 1966, twenty-five days after leaving Delano, the marchers—whose ranks had swelled to 10,000 people—arrived in Sacramento. César Chávez gave a triumphant speech on the steps of the state capitol building. Cheers arose from the crowd as he read from the "Plan de Delano," which outlined the goals of the march:

> Now we will suffer for the purpose of ending the poverty, the misery, and the injustice.... This Pilgrimage is witness to the suffering we have seen for generations.... Across the San Joaquín Valley, across California, across the entire Southwest of the United States, wherever there are Mexican people, wherever there are farm workers, our movement is spreading like flames across a dry plain. Our Pilgrimage is the match that will light our cause for all farm workers to see what is happening here, so that they may do as we have done.

UFW steps up grapes boycott In August 1966, nearly one year into the strike, the DiGiorgio Corporation bowed to pressure and signed a contract with the UFW. While DiGiorgio and Schenley—the two growers targeted by the boycott—had given in to workers' demands, twenty-eight other growers still refused to bargain. The strike leaders decided their next target would be Giumarra (pronounced juh-MAR-rah), the employer of 4,000 workers and the largest grower in the region. The UFW initiated a boycott of Giumarra grapes.

Giumarra first managed to skirt the boycott by marketing its grapes under different labels. Each time Giumarra changed labels, the strikers would have to issue new boycott leaflets. Before long, Giumarra

Teatro Campesino

Teatro Campesino, Spanish for "Farm Workers Theater," was a traveling theater group founded in 1965 by Luis Valdéz. Valdéz was a recent graduate of San Jose State University and a veteran of the 1960s' foremost street theater organization, the San Francisco Mime Troupe. The actors, who included farm workers and their supporters, identified their roles with cardboard signs reading "huelgista" ("striker"), "patroncito" ("boss"), and "esquiról" ("scab"). In some skits, workers ridiculed growers; in others, they acted out the stories of their lives.

Teatro Campesino performed on picket lines, at fundraisers, and along the march route from Delano to Sacramento. Everywhere they went, Teatro's organizers invited farm workers to participate. Many workers relished the opportunity to mock their bosses after the years of poor treatment they had received. It was common for audiences to jump to their feet, laughing and shouting at the performances.

Teatro Campesino was important not only as an avenue of self-expression, but also as a means of political education. Some of the UFW's most effective organizers began their careers as actors in Teatro Campesino.

was changing labels so rapidly that the UFW could not keep up. The UFW decided the only solution was to call for a boycott of the entire California table-grape industry. Only grapes bear-

ing the UFW seal, meaning they had been picked by union workers, would be exempt from the boycott. The boycott was no longer limited to Giumarra but also affected the other twenty-seven growers with no union contracts.

UFW organizers set up chapters throughout the nation and worked with local volunteers to promote the grape boycott. They found the public to be overwhelmingly sympathetic to their cause. People in many cities picketed in front of stores that sold nonunion grapes and pressured supermarkets to stop stocking the products. Mayors, religious leaders, and labor leaders endorsed the boycott in their cities. The action was even supported overseas. In Sweden, England, and France dock workers refused to unload California grapes.

Chávez holds a 25-day fast In February 1968, two and a half years after the strike had begun and six months into the grape boycott, thousands of farm workers were still out of work. Many people were growing impatient with the UFW's nonviolent tactics. Talk turned to sabotage of crops and equipment, as well as to violence against growers and foremen. UFW leader César Chávez, a believer in the power of nonviolence and a follower of the teachings of Indian nationalist leader Mohandas Gandhi (1869–1948) and Martin Luther King Jr. (1928–1968), saw a need to redirect the worker's energies.

Chávez began to fast in order to force people to reflect on how far they had come in the struggle as well as to demonstrate the righteousness of the UFW's cause. He claimed that the only lasting victories came by nonviolent means and that violence only demonstrated the weakness of one's position.

Chávez fasted for twenty-five days, from February 14 to March 10, 1968. Many strikers doubted the sensibility of the fast, which left the UFW without a day-to-day coordinator. Some of the UFW's supporters from other unions abandoned the farm workers' movement in disgust. Yet even when his health faltered, Chávez remained convinced of the spiritual power of the fast. Thousands of supporters filed past the room where Chávez was fasting, to speak with him, to play music for him, or just to look in.

When Chávez broke his fast, he spoke at a mass attended by 4,000 of his supporters. "When we are really honest with ourselves, we must admit that our lives are all that really belong to us," Chávez stated. "So it is how we use our lives that determines what kind of men we are. It is my deepest belief that only by giving our lives do we truly find life. I am convinced that the truest act of courage, the strongest act of manliness ... is to sacrifice ourselves for others."

Victory! In early 1970 there came a turning point in the farm workers' strike. The grape boycott had succeeded to the point that it was causing the growers serious economic harm. Supermarket chains in Detroit, Michigan, New York City, and several other

UFW chief negotiator Dolores Huerta bargained with twenty-six nonunion Delano grape growers in order to draw up a satisfactory worker contract. *Reproduced by permission of AP/Wide World Photos.*

large cities announced their refusal to carry nonunion grapes. (In fact, the strike was 95 percent effective in New York City.) Shipments of grapes to the nation's top grape-consuming cities fell off by 22 percent.

In July 1970—almost five years after the strike had begun— grape growers finally decided to negotiate. The first grower to contact the UFW was Giumarra. The UFW told Giumarra representatives that in order to sign a contract, Giumarra had to first convince all other Delano growers to join them at the table. Giumarra complied. On July 29 the remaining twenty-six nonunion Delano growers sat down to bargain with UFW chief negotiator (and current secretary-treasurer) Dolores Huerta.

By the end of the day, all the growers had signed contracts guaranteeing farm workers $1.80 per hour plus 20 cents per box of grapes picked; protection against pesticides; seniority for striking workers; and a union hiring hall. The contracts covered 40,000 grape workers in all. The UFW victory had demonstrated, not only to farm workers but to all Mexican Americans, that it was possible to fight for their rights and win.

Even as the UFW reveled in its victory, organizers looked ahead to the work before them. The vast majority of farm workers were still without unions and contracts. Almost immediately after the grape strike had ended, lettuce workers with the UFW began another lengthy strike. In the following decades the UFW, together with the Farm Labor Organizing Committee and other farm worker unions, continued to organize farm workers to better their conditions.

Land reclamation in New Mexico

In 1965, while the UFW was fighting for farm worker rights in California, a different kind of battle was being waged in New Mexico. Mexican Americans in New Mexico were fighting to reclaim the land that had been taken from their families since the end of the U.S.-Mexico War (1846–1848). The Treaty of Guadelupe Hidalgo, which marked the end of the war, had guaranteed property rights to Mexicans living on lands conquered by the United States. In the century since the treaty was signed, however, millions of acres had been taken from Mexican landholders.

Most of the Mexicans who had lost their lands were subsistence farmers (the farmers grew the food they needed to eat). The loss of their land meant that the farmers had to find new ways of making a living and feeding their families. Most ended up as hired farm hands or migrant workers.

Another factor, often overlooked, was the spiritual component of the loss of the farmers' land. Mexicans considered their land sacred. In fact, it was common for generations of ancestors to be buried on the family land. "The land, it is everything," explained Sevedeo Martinez, a farmer from Monero, New Mexico, in *Viva la Raza!* "My wife and I, we have grown twenty-eight crops on this land. How can I say what the land means to me?... I would kneel down and take some of the rich black earth in my hands. It would break in my hand, it was rich. 'Estoy encantado con esta tierra,' I would say—I am enchanted with this land.... Yes, I love the land. The land is in my blood, in my heart. The land, it is everything."

Tijerina spearheads land reclamation drive

Anger at having their lands taken had long simmered within Mexican Americans living in New Mexico. The level of that anger came to a boiling point in 1965 when, adding insult to injury, the U.S. Forest Service revoked the grazing rights of Mexican American farmers in the Kit Carson National Forest. The farmers had raised their herds on that land for generations. The situation was ripe for a charismatic and convincing leader to step forward and organize the angry farmers. That person was Reies López Tijerina (pronounced RAY-ayes LO-pez Tee-hay-REE-nah), nicknamed "King Tiger."

Tijerina was born in 1926 in the countryside near Fall City, Texas. He grew up in a family of migrant farm workers. Tijerina's great-grandfather had lost his land to whites in a manner that was common at the time. White ranchers had driven some of their cattle onto the Mexican man's land, then accused him of stealing the cattle. The whites called in the local law enforcement officers—the Texas Rangers (see box)—who hanged Tijerina's great-grandfather. The white ranchers then took over the land.

Tijerina became a preacher with the fundamentalist Assembly of God church at the age of seventeen. After ten years of preaching by night and working in the fields by day, Tijerina moved to Arizona with his wife and sixteen other migrant families. The group pooled their resources, bought a small piece of land, and es-

tablished a community of poor people called "Valle de la Paz" (pronounced vah-yay day la PAHSS), or Valley of Peace. Within a few years, local whites, calling the Valle members gypsies and communists, burned down their houses and drove them out.

Tijerina then traveled to Mexico to study the history of the loss of Mexican lands in New Mexico as well as laws regarding land grants and land ownership. (Most of the descendants of Mexicans in New Mexico had received their land through grants from the Spanish government, prior to Mexican independence.) Tijerina became convinced that the primary cause of poverty among Mexican Americans was the loss of their lands.

In 1960 Tijerina moved to New Mexico and began working with local farmers. Three years later, eight hundred farmers who had lost their land grants to the whites gathered in Albuquerque to form the Alianza Federal de Mercedes (Federated Alliance of Land Grants), "The Alianza" for short. The group sought to reclaim both its lands and its culture. It also advocated bilingual education, civil rights, economic equality, and an end to police brutality.

Many of the Alianza's original members were from the northern New Mexico county of Rio Arriba. The land of that county was formerly communally owned (held in common by everyone who lived there); by 1960, 70 percent of the land was in the hands of the U.S. Forest Service.

Tijerina rallied people to the cause with fiery speeches. "They took

The Texas Rangers

The Texas Rangers were created in 1823—when Texas was still part of Mexico—as an armed force with the stated purpose of protecting white settlers from Mexicans and Native Americans, both groups considered "outlaws" by whites. The Rangers' primary objective was to drive away Mexicans so that white ranchers could take over their lands.

When Texas declared its independence from Mexico in 1836, the Rangers became the armed forces of the Lone Star Republic. Ten years later, about 1,500 Texas Rangers fought alongside U.S. troops in the United States-Mexico War. In 1874 the Texas Rangers' official designation was changed to "peace officers." Their conduct, however, was anything but peaceful.

In the late 1800s and early 1900s the Texas Rangers killed hundreds of Mexicans. "Some of the Rangers have degenerated into man killers," wrote reporter George Marvin in the newspaper *World Work* around the turn of the century. "There is no penalty for killing [Mexicans], for no jury along the border would ever convict a white man for shooting a Mexican."

The Texas Rangers operated beyond the confines of the United States legal system; their brand of law enforcement was known as "frontier justice." The most common "crime" for which Texas Rangers lynched Mexican Americans was defending their land from white land-grabbers; sometimes the "crime" was simply being a Mexican on U.S. soil.

In the early 1920s the level of violence against Mexicans reached its highest point. An estimated 100 to 300 Mexicans per year were killed by the Texas Rangers in border towns during that period. In 1921 the *The New York Times* ran an editorial about the situation, noting that "the killing of Mexicans without provocation is so common as to pass unnoticed."

The Texas Rangers were incorporated into the Texas state highway patrol in 1935. In the 1960s and 1970s the Texas Rangers acted like a private police force serving the growers in South Texas. They broke up farm worker strikes and killed or deported strike leaders. One of the most famous examples of this activity occurred during the 1966 United Farm Workers' strike in the melon fields of Starr County. When 700 melon pickers walked off the job, protesting wages that ranged from forty cents to $1 an hour, the Rangers set out to crush the strike. The Rangers arrested picketers, beat union workers, and served as armed guards for scabs (people brought in to do the work of striking workers).

In one incident the Rangers pistol-whipped a strike leader so brutally that the local doctor described it as "the worst beating I have ever seen given by the police." After that beating the union sued the Rangers for harassment; six years after filing the case, the union won.

your land away and gave you powdered milk!" thundered Tijerina. "They took your trees and grazing away from you and gave you Smokey the Bear! They took your language away and gave you lies in theirs. They took your manhood away and asked you to lie down and be a Good Mexican. They told you were lazy and cowardly and backward, and you believed them."

The Alianza begins land reclamation campaign

The Alianza began its land reclamation campaign with an appeal to the U.S. government to uphold the Treaty of Guadelupe Hidalgo. A delegation of Mexican Americans traveled to Washington, D.C., in 1964 and asked members of Congress to investigate the theft of their lands. The group also tried to arrange a meeting with officials from the Justice Department. Their requests were ignored. The delegation also traveled to Mexico to seek help from that government, but instead were arrested and deported.

In July 1966 the Alianza undertook a fifty-mile march from Albuquerque to Santa Fe, where the group delivered a petition to Governor Jack Campbell. The Alianza requested that the governor endorse its efforts for a congressional investigation into the stolen lands. Campbell responded by hiring a researcher to investigate the matter. The researcher's report was an attempt to discredit the Alianza by claiming that Alianza members were not heirs to land grants. With the governments of the United States, Mexi-

co, and New Mexico all refusing to assist them, the Alianza devised new strategies.

The Alianza occupies national forest
On October 15, 1966, the Alianza dramatically drew attention to its cause with a demonstration at Kit Carson National Forest in Rio Arriba County. About 350 Alianza members took over the Echo Amphitheater campgrounds, claiming that the land was rightfully the communal property of Mexican Americans from the village of San Joaquín del Río de Chama. The demonstrators gave the campground a new name: the San Joaquín Pueblo Republic (People's Republic of San Joaquín). They elected a mayor and village council and posted armed guards around the perimeter of the area. The demonstrators sent a letter to the Forest Service and to President Lyndon Johnson explaining that the United States had been evicted from the area.

The takeover lasted a little over a week. When law enforcement officials entered the campgrounds, Alianza members captured two forest rangers. They subjected the rangers to mock legal proceedings where they found them guilty of trespassing on Mexican American lands. Their sentences suspended, the rangers were free to go. Tijerina and several other men, however, were later charged with assault.

Police block planning meeting In the spring of 1967 the Alianza once again took its grievances to the New Mexico state capitol. Frustrated by the lack of response from the new governor, David Cargo, Alianza members planned their next move, widely rumored to be another land takeover. The group called a mass planning meeting for June 3, 1967, in the village of Coyote in Rio Arriba County.

State law enforcement officials, using a variety of illegal means, set out to prevent that meeting from taking place. U.S. District Court Judge H. Verle Perle demanded that a list of Alianza members be turned over to the Internal Revenue Service (IRS) for investigation. The Alianza skirted this request by dissolving its organization and forming a new one, called La Confederación de Pueblos Libres (The Federation of Free Towns).

On June 2, the night before the meeting, Rio Arriba County Attorney Alfonso Sánchez ordered police to erect roadblocks along the routes to Coyote. That same night, police burst into the homes of several suspected Alianza members and roughed them up. The next day police arrested eight Alianza members in Coyote who had managed to elude the roadblocks, on the charge of unlawful assembly.

Angry members of the Alianza plotted to get even. Twenty men from the Alianza, including Tijerina, were designated "people's deputies." The men set out to make a citizen's arrest of County Attorney Sánchez for violating Alianza members' constitutional right to freedom of assembly and for violating their civil rights. (According to New Mexico state law, a citizen may make an arrest when a criminal act has been committed.) The group was also determined to free its eight compatriots who had been arrested.

Shootout at the Tierra Amarilla courthouse On June 5, 1967, the twenty deputized and armed Alianza members approached the courthouse in Tierra Amarilla. (Tierra Amarilla, the county seat of Rio Arriba, was itself a former Mexican land grant area that had been taken over by Santa Fe businessmen.) The eight arrested men were scheduled to be arraigned that day, and County Attorney Sánchez was expected to be there. The Alianza directed a policeman on the front steps to drop his weapon. When the officer instead reached for his gun, the people's deputies shot him in the chest. A gunfight ensued. The jail-keeper was shot as he tried to escape.

The Alianza members rounded up the sheriff and county commissioners and held them captive while they searched for Sánchez. During the search, they opened the jail and freed all the prisoners. The Alianza members soon learned that Sánchez was not in the building and that their eight compatriots had been freed on bond earlier that day. They then allowed an ambulance to take away the two wounded officials and began leaving the courthouse themselves. The last two Alianza members to leave took with them two hostages—a sheriff's deputy and a white reporter—and rode off in the sheriff's car.

The sheriff's car was soon stopped by a group of police cars. The hostages were released, one of their captors was arrested, and the other—twenty-two-year-old Baltazar Martínez—fled into the hills. That night 1,000 troops from the National Guard and state police were called to Rio Arriba. They filtered through the little villages, harassing the Mexican Americans living there. In one village the troops rounded up forty unarmed Mexican Americans and held them in a muddy sheep corral for twenty-four hours with no food or water. The villagers were then released, and no charges were filed against them.

Eventually all twenty Alianza members from the courthouse raid were arrested or turned themselves in. They were charged with dozens of offenses. The charges against all except Tijerina and Baltazar Martínez were eventually dismissed; Martínez was later found innocent. While awaiting trial, Tijerina traveled to colleges and universities throughout the nation and spoke about the Mexican Americans' land struggle. He also traveled to Washington, D.C., to participate in the 1968 Poor People's March on Washington (see box).

The Alianza's final years In 1969 an all-out assault against the Alianza by law-enforcement authorities and conservative political groups began. The Alianza's meeting hall and cultural center, as well as a health clinic run by the Alianza and several of its members' homes, were destroyed by dynamite blasts. Powdered tear gas was placed in the exhaust systems of

 The Poor People's March on Washington

In the fall of 1967 Martin Luther King Jr. (1929–1968) proposed a multiracial Poor People's March on Washington to be held in the spring of 1968. Although King was assassinated before the march began, it went ahead under the leadership of King's aides, Reverend Ralph Abernathy and Reverend Jesse Jackson. King had personally invited Reies López Tijerina and Rodolfo "Corky" Gonzales, leader of the Denver-based Crusade for Justice (see "The National Chicano Youth Liberation Conference"), to co-chair the Mexican American contingent of the march.

Tijerina explained his decision to help organize the march: "I agreed [to co-chair] on one condition, that the Treaty of Guadelupe Hidalgo be used and mentioned. And I demanded that it be complied with. And it was done." Tijerina and several Alianza members joined the march as it came through Albuquerque. After arriving in Washington in May 1968, the group spent six weeks in a tent city erected on the Mall, which they called Resurrection City. Tijerina developed friendships with Native American and African American civil rights leaders. When he returned to New Mexico, he continued his support for Native American causes.

Alianza members' cars, making them ill. The NBC television network even aired a documentary called "The Most Hated Man in New Mexico" that cast

Tijerina and the Alliance in the worst possible light.

Tijerina ultimately served 775 days in prison, from June 8, 1969, to July 26, 1971. Seven months of that time was spent in solitary confinement. Tijerina's sentence did not spring from his actions at the Tierra Amarilla courthouse (serving as his own counsel, he had beaten those charges). Tijerina's jail time was punishment for the burning of two U.S. Forest Service signs (an act committed by Tijerina's wife and witnessed by many people) and for assault and trespassing at Kit Carson National Forest in 1967. When Tijerina was paroled, it was under the condition that he not serve as an officer of the Alianza for the next five years.

After his release from jail, Tijerina announced a shift in his political priorities. Instead of continuing his efforts around land grants, he was going to work toward reconciliation between people of all races. Tijerina founded a new organization in Albuquerque called the Brotherhood Awareness Center, and the Alianza began a rapid decline.

The Chicano youth movement

The period from 1967 to 1971 was one of great social awakening and political activity on the part of urban Mexican American youth. The young people had been inspired by the California farm worker struggle, the New Mexico fight for land reclamation, and the African American civil rights movement. The youths had become radical-ized in the upheaval surrounding the Vietnam War. They began to find intolerable the injustices in their own lives, particularly the lack of educational opportunities and police brutality.

Mexican American youths invented a new term for describing themselves: Chicano. According to some historians, "Chicano" is derived from the Aztec Indian word "Meshicano." Regardless of its roots, the term "Chicano" was embraced by young Mexican Americans as a label of their own creation. The word came to symbolize their pride in their cultural heritage.

Students respond to injustices

In the mid-1960s only one half of all Mexican Americans had completed eight years of education, and one-third lived in poverty. Unemployment among Mexican Americans was nearly double the national average. There were only four Mexican Americans serving in Congress. Education was seen as the key to social and economic advancement in the United States, yet the educational system was failing Mexican American youth.

In East Los Angeles, which was home to one million Mexican Americans—the largest concentration in the United States—only one in four Chicanos completed high school. Chicanos referred to this statistic not as the "drop-out rate," but as the "push-out rate." They claimed that they were being "pushed out" of the schools by educators who banned their language, ignored their history, and belittled their traditions. Chicano students were directed into vocational classes that prepared them for lives as laborers and seamstresses, while white students were directed into academic classes that prepared them for college.

In early 1968 East L.A. Chicano high school students took a survey and discovered there was a great dissatisfaction among their fellow students. The students indicated that although they wanted to get to college, they received no assistance from teachers and counselors. They also felt that discipline was doled out unfairly, pointing to punishments for speaking Spanish in the classroom. The students had a sense that their teachers did not care whether or not they received a decent education.

The students presented their survey to the Los Angeles Board of Education, along with a list of demands. They asked for bilingual education; Mexican American history classes; an end to corporal punishment (using physical force, such as striking with hands or a stick); improvements to school buildings; and the hiring of more Mexican American teachers and counselors. The survey and demands, however, fell on deaf ears. The refusal of the school board to acknowledge the students served to further politicize them. The students began planning for a walkout.

Walkouts staged At 9:00 A.M. on Friday, March 1, 1968, three hundred students walked out of Wilson High School. The following Monday students walked out of Lincoln High School; on Tuesday the walkout extended to Garfield High School; and on Wednesday, to Roosevelt High School. By Friday, there were more than 15,000 students on strike from sixteen predominantly Mexican American schools (five of them high schools) in Los Angeles.

Students would arrive at school at 9:00 A.M. each morning, only to file out of the buildings and into the streets or parks. The students chanted "Chicano Power" and "Ya Basta" ("Enough"). They held signs reading "We are not Dirty Mexicans" and "Brown is Beautiful."

Toward the end of the week, several thousand students gathered at a park in East Los Angeles and demanded a meeting with school board members. That afternoon a large contingent of police officers came to the park and ordered the students to disperse. As the students retreated, the officers chased after them and clubbed them to the ground with nightsticks. Several students were arrested.

The Mexican American community was outraged at this display of brutality against the students. The students had merely been engaged in peaceful protest. It became clear to Mexican American adults, who had long been subjected to harassment by police, that the police held the youngsters in no special regard; to the police, they were all Mexicans.

School administrators would not grant the students' request for a meeting. Instead, they threatened participants in the walkouts with expul-

The Brown Berets

East Los Angeles high school students were supported in their walkouts by the Brown Berets. The Brown Berets were a young Chicano activist group, among whom were many college students. Similar to the Black Panther Party (see chapter 1, "The Black Panther Party"), the group believed in the use of arms to protect themselves and their community from police brutality. The manifesto of the Brown Berets stated: "We are against violence.... We have gone to the courts.... We have demonstrated peacefully ... only to be met with more violence.... We have to arm ourselves now to protect ourselves."

The Brown Berets were founded in the fall of 1967 by David Sánchez, who the year before had been named "outstanding high school student" by the Los Angeles mayor's Advisory Youth Council. Sánchez had initiated a number of community assistance projects while still in high school. As long as he was gathering food for poor people, the police did not hassle him. When Sánchez established a coffeehouse for Chicano teenagers, however, the police took notice. They felt threatened by the numbers of young Chicanos coming together. The police attempted to close down the coffeehouse and beat Sánchez. That experience radicalized Sánchez; it made him realize that Chicanos needed an armed group that would defend them from the police. Sánchez then came together with other angry and determined youth to form the Brown Berets.

The Brown Berets, which included about 5,000 men and women, had a varied agenda. The Berets fought for improvements in the educational system, for decent housing, and for immigration rights. They also opposed the drafting of Chicanos to

sion or with the cancellation of their college scholarships. The students were encouraged by the support they received from three influential individuals: Senator Robert Kennedy, who visited East Los Angeles and spoke on behalf of the students; Congressman Edward Roybal from Los Angeles, who tried to persuade the police to leave the students alone; and high school teacher Sal Castro, who supported the students' demands for reform and helped them organize the walkouts.

Parents get involved Mexican American parents, frightened for the safety of their children, requested a meeting with the school board. To their surprise, the board denied them. The parents were left with no choice but to support the actions of their children.

Three weeks into the walkouts, the school board bowed to pressure and met with the parents. "We have allowed our children to get the short end of the stick for too long," voiced fight in the Vietnam War (1954–1975). The Brown Berets established community centers where Chicanos could file reports of police brutality and published those reports in their newspaper, "La Causa" ("The Cause").

The Brown Berets were special targets of harassment and surveillance by the police and the FBI's notorious Counter-Intelligence Program (COINTELPRO). Under the guise of combating domestic terrorism, COINTELPRO engaged in information-gathering on activists in a variety of movements, including the Chicano movement and the African American and Native American rights movements.

In August 1967 COINTELPRO operatives were ordered by FBI Director J. Edgar Hoover "to expose, disrupt, misdirect, discredit, or otherwise neutralize the activities of black nationalist, hate-type organizations and groupings, their leadership, spokesmen, membership and supporters, and to counter their propensity for violence and disorder."

The FBI and the police harassed the Brown Berets by taking group members' pictures at demonstrations, arresting them on a variety of false charges, tapping their telephones, and planting drugs and weapons in their cars. FBI agents and police infiltrated the Brown Berets, as well as the high school student strike committee. Undercover operatives encouraged the groups to commit violent or illegal acts, so that police could arrest them. Brown Beret members regularly received death threats, and their headquarters were firebombed. In 1972, when the large number of police informants was making it impossible for the group to function, the Brown Berets disbanded.

one angry parent. The school board agreed to implement the students' demands. The students returned to class, and parents held regular meetings with administrators to make sure the reforms were being implemented.

The "L.A. Thirteen" arrested In early June, with the walkouts long behind them, students seemed satisfied that conditions in the schools were improving. It therefore shocked the community when police came in the middle of the night for thirteen of the parent and teacher leaders. Held at gunpoint by the police, the leaders were handcuffed and thrown into patrol cars. The police refused to tell the activists why they were being arrested.

Conspiracy indictments were brought against the arrested people, who came to be known as the "L.A. Thirteen." If convicted of the felony offense, each person faced up to sixty-six

Mexican American congressman Edward Roybal supported the student walkouts in East Los Angeles. *Reproduced by permission of the Library of Congress.*

High School and one of the thirteen people arrested and charged with conspiracy, was fired by the school board. The board maintained that since Castro had been arrested (even though the case had not yet gone to trial) he would not be allowed in the classroom. Students and parents rallied to Castro's defense.

Castro had been one of the very few educators to openly support the students' demands for change. While the school board blamed Mexican American parents for their children's failures, Castro placed the blame squarely on the schools. Castro made the students feel proud of their Mexican heritage. For his actions, Castro was considered a hero in the Mexican American community.

Following Castro's firing, the parents of Chicano students held daily pickets in front of Lincoln High School. They also went to every school board meeting and appealed for Castro's reinstatement. The parents demanded a role in determining who could teach in their children's schools. Realizing that these actions were ineffectual, ten days after beginning their pickets the parents held a sit-in. They went to a school board meeting and refused to leave until Castro was given his job back.

The sit-in lasted seven days. During that time the parents discussed strategy, sang, read books, and held mass. The school board tried to make the group leave by turning off the air conditioning and the phones. The school board finally sent in the police,

years in prison. The L.A. Thirteen were released on bail, and the American Civil Liberties Union (ACLU) agreed to represent them. The ACLU argued that the case was about free speech—that the parents' and teachers' activities had been protected by the First Amendment. After two years of courtroom battles, the L.A. Thirteen were cleared of all the charges against them.

The fight to reinstate Sal Castro Sal Castro, a history teacher at Lincoln who arrested thirty-five of the parents. The parents' message, however, had been heard. At their next meeting the school board voted to reinstate Castro.

Student walkouts sweep the nation
Within eighteen months of the East Los Angeles strike, student walkouts took place in almost every large Mexican American community and in many small ones. A sampling of cities where walkouts occurred include Denver, Colorado; Phoenix, Pueblo, and Tucson, Arizona; San Antonio and Crystal City, Texas; Albuquerque, New Mexico; and the midwestern cities of Milwaukee, Wisconsin, and Chicago, Illinois.

Two years after the original East Los Angeles walkouts, students in the area concluded that conditions in the schools had not measurably improved. Thus, the East Los Angeles walkouts began anew. Dozens of students and parents were arrested, and several were beaten in the school boycotts of 1970.

The National Chicano Youth Liberation Conference

From March 27 to March 31, 1969, Denver, Colorado, was the site of the National Chicano Youth Liberation Conference. Just a few days before the conference, Denver had witnessed a walkout by hundreds of high school students and a violent response by the police. It was in that air of resistance and determination that more than 1,500 young Chicanos from all over the nation came together to draft the guiding platform of their movement.

 ### I am Joaquín

In 1967 Chicano activist Rodolfo "Corky" Gonzales wrote an epic poem called *I am Joaquín*. (Joaquín is a common Mexican name; it was often used by police officers to address Mexican Americans whose real names the officers did not know.) *I am Joaquín* captured the spirit of Chicano nationalism and is credited with creating a widespread spiritual and cultural awakening in a generation of Mexican Americans. Much as "We Shall Overcome" became the anthem of the African American civil rights movement, *I am Joaquín* became the anthem of the Chicano rights movement.

The Youth Liberation Conference was sponsored by a Denver Chicano organization called the Crusade for Justice. The Crusade for Justice had been founded in 1965 by Rodolfo "Corky" Gonzales, a former boxer, businessman, and director of Denver's War on Poverty program (the "War on Poverty" was a series of social programs intended to combat poverty, initiated by President Lyndon B. Johnson in 1964).

As a Democratic Party insider, Gonzales had become disillusioned with the corruption that ran rampant in government programs and with the discrimination that kept most Mexican Americans from getting ahead economically, socially, and politically. Gonzales finally broke with the political estab-

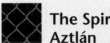

The Spiritual Plan of Aztlán

The young Chicanos' political manifesto, developed during the National Chicano Youth Liberation Conference, was entitled the Plan Espiritual de Aztlán (Spiritual Plan of Aztlán). The fifteen-point plan called for community control of schools; a community-controlled economic network of food cooperatives and land banks; an independent Mexican American political party; and cultural expression in the form of art and writing.

The preamble to the Plan was a poem, written by Chicano poet Alurista:

> Brotherhood unites us, and love for our brothers makes us a people whose time has come and who struggles against the foreigner 'Gabacho' [Gabacho is Mexican slang term for "white man"] who exploits our riches and destroys our culture. With our heart in our hands and our hand in the soil, we declare the independence of our Mestizo Nation [a mestizo is a person of mixed Indian and Spanish blood]. We are a bronze people with a bronze culture. Before the world, before all of North America, before all our brothers in the Bronze continent, we are a nation, we are a Union of free pueblos [people], WE ARE AZTLÁN.

lishment and founded the Crusade, an organization that fought for the rights of Chicanos on the streets (from police brutality), in the schools, in the jails, and in the welfare system, and promoted the ideals of ethnic pride and economic self-reliance.

At the Youth Liberation Conference, participants held political discussions and attended cultural workshops on Mexican poetry, literature, song, dance, and theater. They struggled to define their role in the United States and to identify a place they considered their home—a place where they felt rooted in the land and culture. With the latter quest, a poet named Alurista offered an answer: Aztlán, the mystical homeland of the Aztec Indians.

The Aztecs were an indigenous civilization that flourished in Mexico from the twelfth to the sixteenth centuries. By some accounts, the Aztecs defined Aztlán as the region that is now Mexico City; by other accounts, Aztlán was described by the ancient Aztecs as being somewhere in the southwestern United States; still others believed that Aztlán meant "the place beyond" and could not be defined in geographic terms—it could be any place. To the young Chicano activists, Aztlán came to represent their own homeland in the southwestern United States.

At the close of the conference, the Chicanos in attendance marched to the state capitol building. There they lowered the Colorado flag and raised the Mexican flag. To Chicanos, that action symbolized the fact that they were here to stay. They were not foreigners; they were home.

Chicano college and university students press for reforms

While Chicano high school students were protesting conditions in their schools with walkouts, Chicano college and university students were also organizing to improve the quality of their educational experience. The students at institutions of higher learning pressed for the hiring of more Hispanic faculty members, the admittance of greater numbers of Chicano students, and classes on Hispanic history and culture. Students at colleges and universities throughout the Southwest pressed their demands at mass demonstrations and at sit-ins in administrative offices.

There were several Chicano college organizations founded in the mid-1960s. In California the Mexican American Student Association (MASA) was organized at East Los Angeles Community College, and United Mexican American Students (UMAS) was organized at Loyola University in Los Angeles. Students formed the Mexican American Youth Organization (MAYO) in Texas and the Chicano Associated Students Organization (CASO) in New Mexico.

The assemblage of college and university student groups came together for a 1969 conference at the University of California, Santa Barbara. At the conference the students formed a coalition called the Movimiento Estudiantil Chicano de Aztlán (MECHA), which translates as the "Chicano Student Movement of Aztlán." The students developed the "Santa Barbara Plan," which called for the design and implementation of Chicano studies programs, over which students would have control. The group explained the guiding principle of Chicano studies, which they called "Chicanismo," as such:

> Chicanismo involves a crucial distinction in political consciousness between a Mexican American and a Chicano mentality. The Mexican American is a person who lacks respect for his culture and ethnic heritage. Unsure of himself, he seeks assimilation as a way out of his 'degraded' social status. Consequently, he remains politically ineffective. In contrast, Chicanismo reflects self-respect and pride in one's ethnic and cultural background.... The Chicano acts with confidence and with a range of alternatives in the political world.

Due to the efforts of MECHA and other organizations, Chicano studies programs—offered as major or minor fields of study or graduate programs—were established at numerous colleges and universities. The student activists also made strides in increasing the numbers of Hispanic teachers, students, and administrators. In New Mexico, students secured the nation's first appointment of a Mexican American university president, Dr. Frank Angel at New Mexico State University. MECHA chapters continue to operate at virtually every college and university throughout the Southwest.

Crystal City residents seek power

The Mexican American civil rights campaigns of the 1960s and 1970s not only took on issues of employment, land, and education but also of voting and political representation. Historically, Mexican Americans have been seriously under-represented in the government. In the early 1960s no place better exemplified this shortcoming than Crystal City, in southern Texas. Mexican Americans in Crystal City—many of whom were migrant workers—accounted for 85 percent of the population. Despite this large percentage, the workers did not have a single representative in any branch of city government.

Until the mid-1960s Mexican Americans in Crystal City and elsewhere in Texas were kept from voting by the poll tax and the literacy test, among other means. (The poll tax was a fee people had to pay in order to vote. Voters had to display their payment receipt in order to enter the voting booth. The literacy test was a piece of legislature adopted by many southern states that required all voters be able to read and interpret a section of the state constitution.)

Most Mexican Americans could not afford to pay the poll tax (the average annual income of a Mexican American family in Crystal City in 1970 was about $1,750 per year). Even for people who could afford it, paying the tax to vote was seen as a waste of money for a candidate who would not represent the interests of Mexican Americans. And for people who were largely uneducated and whose first language was Spanish, there was little hope of passing an English-language literacy test.

Political constituency formed

In the early 1960s Mexican Americans in Crystal City came to the conclusion that without political power they would forever be held to the status of second-class citizens. The residents thus began the process of molding the Mexican American community into a political constituency. In the early 1960s they worked within the Democratic Party; by the end of the 1960s they had formed their own political party called "La Raza Unida."

In 1963 Mexican Americans ran a slate of candidates for city council and mayor of Crystal City. The candidates held fundraisers to finance the campaigns and sponsored voter registration drives. To the surprise of the entire community, the five candidates, known as "Los Cinco" ("The Five"), won every seat up for election. For the first time in a century, Mexican Americans controlled the city council of Crystal City.

The white political power structure did not yield easily to the newly elected officials. The first act of resistance occurred when Texas Ranger Captain Alfred Y. Allee refused to grant the mayor and council members access to city hall. The elected officials only received the keys after Allee received orders from Texas Governor John Connelly.

Once the members of Los Cinco had taken their seats at the council table, Crystal City's business community began a relentless drive to get the five officials to step down. Some representatives were fired from their jobs. One council member was indicted on charges of having bounced a check. There were attempts to unseat other members for late payments of utility bills.

Ultimately, the business community's tactics worked. By 1965, when the next elections took place, Los Cinco were worn down, and political organizing in the Mexican American community had fallen into disarray. The outcome of the 1965 election was a return to an all-white city council and mayorship. It was not until 1969, in the aftermath of a Chicano student walkout, that political organizing was revitalized in Crystal City.

Walkout at Crystal City High School

In South Texas high schools, Chicano students faced many of the same objectionable conditions as did their counterparts in Los Angeles and elsewhere. South Texas students were presented with a curriculum that ignored Mexican American history; teachers and administrators who were not concerned about the academic success of Mexican American students; and textbooks that offered stereotypes of Mexicans as either being lazy (asleep under a sombrero) or criminal (the bandito). Speaking Spanish in school was grounds for being beaten with a paddle. Chicano students had a dropout rate of 71 percent.

While these conditions fostered a general dissatisfaction within the Mexican American student body at Crystal City High School, it took an unfair policy regarding cheerleaders to get the students to walk out. In a high school with eight times as many Chicano students as white students, only one Chicana (Mexican American girl) each year made the cheerleading squad. When a student named Diana Palacios decided to challenge this policy in 1969 and tried to become the second Chicana on the cheerleading squad, she was rejected by a teachers' committee.

The message to Mexican American students was that, with the exception of a token Chicana, only whites were beautiful enough to be cheerleaders. The policy symbolized the whites' control over the school. The students filed complaints with the school board, but received no response.

On December 9, 1969, 700 Chicano students walked out of their high school classes. They were joined by an additional 1,000 students from the middle schools and elementary schools. The students demanded more Mexican American cheerleaders, teachers, and counselors; the removal of racist teachers; courses in Mexican American history; the right to speak Spanish in school; and improvements to the school buildings.

The Mexican American parents supported their children's action. They provided volunteer teachers to hold classes for striking students in "liberation schools." Representatives of the U.S. Department of Justice were called in to mediate. Three months after the walkout had begun, nearly all of the students' demands were met. Palacios was named head of the cheerleading squad, and the Chicano students returned to the public schools.

La Raza Unida founded

Political organizers in Crystal City capitalized on the momentum of the students' victory by launching a new political party: La Raza Unida (The People United). Instrumental in organizing the party was José Angel Gutiérrez, a student activist who had founded the Mexican American Youth Organization (MAYO) at St. Mary's College in San Antonio, Texas.

Gutiérrez and other Chicano activists around the country had become convinced of the need for their own party after concluding that neither the Democratic Party nor the Republican Party could be counted on to champion the interests of Latino people. As Corky Gonzales, a former Democratic Party organizer and head of the Crusade for Justice in Denver, Colorado, stated in 1970, "The two-party system is one animal with two heads eating out of the same trough."

"The ruling class of this country uses the two parties to deceive us into believing that we have a choice," California Chicano activist Frobén Lozada once commented. "It is like two baseball teams disguised in different uniforms and pretending to be enemies, but all along being owned by the same man. In this ball park, we Chicanos are relegated to the role of water boys, with no voice, no decision-making power."

The La Raza Party was organized largely around economic issues and policies that would bring relief to working-class Mexican Americans. In addition to bilingual education, the La Raza Unida platform called for the regulation of public utilities (to prevent gas and electricity companies from enacting steep price increases), farm subsidies, and a tax structure that favored low-income people.

Hard work pays off In early 1970 La Raza Unida organizers in Crystal City threw their energies into a voter registration drive. That April the group's hard work paid off. La Raza candidates swept the majority of races for city council and school board. In neighboring towns La Raza candidates also fared well. The new Crystal City government passed legislation stating that the Texas Rangers no longer had authority within city limits.

The new school board (of which Gutiérrez was a member) implemented bilingual education and a free breakfast and lunch program; they also ordered new textbooks that accurately described the role of the Mexican people in history. The school board directed school cafeteria workers to purchase only union lettuce (lettuce bearing the United Farm Workers seal).

Negative community reaction The white community reacted with shock and dismay. It accused the new Mexican American leaders of unfair treatment toward the white minority. More than thirty white teachers and administrators resigned from the Crystal City public schools. White-owned newspapers denounced La Raza Unida, calling it a "destructive force."

"The Anglo community never gave up," stated Gutiérrez. "Their reaction was similar to what happened in the black south when integration and the end of segregation occurred.... They [the whites] created their own private schools ... transferred to neighboring school districts ... many of them fired people [La Raza Unida supporters] to see if that would scare us with economic sanctions.... It just made us stronger because we were enjoying the power."

La Raza Unida supports gubernatorial candidate After the Crystal City victories, support for La Raza Unida spread throughout Texas. In 1972 La Raza Unida decided to run a candidate for governor, Ramsey Muñiz, an attorney and former football star for Baylor University. Despite Muñiz's diligent campaigning, the Democratic Party refused to take his challenge seriously. Muñiz lost to the Democratic contender that fall, yet he surprised his opponents by taking nearly a quarter of a million votes. For the first time in a century, the Texas Democrats had won the governorship with less than a majority of votes.

"We didn't just put buttons on people's chests," Gutiérrez later commented about La Raza's campaigns. "We created a new kind of feeling and real action. We used what is natural to our culture—the family—to organize. If one person is badly treated by the gringos, everybody is. By moving in this spirit, we can all move together against the ranchers and the *rinches* [the Texas Rangers]."

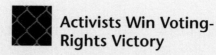

Activists Win Voting-Rights Victory

At the same time that the La Raza Unida national convention was taking place, Mexican Americans scored a significant voting-rights legal victory. The Mexican American Legal Defense and Education Fund (MALDEF), an organization formed in 1968 to promote the civil rights of Mexican Americans through the legal system, won a suit against the government of Bear County, Texas, in the Supreme Court.

MALDEF contended that Bear County's policy of electing representatives on an "at large" basis discriminated against Mexican Americans. ("At large" candidates are elected from an entire municipality, rather than from geographically defined districts.) The group claimed that a Mexican American candidate stood little chance of being elected under that system, since whites formed the majority in the municipality; however, if elections were conducted on a district-by-district basis, Mexican Americans would have a chance of being elected in districts where they formed the majority.

This voting rights case, called *White v. Register,* set a legal precedent. Before similar suits could be filed, numerous other city, county, and state governments voluntarily ended their at-large systems.

The La Raza Unida national convention The Ramsey Muñiz campaign thrust La Raza Unida into the national spotlight. The party took hold in Colorado in 1970, in California and Arizona in 1971, and in New Mexico in 1972. By the end of 1972, chapters had been established in sixteen states.

All La Raza Unida chapters conducted voter registration drives, and most ran candidates for office. The strategies of the party varied from chapter to chapter, depending on the proportion of Mexican Americans living in the area. Where Mexican Americans formed a majority, the goal was to win elections; where they formed a minority, the goal was to advocate for the rights of Mexican Americans and to pressure the major party candidates for concessions.

From the first through the fourth of September 1972 (a presidential election year), the La Raza Unida party held its first national convention in El Paso, Texas. More than 3,000 Chicano activists came from the sixteen states with existing party chapters. One of the main questions participants grappled with was whether La Raza Unida should participate in the two-party system, throwing its votes behind whichever presidential candidate best articulated its concerns, or remain an independent third party.

Delegates cast their votes in favor of remaining an independent political party and chose not to endorse either major-party presidential candidate. Participants also passed resolutions opposing the war in Vietnam and police brutality and called for greater access to housing and jobs.

They chose José Angel Gutiérrez as the party's national leader.

The decline of La Raza Unida In the two years that followed the national convention, La Raza Unida activists lost their momentum. The party continued to field candidates in Texas, but without success. By 1974 Crystal City was the only place in the nation where La Raza Unida held power. (Gutiérrez won a judgeship in Zavala County, Texas, in 1974; he resigned seven years later to become a teacher.)

Although it was short-lived, La Raza Unida added large numbers of Mexican Americans to voter rolls and trained many Mexican Americans to be political organizers. The party did a great deal to combat the stereotype of Mexican Americans as being passive, incapable of governing, and uninterested in politics. Several La Raza Unida organizers went on to become active in the Democratic or Republican parties.

Most important, La Raza Unida spearheaded an ongoing push for Mexican Americans' participation in electoral politics. From 1974 to 1994 some two million new Latino voters were registered (this was partly because of a 1975 congressional act that extended the protections contained in the 1965 Voting Rights Act to Hispanics). There are now nearly 5,000 Hispanics holding elected offices in the United States—roughly half of them are from Texas. Even with these advances, in 1994 Hispanics were still grossly under-represent-

On August 29, 1970, between 25,000 and 30,000 Chicanos gathered in East Los Angeles to protest the Vietnam War. What began as a peaceful demonstration turned into a riot after policemen in riot gear entered Laguna Park and began forcing people out. *Reproduced by permission of AP/Wide World Photos.*

ed, holding fewer than 1 percent of the nation's elected offices.

The Chicano Moratorium against the Vietnam War

In 1969 the Mexican American community was overwhelmingly opposed to the U.S. war in Vietnam. Mexican Americans resented discriminatory draft laws that granted middle-class people deferments but sent poor people to fight. While Mexican Americans made up 12 percent of the population of the southwestern United States, they accounted for 20 percent of the region's deaths in the war.

The Mexican American community had traditionally held the U.S. armed forces in high regard. For many, the military was seen as the only way to escape from the poverty so pervasive in Mexican American neighborhoods. During the Vietnam War (1954–1975), however, that long-held respect for the military was called into question. Many Mexican Americans felt they had

One Chicano's Refusal to Fight in Vietnam

"Today, December 8, 1969, I must refuse induction into the Armed Services of the United States," wrote Manuel Gomez to his draft board in Temescal, California. Gomez continued: "My people have known nothing but racist tyranny and brutal oppression from this society. Your educational system has butchered our minds, strung our hearts, and poisoned our souls. You cut our tongue and castrated our culture, making us strangers in our own land. The sweat of my people watered the fields and their aching bones harvested your food....

I see rabid leaders of this land live in luxury and comfort while they send my poor brothers to kill in a war no one wants or understands. The helpless and the inno-

cent have lost on both sides, as has been the case in all wars. My ears hear the screams of the fatherless children, my heart hurts with the tears of mothers mourning for their sons, my soul shrinks from the knowledge of the unspeakable horrors of Song My and the rest to come. For the Vietnamese people, I refuse to accept your induction papers.

I cannot betray the blood of my brothers. We are all branches of the same tree, flowers of the same garden, waves of the same sea. The Vietnamese people are not my enemy, but brothers involved in the same struggle for justice against a common enemy. We are all under the same sky. East and West are one."

more in common with the Vietnamese, most of whom were poor farmers, than they did with the Washington politicians who were running the war. Chicanos were no longer willing to fight for a country that treated them like second-class citizens. Mothers and fathers were no longer willing to send their sons overseas to die.

The Chicano Moratorium Committee was formed in 1969 as a nationwide network of Chicanos opposed to the Vietnam War. In 1970 the committee organized a series of large

demonstrations against the war in Chicago, San Francisco, Austin, Houston, and other cities. The final, and largest, demonstration took place in Los Angeles.

Police break up Los Angeles demonstration On August 29, 1970, between 25,000 and 30,000 Chicanos gathered in East Los Angeles to protest the Vietnam War. They were also protesting police brutality. According to organizers, the police had killed nine Chicanos in Los Angeles since the start of the year. Demonstrators marched along a four-and-a-half mile-route through the city, then gathered for a rally in Laguna Park. The atmosphere in the park was festive. People chatted with old friends, and families picnicked while listening to music and speakers.

The Los Angeles police were anxious for the rally to end. At around 3:00 P.M. they made their move. By some accounts, police sent undercover agents to provoke a disturbance in one corner of the park; by other accounts, the disturbance began in a nearby liquor store where some marchers stole pop and beer. In response to whichever provocation, 500 police officers in riot gear entered the park and, without warning, began chasing people out. The police fired tear gas canisters and beat people of all ages with their nightsticks.

According to march organizer and UCLA student body president Rosalio Muñoz, "People were trapped there [between the wall of police and the stage] ... and kids were climbing out through the stage.... People were climbing and tossing babies over to the other side.... Then the cops started throwing tear gas, making it worse. And so then the people started throwing things back."

Once in the streets, some demonstrators vented their anger by smashing windows and setting fire to buildings. By nightfall 200 Chicanos had been arrested, sixty had been wounded, and three had been killed by the police. The events of the day were characterized by Chicanos as a "police

The Death of Journalist Rubén Salazar

One of the three Chicanos killed during the anti-Vietnam War demonstration in Los Angeles on August 29, 1970, was respected *Los Angeles Times* journalist and television commentator Rubén Salazar. Salazar had been present at the second National Chicano Youth Liberation Conference in Denver earlier that year and had been profoundly moved by the commitment of the young activists to their people's cause. Salazar was regarded as the only mainstream news reporter sympathetic to the Chicano movement.

Salazar had been present in Laguna Park, covering the demonstration, when the police had cleared people out. Salazar sought refuge from stampeding police in the nearby Silver Dollar Café. A police officer who had seen demonstrators enter the café stood in the doorway and fired a tear gas canister toward the back of the room. The ten-inch-long canister struck Salazar in the head, killing him instantly and nearly decapitating him. At the time of his death, Salazar had been working on a series of articles about six Chicanos who had died while in police custody earlier that year. No charges were filed against the police officer responsible for Salazar's death.

riot" and by the police as a "Chicano riot." To Chicano activists, the police conduct underscored the notion that *their* war was not in Vietnam; it was in the streets of their own cities.

"Undocumented Worker" and "Illegal Alien"

There are many foreign workers in the United States. They are often referred to in the press as "illegal aliens," or people who are not in compliance with official immigration guidelines. Some of these people do not have the appropriate papers to be in the United States; others have outlasted their temporary work permits or student visas.

In 1974 the International Labor Organization resolved that it is more appropriate to call these individuals "undocumented workers" than it is to call them illegal aliens. The organization noted that "illegal" has a negative connotation and is generally used to describe criminals. Immigration into the United States without the proper papers is a civil, not a criminal, offense.

The current status of Mexican Americans

The Chicano movements of the 1960s and 1970s succeeded in advancing the cause of Mexican American civil rights in several important ways. The farm worker strikes and grape boycotts led to improvements in the living and working conditions of many migrant workers. The youth movement brought to the fore the need for bilingual education and created greater educational opportunities for Mexican American students. The La Raza Unida party spearheaded increased Mexican Ameri-

can involvement in electoral politics. The Chicano movement not only expanded the definition of civil rights in the United States, it also encouraged Mexican Americans to reclaim their culture through art, literature, poetry, and music.

The 17 million people of Mexican origin in the United States today, however, continue to be largely shut out of the educational and employment mainstream. At present, just 5.9 percent of Mexican Americans age twenty-five or over have completed at least a bachelor's degree (for Puerto Ricans in the United States, this figure is 8 percent; for Cuban Americans it is 16.5 percent). In addition, nearly one-third of Mexican Americans lived below the poverty line in 1992, as compared with 14.5 percent of the U.S. population overall.

While Mexican Americans are still fighting the traditional battles over discrimination in schools and workplaces, they also find themselves on the defensive in other areas. Some of the most highly publicized issues affecting the civil rights of Mexican Americans today are U.S. immigration policy and its enforcement; the consequences of the North American Free Trade Agreement (NAFTA); and California ballot initiatives ending government assistance to undocumented workers and prohibiting affirmative action and bilingual education.

Immigration laws and border battles

Throughout the 1970s, 1980s, and 1990s, immigration policies regulating the influx of Mexicans into the United States have remained a politically charged topic. The constantly changing immigration policies are driven both by employers' needs for cheap labor and by politicians' needs for outside elements on which to blame the nation's economic problems.

Mexican workers are crucial to the U.S. economy because they are willing to perform difficult and dangerous tasks, work many hours a day, and receive low wages. In other words, they fill jobs that very few U.S. citizens would want. In the early 1980s, however, an economic recession led to a "brown scare"—a perception, fanned by many politicians, that the U.S. economic problems were caused by undocumented Mexican workers taking "American jobs." It was more convenient to blame the problem on outsiders than to search deep within our own nation's economic structure for the true factors driving the recession. The battle cry of many politicians was "close the border!"

The Immigration Reform and Control Act The 1986 Immigration Reform and Control Act (IRCA) simultaneously restricted the flow of Mexican immigrants and ensured a supply of cheap agricultural laborers. While providing for sanctions against employers who hired undocumented Mexican workers, the act also allowed U.S. employers to legally import up to one-third of a million agricultural workers yearly.

Violence on the border In 1980 newly elected president Ronald Rea-

gan (1911–) promised to "regain control of our borders." As the Border Patrol (the arm of the Immigration and Naturalization Service that polices the border) was beefed up, incidents of anti-Mexican racism and violence sharply increased. The hostility was not only directed at illegal immigrants but also at U.S. citizens of Mexican descent. Anti-Mexican sentiment was not limited to the border but was expressed wherever large numbers of Mexican Americans resided. All Latinos—whether in the United States by legal or illegal means—were subjected to interrogation and harassment during workplace sweeps by the Immigration and Naturalization Service (INS).

Racist violence against Mexicans in California reached shocking proportions in the mid-1980s. In San Diego County, a 1985 television report focused on white suburban teenagers shooting at Mexicans "for sport." The Christopher Commission Report, a document written in 1991 by a congressional committee chaired by Representative Warren M. Christopher, chastised the Los Angeles Police Department for having committed hundreds of "beatings and other excessive uses of force." The report quoted racist references made by police officers on their radios regarding the city's Mexican residents. These comments included: "Sounds like monkey slapping time"; "We're huntin' wabbits"; "I almost got me a Mexican last night"; "Capture him, beat him and treat him like dirt"; and "A full moon and a full gun make for a night of fun."

United States Border Patrol agents load undocumented workers into a van for deportation during "Operation Gatekeeper." *Reproduced by permission of AP/Wide World Photos.*

In the 1980s the border became a virtual war zone. Bands of Ku Klux Klansmen joined Border Patrol Agents in the search for Mexicans wading across the Rio Grande. In 1985 a twelve-year-old Mexican boy was shot and critically wounded by border patrol agents near San Ysidro, California. In 1993 a Border Patrol agent shot and killed an unarmed man attempting to cross the border and tried to hide the body. And in 1997 eighteen-year-old Esequiel Hernandez Jr. was shot to death at the border south of Redford, Texas, by Marines conducting drug surveillance.

In every case, the perpetrators were cleared of all charges.

Groups release reports In 1993 the human rights organization Americas Watch released a report entitled "Frontier Justice," in which the group sharply criticized the U.S. Border Patrol for hundreds of incidents of brutality. In 1997 the U.S. Civil Rights Commission issued a report entitled "Federal Immigration Law Enforcement in the Southwest: Civil Rights Impacts on Border Communities" in which the Commission expressed "deep concern" about violations of Latinos' civil rights by Border Patrol agents and found "that a pattern of abusive treatment by Border Patrol officials may exist." The Commission called on Congress to investigate cases of alleged abuse.

According to the California Rural Legal Assistance Foundation, 173 Mexicans died trying to cross the U.S. border in 1998 and early 1999. That same year, Amnesty International released a report entitled "Human Rights Concerns in the Border Region with Mexico." This document criticized the treatment of Mexicans and Hispanics by the Immigration and Naturalization Service and the Border Patrol. "Reports of cruel, inhuman or degrading treatment were collected along the length of the 2,000-mile border and present a disturbing picture of unprofessional conduct," the report stated. "There is credible evidence that persons detained by [the Immigration and Naturalization Service] have been subjected to cruel, inhuman, or degrading treatment, including beatings, sexual assault, denial of medical attention, and denial of food, water and warmth." The report pointed out that the abuse was not limited to people trying to cross the border illegally, but also to U.S. citizens of Latin American descent, to legal permanent residents of the United States, and even to members of four Native American nations with tribal lands near the border.

In 1997 the Border Patrol had more than 6,300 agents. A current policy calls for escalating the number of Border Patrol agents by 1,000 per year through the year 2001.

The consequences of NAFTA

In 1993 the U.S. Congress narrowly ratified the North American Free Trade Agreement (NAFTA), which provided a new method of dealing with immigration issues and employers' needs for labor. The architects of NAFTA argued that by creating a common market between Canada, the United States, and Mexico, incomes in Mexico would rise and the numbers of Mexicans crossing the border into the United States would decline. U.S. factory owners supported NAFTA because it would allow them to more easily relocate factories (in Spanish, "maquiladoras") to Mexico where labor costs one-seventh what it does in the United States.

As NAFTA's critics pointed out, the proposed agreement had several drawbacks. For one, it contained only flimsy (and as many argued, unenforceable) provisions guaranteeing the rights of Mexican workers to decent wages and working conditions. NAFTA's critics also pointed out that many people in the United States would lose their jobs as factories moved south across the border. There were other concerns about environmental degradation in the border area, which was already home to nearly 2,000 maquiladoras. Although a side agreement regarding environmental protection was included in the final version of NAFTA, environmentalists

A maquiladora in Mexico. *Photo by Mario Villafuerte. Reproduced by permission Reuters/Archive Photos.*

considered it too weak to prevent worsening pollution.

A surge in child labor Indeed, many of the predictions of NAFTA's critics have come to pass. As U.S. growers have moved portions of their vegetable operations south of the border (particularly into the strip of land on Mexico's western edge called "Baja California") there has been a surge in child labor in Mexico. The rise of export-oriented agriculture, largely fostered by the influx of U.S. employers into Mexico, contributed to an economic crisis in Mexico that has cut the incomes of most Mexicans in half. As a result, more children than ever before are being forced to contribute to their families' income.

More than 2.5 million children between the ages of six and fourteen do not attend school, and a good number of them can be found in the Mexican fields of U.S. growers. These child-workers are being called the "hidden victims of NAFTA."

"Our laws say one thing ... about child labor, but the reality is another," stated Pedro Gonzalez Hernandez, a teacher in a rural Mexican school that has seen many of its students leave for the fields. "The companies come here, and they create jobs, which the Mexican government isn't doing. But I just wish they would pay more, so it didn't have these consequences for children."

Environmental conditions worsen Another legacy of NAFTA has been the worsening of environmental conditions along the border, where the vast majority of maquiladoras are located. Even before the passage of NAFTA, employers had been taking advantage of Mexico's lax environmental regulations and dumping hazardous chemical wastes on the ground, into the air, and in the waters of the Rio Grande.

A 1991 study conducted by the National Toxics Campaign Fund determined that the border was being turned into a "2,000-mile-long Love Canal" (in reference to the area near Niagara Falls, New York, where high levels of toxic chemicals forced the evacuation of residents in 1980). A report by the American Medical Association in the same year characterized the border as "a virtual cesspool and breeding ground for infectious disease."

Since NAFTA's passage, the number of maquiladoras has risen sharply, and wastewater from the plants often overwhelms municipal sewage systems. Alarming levels of lead and arsenic, as well as other toxic chemicals, have been found in the waters of the Rio Grande and on the beaches of southern California.

California's Propositions 187, 209, and 227

In the mid-1990s a surge in racism and xenophobia (fear or hatred of foreigners) that swept the United States manifested itself in two (and by some definitions, three) successful California ballot initiatives. Proposition 187, favored by 59 percent of vot-

Students in San Francisco protest Proposition 187. This ballot initiative ended government assistance to undocumented workers and their children. *Reproduced by permission of Reuters/Lou Dematteis/Archive Photos.*

ers in 1994, ended government assistance to undocument workers or the children of undocument workers. That assistance took the forms of health care, education, welfare, and other social services. The constitutionality of that measure was challenged, and its fate remains in the hands of the U.S. Supreme Court.

The 1996 passage of the second initiative, Proposition 209, ended the policy of affirmative action in California government agencies. That prohibition applies to the areas of employment, contracts, and admissions to

publicly funded colleges and universities. The passage of Proposition 209 solidified and expanded upon the 1995 decision of the regents of the University of California to drop its affirmative action program (see chapter 1, "Gains and losses in the modern era").

The passage of Proposition 227 in 1998 effectively ended bilingual education in California. Called "English for the Children," the law replaces the dual-language instruction policy, which has been a hallmark of California's education system for nearly three decades, with a one-year English immersion program after which students are placed in English-only classrooms.

It would be an oversimplification to characterize Proposition 227 as racist or anti-Latino (it was not promoted by the same groups that put forth Propositions 187 and 209). In recent years the question of whether bilingual education is helping or hurting limited-English speakers has been the subject of intense debate among educators. Latino voters themselves were split on the proposition and, according to some polls, the majority of Latinos supported its passage.

The proposition, however, was opposed by the Mexican American Legal Defense and Education Fund, the California Teachers Association, and the Clinton Administration. Following the proposition's passage, MALDEF filed a lawsuit to prevent the new law from taking effect. According to MALDEF, Proposition 227 is unconstitutional because it denies non-English-speaking students equal access to education.

Puerto Ricans in the United States

There are approximately 6.5 million people of Puerto Rican descent in the world. More than 3.5 million of them live on the 110-mile-long, 35-mile-wide island of Puerto Rico, which is situated to the east of the Dominican Republic and Haiti in the Caribbean Sea. There are about 2.7 million Puerto Ricans living in the United States. The largest concentration of Puerto Ricans in the United States, numbering 900,000, is in New York City. Around 200,000 Puerto Ricans reside in Chicago and nearby cities. Other states with substantial populations of Puerto Ricans are New Jersey, Connecticut, Massachusetts, Ohio, Pennsylvania, Florida, and California.

The island of Puerto Rico is in the possession of the United States. Puerto Ricans are therefore U.S. citizens and can come and go at will between the island (Puerto Rico) and the mainland (the United States). Ease of immigration, however, stands alone as an advantage that Puerto Ricans hold over other Latino groups. Puerto Ricans in the United States, with an average family income of about $25,000, are the poorest of all Latino groups. In 1992 more than a third of Puerto Ricans in the United States were living below the poverty level. Substandard housing, unemployment, and crime are common features of many Puerto Rican communities.

Puerto Rico becomes U.S. protectorate

Puerto Rico was a colony of Spain for nearly four centuries, beginning with the conquest of the island by Spanish forces in 1509. Puerto Rico was taken out of Spanish control and into the possession of the United States in 1898.

The Spanish-American War began on April 28, 1898, following the sinking of the battleship *U.S.S. Maine* in Havana Harbor, Cuba. The United States identified Spain as the responsible party, a charge that Spain denied. When Spain refused to pay reparations (compensation) for the sunken ship, the United States invaded Spanish army strongholds in Puerto Rico. U.S. forces defeated Spanish forces in a series of battles over a five-month period. On December 10, 1898, the United States and Spain signed the Treaty of Paris, which ended the war and transferred control of Puerto Rico, Cuba, and the Philippines from Spain to the United States.

Acts define status, government structure

Two years after the war the U.S. Congress passed the Foraker Act. This act defined Puerto Rico as a U.S. protectorate—a territory over which the U.S. maintained control—and outlined a plan for the U.S. military government on the island to be replaced by a civilian government. According to the terms of the Foraker Act, the civilian government would be made up of thirty-five elected representatives, with a governor appointed by the U.S. president. The Puerto Rican people would also elect a commissioner to serve as a nonvoting observer in the U.S. Congress. English was declared the official language in Puerto Rico's schools, a rule that was enormously unpopular on the Spanish-speaking islands.

In 1917 the U.S. Congress passed the Jones Act, a law that revamped the Puerto Rican government structure. The Jones Act described a new government for Puerto Rico consisting of two houses (similar to the U.S. government's Senate and House of Representatives). All representatives would be elected by the Puerto Rican people. The positions of governor, commissioner of education, attorney general, and members of the Supreme Court of the island, however, would still be appointed by the president of the United States.

The Jones Act also conferred U.S. citizenship on all Puerto Ricans. As citizens, Puerto Ricans were allowed unhindered travel between the island and the mainland. Puerto Ricans living on the island could not vote in U.S. elections, however, and were not subject to U.S. income tax (most Puerto Ricans on the island did not make enough money to be taxed). In contrast, Puerto Ricans living on the mainland were entitled to vote and were taxed.

Citizenship also carried with it the duty of Puerto Rican men to serve in the U.S. Army. Whether by design or coincidence, Puerto Ricans were made citizens just one month before the United States entered World War I (1939–1945); 18,000 young Puerto Ricans were drafted and served overseas in segregated units.

The Puerto Rican government

In 1948 Puerto Ricans were given their first opportunity to elect their own governor. (They elected Luis Muñoz Marín, whose Partido Popular

Democrático [PPD] advocated greater autonomy and social and economic development for the island.) The governor was charged with naming all the top officials previously appointed by the U.S. president, except members of the Supreme Court (that responsibility remained with the U.S. president). In 1948 the United States also allowed Puerto Ricans to resume using Spanish in their classrooms.

The Constitution Act In 1950 the U.S. Congress passed the Constitution Act, which gave Puerto Ricans permission to draft their own constitution and design their own form of government. The ninety-two delegates to the Puerto Rican constitutional convention crafted a constitution and structure of government similar to those of the United States. The government that was formed in 1952—and that exists to this day—consists of a governor, a Senate with twenty-seven members, and a House of Representatives with fifty-one members. The officials are elected by residents of the island.

At the constitutional convention, Puerto Ricans redefined their island as a Free Associated State, also called a commonwealth—a self-governing political entity with ties to the United States. As a commonwealth, Puerto Rico handles its own domestic affairs, but relies on the United States for defense and matters of foreign policy. The commonwealth status was reaffirmed by Puerto Ricans in votes held in 1967, 1993, and 1998.

Early Puerto Rican immigration to the United States

Puerto Ricans have been coming to the United States mainland since the late 1800s, with the largest wave of immigration occurring after World War II (1939–1945). Over the years the U.S. mainland has served as a safety valve, relieving overcrowding and unemployment in Puerto Rico.

Between 1870 and 1900, a period of high unemployment on the island, many Puerto Ricans left for other islands in the Caribbean or for the United States. In 1870 Spanish rulers bowed to the demands of Puerto Ricans and abolished slavery. The surge of recently-freed slaves into the general labor market, combined with a shift in production from coffee to less labor-intensive sugar and a sudden growth in population, resulted in Puerto Rico having more workers than jobs. By 1910 about 1,500 Puerto Ricans were living in the United States, two-thirds of them in New York City.

The second wave of immigration—again the result of unemployment on the island—came after the passage of the Jones Act of 1917. Investors from the United States, drawn to Puerto Rico by the cheap cost of labor (about one-fourth of that in the U.S.) and the absence of taxes, acquired large sugar plantations. The U.S. owners brought with them machinery, which made the sugar-harvesting process more efficient while requiring fewer workers. At the same time, independent craftspeople and shoemakers found that they could not compete with low-cost manufactured goods from the United States that were suddenly flooding the island. Many workers, finding themselves out of work, left their homes for the United States.

Puerto Rican immigrants were not greeted warmly. New Yorkers viewed the newcomers as unwelcome competition for jobs. Newspapers and magazines helped create a stereotype of Puerto Ricans as lazy, violent, and sexually promiscuous. In 1926 anti-Puerto Rican sentiment boiled over. Gangs of whites attacked Puerto Ricans in an incident known as the Harlem Riots.

Despite the hostility Puerto Ricans encountered, their presence in New York continued to grow. By 1930 there were more than 53,000 Puerto Ricans in the United States; 45,000 of them were in New York City, mostly in East Harlem, Brooklyn, and the Bronx.

The direction of Puerto Rican migration reversed during the Great Depression of the 1930s, as jobs became scarce in the United States. Puerto Ricans were often blamed by jobless whites for the dismal economic conditions in New York City. Twenty percent of Puerto Ricans on the mainland returned to the island between the years 1930 and 1934.

Puerto Rican immigration after World War II

The largest migration of Puerto Ricans to the United States began in 1945, at the conclusion of World War II. Again, the migration was due to a reduction in the number of jobs on the island. At the same time, the United States was in the middle of an economic boom. The shrinking of the job market in Puerto Rico, particularly in agriculture and light industry, came as the result of a new economic policy called Operation Bootstrap. Implemented in the 1940s, this policy was designed to boost the standard of living of the poorest Puerto Ricans. It shifted the emphasis in production from agriculture to manufacturing.

Around 600,000 Puerto Ricans came to the United States between 1945 and 1955. Many of them took advantage of the cheap airfare from Puerto Rico to New York—just $40 for a one-way ticket in the 1950s. The airfares were offered by new airlines, more than twenty of which sprang up in the postwar years. The airlines ferried passengers between San Juan (Puerto Rico's capital) and New York City, and between San Juan and Miami, Florida, in converted World War II cargo planes.

Most of the new arrivals from Puerto Rico found housing in large, crowded barrios (neighborhoods) in New York City. As Puerto Ricans arrived, they moved to public housing projects in a section of Harlem that came to be known as "Spanish Harlem." Puerto Ricans also made their way to textile mill towns in Rhode Island and Connecticut and to steel mill towns in Pennsylvania, Ohio, and Indiana. Large numbers of Puerto Ricans also found jobs in the factories of Chicago.

Puerto Ricans In Government

Once literacy tests were outlawed by the Voting Rights Act of 1965, Puerto Ricans began to participate in electoral politics in greater numbers than ever before. Puerto Rican representation at all levels of government increased as well. In 1965 Herman Badillo (1929–), a Puerto Rican, was elected to the presidency of the Bronx. (New York City is divided into five districts called boroughs, one of which is the Bronx.) In 1970 Badillo became the first Puerto Rican congressman when he was elected to represent the Twenty-first Congressional District of New York.

Badillo lost reelection to another Puerto Rican candidate, Robert García (1933–), in 1978. In 1967 García had been elected the first Puerto Rican state representative in New York and, in 1968, New York's first Puerto Rican state senator.

Three Puerto Ricans were elected to the U.S. Congress in 1992: Luis Gutiérrez from Chicago and José Serrano and Nydia Velázquez, both from New York City. Upon her election, Velázquez became the first female Puerto Rican member of Congress. Miami elected its first Puerto Rican mayor, Maurice Ferré, in 1973. Ferré served until 1985. In 1989 a female Puerto Rican physician named Antonia Novello was appointed U.S. Surgeon General by President George Bush.

Since 1992 there has been a voting member in Congress from the island of Puerto Rico. The current Puerto Rican representative is Carlos Romero Barceló.

Political organizing in New York City

Puerto Ricans arriving in New York City from the early 1900s onward faced discrimination in housing, jobs, and the criminal justice system. For the most part, landlords would only accept Puerto Ricans as tenants in overcrowded and run-down buildings. Employers would only hire Puerto Ricans for menial and low-paying jobs such as janitors, sweatshop laborers, or farm workers. Police brutality was a daily hazard for the new immigrants.

"The tragedy of Puerto Ricans began the moment they chose New York City," wrote historian Earl Shorris in *Latinos: A Biography of the People.* Shorris continued: "[The city] condemned [Puerto Ricans] to live as the objects of invention even as it set them to furious dreaming. They ceased to be who they were.... In Puerto Rico they had been conquered by force of arms and politics; in the new city they fell victim to disappointment.... New York is a business town, a plantation; the Puerto Ricans came to work—but not to live. New York killed them; it took their health and their hopes; it locked them up in dark rooms; it gave them to the landlords for a gift, a sacrifice. Even worse, it told them who they were and made it impossible for them not to accept that external definition."

Marcantonio's election In response to the injustices around them, Puerto Ricans took to political organizing. One of their first and most substantial victories—for which they cooperated with African Americans, Italian Americans, and Jews—was the election of Vito Marcantonio to the United States Congress. Marcantonio served as congressman from East Harlem from 1934 to 1936 and from 1938 to 1950 (he was denied his base of support and lost the election when district lines were redrawn in 1950.) Although an Italian American by birth, Marcantonio fought for the rights of all oppressed peoples. Marcantonio earned the nickname "the Puerto Rican Congressman" because of his dedication to the concerns of the Puerto Rican community.

Until the passage of the Voting Rights Act of 1965 (see chapter 1, "Passage of the 1965 Voting Rights Act") Puerto Ricans had to pass a literacy test, administered in English, in order to vote. The literacy requirement succeeded in keeping most Puerto Ricans in the United States from voting. Puerto Ricans in Harlem overcame that hurdle, however, with the help of sympathetic whites, many of whom were Jewish. The activists helped prepare the Puerto Ricans to pass the literacy tests, and by 1950 there were 63,000 registered Puerto Rican voters in Harlem.

Puerto Rican civil rights organizations

In addition to becoming active in electoral politics, Puerto Ricans joined together in numerous organizations to defend their rights. One of the most prominent organizations, founded in New York City in the mid-1950s to fight discrimination and poverty, was the Puerto Rican Forum. In 1965 the Puerto Rican Community Development Project was organized as a part of President Lyndon Johnson's War on Poverty to expand job opportunities for Puerto Ricans. The Puerto Rican Legal Defense and Education Fund was founded in 1972 to counter discrimination in housing, employment, and education, as well as to provide legal assistance to Puerto Ricans.

Numerous organizations were created to improve living conditions for Puerto Ricans. For example, the Puerto Rican Association for Community Affairs set up daycare centers, health clinics, and bilingual education programs in New York. The East Harlem Council for Human Services and the Emergency Tenants Council in Boston both succeeded in forcing government agencies to make improvements to public housing structures.

Aspira In 1961 the Puerto Rican Forum and the Puerto Rican Association for Community Affairs teamed up to sponsor a program called Aspira (the Spanish word for strive, or achieve). Aspira assisted Puerto Rican youth to complete high school and encouraged them to continue on to college. Aspira workers taught Puerto Rican students about their cultural background and provided training in leadership and community activism. It was a goal of Aspira to produce a core of young Puerto Ricans prepared to help solve their community's problems. Aspira continues to operate chapters in New York City, Washington, D.C., Miami, and Puerto Rico.

The National Welfare Rights Organization In the 1960s and early 1970s many Puerto Ricans, especially women, joined the National Welfare Rights Organization (NWRO). Recipients of welfare were frequently subjected to harassment and humiliation, and through the NWRO they fought back. The NWRO won several important victories in federal court, among them access to welfare benefits by foreigners legally residing in the United States; the provision of legal assistance for poor people; and a prohibition against unannounced visits by social workers (social workers often came to the doors of welfare recipients to see if they had purchased any new items that could disqualify them from continued benefits).

The Young Lords Party While adult members of the Puerto Rican community were striving to better their conditions through reformist groups, Puerto Rican youth organized themselves into a militant group called the Young Lords Party. The original members of the Young Lords Party came from rival Puerto Rican gangs. The gangs decided to make peace and work for the betterment of their people.

Similar to the African American Black Panther Party (see chapter 1, "The Black Panther Party") and the Chicano Brown Berets, the Young Lords Party engaged in armed self-defense of their communities and held protest actions (such as strikes, sit ins, and boycotts) over living conditions in poor neighborhoods. The platform of the Young Lords Party called for Puerto Rican independence, the inclusion of Puerto Rican culture and Spanish language in the public education system, an end to the Vietnam War (1954–1975), equality for women, and political and economic self-determination. The Young Lords promoted a sense of pride in their Puerto Rican heritage.

First organized in Chicago in 1966, the Young Lords Party quickly spread to Milwaukee; a New York chapter was begun in 1968. In 1970 Young Lords Party members participated in a takeover of Lincoln Hospital in the South Bronx. The group established a day care center in an unused building and demanded improved facilities and services. The Young Lords Party also pushed for improved garbage-collection services in the barrios and set up free health clinics and breakfast programs throughout New York City.

The Puerto Rican independence movement

Since the 1920s a small but vocal group has advocated that Puerto

The Division Street Riot

Overcrowded housing conditions, unemployment, and poverty all contributed to the tension that pervaded Chicago's Puerto Rican neighborhoods in the mid-1960s. In the summer of 1966, just one year after riots by African Americans in the Watts section of Los Angeles claimed thirty-four lives, the tension in Chicago erupted in riots.

The shooting of a twenty-year-old Puerto Rican man named Arcelis Cruz by a white police officer on June 12 set off three days of rioting. Hundreds of young Puerto Ricans protested the shooting by smashing store windows and setting fire to businesses (especially those owned by whites) on Division Street, in the Westtown neighborhood of Chicago. The police responded by beating rioters and setting attack dogs on them.

One Puerto Rican youth was quoted in *The New York Times* of June 14 as saying, "Tell the police we are not supposed to be beaten up like animals. Till you show us you are going to do something to stop this, this thing can't stop because we are human beings." By the time order was restored on June 15, there had been sixteen people wounded, forty-nine people arrested, more than fifty buildings destroyed, and millions of dollars in property damage.

Rico become an independent nation. Advocates of independence, known as *independentistas*, believe that Puerto Rico's association with the United States hinders the island's cultural and economic development.

The sentiments of the *independentistas* are summarized in this passage by Earl Shorris in *Latinos: A Biography of the People*:

> In no remembered, recorded time did the people of Puerto Rico control their destiny; they have always belonged to someone, been a possession, nothing more. Had they been able to escape the monolith of their history by coming to the mainland, they might have freed themselves from the prison of colonialism, but coming to the mainland was not an act of immigration. The Puerto Ricans merely migrated; they remained colonized.

The *independentistas* have operated both on the island and on the mainland, and have employed both legal and extralegal means. The governments of Puerto Rico and the United States have long regarded the independence movement as traitorous. Consequently, the activity of *independentistas* has been repressed through a series of laws. Many independence activists have been jailed; their fate serves as a warning to any Puerto Rican considering joining the independence movement.

The father of the independence movement The father of the independence movement was Pedro Albizu Campos (1891–1965), a Harvard-educated lawyer affectionately called "El Maestro" ("The Teacher"). Albizu Campos founded Puerto Rico's Nationalist Party in 1928, the slogan of which was "Puerto Rico for the Puerto Ricans." The Nationalist Party lost the 1932 elections, which it claimed were unfair because of the presence of thousands of gun-toting U.S. troops.

In 1936 Albizu Campos was arrested for advocating the "overthrow of the government of the United States established in Puerto Rico." After being acquitted by one jury, he was convicted by a second jury and spent twenty-five of the final twenty-nine years of his life behind bars. Albizu Campos's conviction sparked widespread protests throughout the island and Puerto Rican communities on the mainland.

Movement marked by violence On March 21, 1937, U.S. soldiers cracked down on Nationalist Party supporters in Ponce, Puerto Rico, where the party was headquartered. The soldiers opened fire on Ponce citizens headed to a mass on Palm Sunday. At least twenty people were killed, most of them children, and more than 100 people were wounded. The Ponce Massacre set off fresh rounds of demonstrations by some 10,000 Puerto Ricans in New York City.

In 1950, when the Nationalist Party was being suffocated by a group of new anti-independence laws, two *independentistas* attempted to assassinate President Harry S Truman. Truman escaped unharmed, but a police officer and an *independentista* were killed. Just two days earlier, five *independentistas* had tried to kill Puerto Rican Governor Luis Muñoz Marín.

Although the governor had escaped unharmed, the five nationalists were killed—but not before they had blown up the governor's residence.

In 1954 a group of *independentistas* opened fire from the visitors' gallery of the U.S. House of Representatives, yelling "Free Puerto Rico now!" The gunmen wounded five members of Congress before being subdued.

The Macheteros

The year 1978 saw the founding of the Macheteros (machete-wielders; a machete is a long knife used to cut sugar cane), a militant group of Puerto Rican independence fighters. The Macheteros, active through the 1980s, conducted their affairs as if they were at war with the United States government. The Macheteros undertook numerous attacks against U.S. government and military personnel in Puerto Rico as well as Puerto Rican security forces protecting U.S. interests.

The Macheteros have also conducted a series of robberies to finance their operations. The most famous robbery occurred in 1983: a Machetero named Victor Genera, who was working as a guard for the Wells Fargo armored car company in West Hartford, Connecticut, stole $7 million from the Wells Fargo depot. It was later discovered that Genera was a member of the Macheteros and that the robbery had been planned by a network of *independentistas* in both Puerto Rico and the United States. By the end of the 1980s many of the Machetero's leaders were either dead or in jail.

The Puerto Rican Independence Party
The Puerto Rican Independence Party (PIP) is the foremost organization advocating independence for Puerto Rico. According to an opinion poll conducted on the island in 1995, just 7 percent of Puerto Ricans would support a PIP candidate for president.

The continuing debate over Puerto Rico's status

Puerto Rico's status as a commonwealth associated with the United States is a matter of continual debate. In three nonbinding referendums, Puerto Rican voters have opted to remain a commonwealth (rather than becoming a state of the United States or becoming an independent nation). The first time the question was put to voters in 1967, 61 percent favored continuing as a commonwealth. Thirty-nine percent favored statehood. Proponents of independence boycotted the vote, calling it a mere "opinion poll" rather than a binding answer to the island's fate. The results of the second referendum, held in 1993, were: 48 percent for commonwealth; 46 percent for statehood; and 4 percent for independence. In a November 1998 referendum, 50.2 percent of voters opted for commonwealth and 46.5 percent opted for statehood.

The current representative in U.S. Congress from Puerto Rico, Carlos Romero Barceló, is from the New Progressive Party, which favors statehood. Barcelós's party points out that if Puerto Rico were a state, it would be entitled to seven members in the U.S. House of Representatives and two members in the Senate, and residents of Puerto Rico could participate in presidential elections. Additionally, he claims that statehood would result in greater economic and political security for Puerto Rico.

Opponents of statehood argue that as a state Puerto Rico would lose its tax exemptions that attract so many U.S. manufacturers. Those manufacturers may then move to Mexico or other third-world countries where production costs are low. The U.S. Congressional Budget Office has estimated that statehood would cost Puerto Rico 100,000 jobs over ten years.

Proponents of continued commonwealth status point out that as a commonwealth, Puerto Rico maintains its cultural identity while benefitting economically from its close association with the United States. Undoubtedly, Puerto Rican voters will again be faced with deciding their homeland's status in the future.

Cubans and Dominicans in the United States

People from Cuba and the Dominican Republic represent the two next largest groups of Hispanic Americans, after Mexicans and Puerto Ricans. Among the Cuban and Dominican immigrants are many refugees—people who came to the United States to escape political conditions not to their liking, or outright political persecution, in their respective homelands.

Cubans have historically received a much warmer welcome in this country than have Dominicans. The disparity between the groups regarding ease of immigration and assistance once in the United States is intricately connected to U.S. foreign policy toward each group's home nation.

There are more than 1.1 million Cubans in the United States, the majority of them in the greater Miami area. With a 1992 average household income of $35,594, Cubans earn more money than any other Hispanic group. And with 16.5 percent of all Cubans in the United States age twenty-five or older holding a bachelor's degree or higher, Cubans are the best-educated of all Hispanic groups.

Since 1994 U.S. immigration quotas have allowed 20,000 Cubans per year into the United States. Prior to 1994 Cuban immigration into the United States was not only limitless but was encouraged.

Cuban immigration to the United States

Cuban immigration into the United States—particularly into Florida, the southern tip of which is only ninety miles north of Cuba—began in 1830. The first Cubans in the United States were cigar manufacturers who opened factories in Key West, Florida, and brought along their Cuban workers. From the 1830s until 1959, about 70,000 Cubans moved to Florida. Most of these immigrants left Cuba during its many periods of political

After assuming power in 1959, Fidel Castro sought to improve the standard of living for Cuba's poorest citizens by redistributing land and nationalizing the island's natural resources and industries. *Reproduced by permission of Archive Photos.*

unrest, the most recent being the 1952–1959 reign of U.S.-backed dictator Fulgencio Batista.

Castro's rise to power The most significant period of Cuban immigration, during which around one million Cubans came to the United States, began with the Cuban Revolution in 1959. The revolution against Batista's corrupt and abusive government was led by a young lawyer with a penchant for rousing speeches named Fidel Castro (1927–). Upon taking power, Castro sought to improve the standard of living for Cuba's poorest citizens by redistributing land and nationalizing (taking government control of) the island's natural resources and industries. Cubans who criticized or attempted to sabotage the government's plans were jailed or even sentenced to death.

Politicians, businessmen, and wealthy tourists in the United States were outraged at Cuba's economic restructuring; they also voiced opposition to Cuba's human rights abuses. Under Batista, U.S. investments had been protected and investors had turned a handy profit. Castro shut down these opportunities. To make matters worse (in the eyes of the U.S. power structure), Cuba had entered into an alliance with the Soviet Union at the height of the Cold War. (The Cold War was the period of tense relations, lasting from 1945 to 1990, between the former Soviet Union and the United States.)

Ever since Castro took power, the United States has attempted to topple the Cuban government using a variety of economic and political means. One strategy used by the United States from 1959 to 1994 was to encourage wealthy, middle-class, and professional Cubans to leave the island. Policymakers in the United States anticipated that the exodus of wealth and knowledge would be a setback to Castro's Cuba. President Dwight D. Eisenhower, who held office from 1953 to 1961, spearheaded

an effort to organize Cuban refugees into a military force to overthrow Castro. That effort was brought to fruition in 1961 by President John F. Kennedy, in the unsuccessful invasion by Cuban exiles—trained and armed by the United States—at the Bay of Pigs.

In the first ten years of Castro's rule, nearly 500,000 Cubans came to the United States. Many of these refugees were businesspeople, technicians, doctors, teachers, and other professionals. Under the Cuban Refugee Program, the U.S. government provided the newcomers with nearly one billion dollars of assistance in housing, English-language instruction, small business loans, job placement services, medical care, and college scholarships for Cuban youth.

"When you said that you were a Cuban," commented one refugee in Miami, "it sounded like a magic word that opened every door. Employers demonstrated their willingness towards Cubans.... Landlords gladly rented out their apartments.... Colleges and universities started to hire Cuban professors, and adolescents in the high schools were winners of outstanding awards."

The Mariel Boatlift In the 1970s and 1980s the Cuban government first loosened, then lifted, its restrictions on leaving the island. These policy changes sparked a new wave of Cuban migration to the United States. The largest exodus of Cubans was in April 1980, when Castro gave blanket permission for anyone who wished to

A street in Miami, Florida's "Little Havana." *Photo by Russell Thompson. Reproduced by permission of Archive Photos.*

leave Cuba. The Cuban community in Florida obtained a fleet of forty-two boats and, in an operation called the Mariel Boatlift, transported more than 125,000 Cubans (known as Marielitos) to the United States by the end of 1980.

Whereas the earlier group of Cuban refugees had been largely wealthy and white, the Marielitos were a mixed group containing many poor and dark-skinned people. And, as U.S. officials later learned, among the Marielitos were convicted felons released from Cuban prisons. The Marielitos did not receive the same hospitality as the earlier Cuban immigrants. After being herded through processing centers, the Marielitos were housed in tent cities and even in a Miami football stadium. There they had to wait for months and sometimes years until U.S. citizens agreed to sponsor them. The wait was longest for Marielitos who did not have family members already in the United States.

Immigration policy changes in 1994
In 1994 the Clinton Administration placed restrictions on Cuban immigration for the first time in U.S. history. The move was prompted by a mass exodus of Cubans in August 1994. Wishing to leave behind the island's depressed economy, the refugees boarded rafts and makeshift boats for the ninety-mile ocean crossing. The governor of Florida expressed fears about the disruption that would be caused by the sudden arrival of 26,000 refugees. In response, President Bill Clinton ordered the U.S. Coast Guard

to intercept the refugees at sea and to take them to the U.S. Naval base at Guantánamo Bay, Cuba.

The refugees were held in deplorable conditions at makeshift camps at Guantánamo Bay for several weeks until a pact was reached between President Clinton and President Castro. Castro agreed to stop future boat migrations, and Clinton agreed to allow 20,000 Cubans per year to enter the United States.

The United States' present-day immigration policy toward Cuba is motivated by different factors than it was in previous decades. While U.S. politicians are still committed to undermining Castro's government, they no longer believe that encouraging immigration furthers that goal. Most Cubans wishing to leave the island today are neither wealthy nor professionals. Moreover, immigration to the United States has become something of a safety valve for the Cuban government—it serves to lessen the impact of unemployment and shortages of resources. Another factor in the shift in today's U.S. immigration policy regarding Cubans is the general anti-immigrant attitude that exists in the United States. While Cubans are still treated better than any other group of Latino immigrants, they no longer reap the same benefits enjoyed by their predecessors.

Dominican immigration to the United States
The Dominican Republic is situated on the eastern two-thirds of the

Caribbean island of Hispaniola (Haiti occupies the western third). Recent estimates place the number of immigrants from the Dominican Republic in the United States, including those here "illegally," at over one million. Dominicans now rival Cubans as the third-most-populous Latino group in the nation.

Many Dominican immigrants live in New York City, New Jersey, Florida, Washington, D.C., and cities throughout the northeastern United States. The largest concentration of immigrants from the Dominican Republic is in New York City's Washington Heights, a fifty-block area in upper Manhattan. There are also large numbers of Dominicans in Puerto Rico. Many Dominicans, posing as Puerto Ricans (who can freely migrate to the United States), use the island as a jumping-off point for the United States.

Twenty thousand Dominicans are allowed to legally enter the United States each year. Many of them are given temporary student visas or are admitted under policies that allow immigrants to join their families in the United States. Most of these "legal" immigrants are from the middle or professional classes.

In recent years the number of undocumented Dominicans in the United States has grown dramatically. Around 20,000 of these "illegal" immigrants each year, desperate to escape the oppressive political and economic conditions on the island, risk death by traveling in flimsy boats through eighty miles of shark-infested waters to Puerto Rico. About 10 percent of these "boat people" do not survive the journey. About 60 percent of the people who make it to Puerto Rico are deported back to the Dominican Republic. Of the remaining 30 percent, some refugees remain in Puerto Rico. Others make their way to the United States where they find work in textile sweatshops, restaurants, and hotels, or as migrant farm workers along the East Coast, living in constant fear of deportation.

Despite overwhelming evidence that Dominicans are fleeing political repression in their homeland, the United States does not recognize Dominicans as "political refugees." The U.S. government has been accused of employing a double standard in its definition of "political refugee," especially regarding its treatment of Cubans and Dominicans. The Cubans, who are fleeing a government that the United States opposes, are considered political refugees; the Dominicans, who are fleeing a government the United States supports, are not.

The first Dominican immigrants

Dominican immigration to the United States began around 1900. The first Dominican immigrants were farmers who had been forced off their land by foreign investors (mostly from the United States) who were setting up sugar and coffee plantations. In 1916 the U.S. Marines occupied the Dominican Republic in order to protect the lands of U.S. investors. During the eight-year occupation, the living standards of Dominicans dropped dramatically, and the public education system fell into disarray.

By the time the Marines left the island in 1924, more than one-quarter of all land was in the hands of foreign-owned sugar companies—80 percent of those companies were based in the United States. In 1924 Americans controlled 33.7 million dollars worth of property on the island, while Dominican assets totaled just 1.4 million dollars. Before they left the Dominican Republic, the Marines trained and left in their place the Dominican National Guard. From 1930 to 1961 the Dominican National Guard backed dictator Molina Trujillo. Trujillo presided over one of the most brutal regimes in Latin America.

Violence and political upheaval

Dominican emigration slowed significantly during the first two decades of Trujillo's reign, largely due to policies making emigration illegal. During Trujillo's final eleven years, however, nearly 10,000 Dominicans found a way off the island.

Trujillo was assassinated in 1961. The following year the Dominican Republic saw its first democratically elected government, headed by President Juan Bosch. The Dominican Republic's experiment with democracy, however, was short-lived. Bosch was overthrown by a U.S.-backed military coup in 1963. In 1965 the U.S. Marines occupied the Dominican Republic to prevent Bosch's return to power.

The following period was one of the bloodiest in the history of the Dominican Republic. Military units called "death squads" hunted and killed many pro-democracy activists. The 1960s and 1970s saw the exodus of hundreds of thousands of Dominicans for U.S. shores. In the early 1980s the Dominican army used force to put down a series of strikes and demonstrations. Around half a million Dominicans came to the United States during the 1980s.

Discrimination in New York City

Dominican immigrants in New York City, especially those who are poor and dark-skinned, face a daily battle against racism and discrimination. Dominicans, who have been stereotyped as drug dealers, have even been spurned by members of other Latino groups.

In 1992 a policeman in New York City's Washington Heights section shot and killed a Dominican suspected of selling crack cocaine. The shooting provoked riots by the Dominican community. The social justice organization Alianza de Dominicanos Progresistas (Alliance of Progressive Dominicans) extracted promises of improved police conduct in Dominican neighborhoods. The following year police shot a Dominican bicyclist. That incident set off a new rash of protests against police brutality.

Sources

Books

Boswell, Thomas D. and James R. Curtis. *The Cuban American Experience: Culture, Images and Perspectives*. Totowa, NJ: Rowman & Allanheld Publishers, 1983.

Chomsky, Noam. *Turning the Tide: U.S. Intervention in Central America and the Struggle for Peace*. Boston: South End Press, 1985.

Cockroft, James D. *The Hispanic Struggle for Social Justice*. New York: Franklin Watts, 1994.

Cockroft, James D. *Latinos in the Making of the United States*. New York: Franklin Watts, 1995.

De Varona, Frank. *Latino Literacy: The Complete Guide to Our Hispanic History and Culture*. New York: Henry Holt, 1996.

Fernandez, Ronald. *Los Macheteros: The Wells Fargo Robbery and the Violent Struggle for Puerto Rican Independence*. New York: Prentice-Hall Press, 1987.

Fitzpatrick, Joseph P. *Puerto Rican Americans: The Meaning of Migration to the Mainland*. Englewood Cliffs, NJ: Prentice-Hall, Inc., 1971.

Fox, Geoffrey. *Hispanic Nation: Culture, Politics, and the Constructing of Identity*. Secaucus, NJ: Birch Lane Press Book, 1996.

Frost-Knappman, Elizabeth, Edward W. Knappman, and Lisa Paddock, eds. *Courtroom Drama*. Detroit: U•X•L, 1998, pp. 215–220.

Garcia, Chris F., ed. *Pursuing Power: Latinos and the Political System*. South Bend, IN: University of Notre Dame Press, 1997.

Graham, Hugh Davis, ed. *Civil Rights in the United States*. University Park, PA: Pennsylvania State University Press, 1994.

Kanellos, Nicholás and Bryan Ryan, eds. *Hispanic American Chronology*. Detroit, MI: U•X•L, 1996.

Karst, Kenneth L., Leonard W. Levy, and Dennis J. Mahoney, eds. *Civil Rights and Equality*. New York: Macmillan Publishing Company, 1986.

Mapp, Edward, ed. *Puerto Rican Perspectives*. Metuchen, NJ: The Scarecrow Press, 1974.

Martinez, Elizabeth Sutherland and Enriqueta Longeaux y Vásquez. *Viva la Raza!: The Struggle of the Mexican-American People*. Garden City, NY: Doubleday & Company, Inc., 1974.

Oboler, Suzanne. *Ethnic Labels, Latino Lives: Identity and the Politics of (Re)Presentation in the United States*. Minneapolis: University of Minnesota Press, 1995.

Padilla, Felix M. *Puerto Rican Chicago*. South Bend, IN: University of Notre Dame Press, 1987.

Rosales, F. Arturo. *Chicano! The History of the Mexican American Civil Rights Movement*. Houston, TX: Arte Público Press, 1997.

Ryan, Bryan and Nicolás Kanellos, eds. *Hispanic American Almanac*. Detroit: U•X•L, 1995.

Ryan, Bryan and Nicol's Kanellos, eds. *Hispanic American Chronology*. Detroit: U•X•L, 1996.

Shorris, Earl. *Latinos: A Biography of the People*. New York: W.W. Norton, 1992.

Sigler, Jay A., ed. *Civil Rights in America: 1500 to the Present*. Detroit: Gale, 1998, pp. 159–218.

Steiner, Stan. *La Raza: The Mexican-Americans*. New York: Harper & Row, 1969.

Thernstrom, Abigail M. *Whose Votes Count?: Affirmative Action and Minority Voting Rights*. Cambridge, MA: Harvard University Press, 1987.

Periodicals

"Amnesty Criticizes U.S. Border Patrol." Associated Press. May 20, 1998.

Bacon, David. "Mexico's New Braceros." *The Nation*. January 27, 1997: 18–21.

"California: Judge Won't Block Proposition 227." *The Ann Arbor News*. July 16, 1998: A3.

Fox, Ben "Promised Land: U.S. Efforts Force Migrants onto Dangerous Routes." *The Ann Arbor News*. April 15, 1999: A8.

"Group Fights to Keep Bilingual Education." *The Ann Arbor News.* June 4, 1998: A3.

"Probe Finds Violations at Vineyards." Associated Press. September 16, 1998.

"Puerto Rico: Voters Reject Nonbinding Referendum on Statehood." *The Ann Arbor News.* December 14, 1998: A3.

"Rights Group Focuses on Immigrants' Death." *The Ann Arbor News.* February 11, 1999: A3.

Rodriguez, Gregory. "English Lesson in California." *The Nation.* April 20, 1998: 15–19.

Ross, Sonia. "Race Panel Cites 'White Privilege'." Associated Press. September 19, 1998.

"Teenage Boy Killed Shot and Killed by Marines." Associated Press. September 10, 1998.

"United States Has More Hispanic than Black Children." Associated Press. July 15, 1998.

"White House Opposes Bilingual Education Ban." Associated Press. April 27, 1998.

Wieland, Robert G. "PBS Revisits 'Forgotten' War Between U.S., Mexico." *The Ann Arbor News.* September 12, 1998: D8.

Web Sites

Amnesty International. "From San Diego to Brownsville: Human Rights Violations on the USA-Mexico Border" May 20, 1998. [Online] Available http://www. amnesty.org//news/1998/25103398.htm. (last accessed March 31, 1999).

César Chávez School. "Prop 227 Updates." [Online] Available http://www.sfusd.k12. ca/us/schwww/sch603/227.htm. (last accessed March 28, 1999).

Jackson, Bernice Powell/Commission for Racial Justice of the United Church of Christ. "Border Justice." [Online] Available http: //www.ucc.org/justice/crj/cr060997 (last accessed March 31, 1999).

MSNBC. "LAUSD Exposes Prop 227 Strategy." July 21, 1998. [Online] Available http:// www.msnbc.com/local/KNBC/1114701. asp (last accessed March 31, 1999).

Pringle, Paul. "California Bilingual Vote Reverberates." *The Dallas Morning News.* June 4, 1998. [Online] Available http:// www. dallasnews.com/in-the-news-nf/nat18. html (last accessed March 31, 1999).

Saldana, Lori/Sierra Club (San Diego Chapter). "The Downside of the Border Boom." [Online] Available http://www. sierraclub.org/trade/SALDANA.HTML (last accessed March 31, 1999).

Other

Chicano! The History of the Mexican American Civil Rights Movement (four episodes; videocassette). Los Angeles: NLCC Educational Media, 1996.

Civil Rights of Native Americans

Civil rights for Native Americans are defined somewhat differently than they are for other racial minority groups in the United States. Native Americans are citizens not only of the United States, but of their respective tribes. Accordingly, Native American civil rights are not only about individual rights—such as the right to vote or the right to obtain housing or employment free from discrimination—but are also about collective rights, such as the right of tribes to govern themselves or the right to tribal lands guaranteed by treaty.

Native Americans' dual role as people of color as well as tribal citizens has often worked against them. Like other racial minorities, Native Americans have been, and continue to be, subjected to a range of racist and discriminatory policies on the part of individuals and government agencies. Native Americans have been prevented from voting, have been made to attend segregated schools, and have been denied access to decent jobs and housing. And because of the tribes' official designation as "wards of the state," Native Americans have been subjected to a series of government policies that have stampeded over Indian lives, lands, cultural values, and traditions.

Indian people have managed to maintain a viable and cohesive social order in spite of everything the non-Indian society has thrown at them in an effort to break the tribal structure. At the same time, non-Indian society has created a monstrosity of a culture where people starve while the granaries are filled and the sun can never break through the smog.

Vine Deloria Jr., in the New York Times Magazine, *March 8, 1970*

A Discussion of Labels

There is no one universally agreed-upon term to describe the original inhabitants of the land that is now the United States. While some people prefer the term Native American, others prefer Native American Indian, American Indian, Indian, or native peoples. The legal term, used by the federal government and most federally-recognized tribes in their official names, is Indian.

As is the case with Hispanic Americans, Native Americans are not a single group of people with common roots—rather, they come from many different nations, also called tribes. While many native groups have shared values and cultures, their members practice many different religions, speak many different languages, and observe many different traditions. For these reasons, the most appropriate labels for Native American peoples are the names of their particular tribes, such as Sioux, Cherokee, Cree, Menominee, Hopi, and Navajo.

Throughout history, there has been a great deal of confusion regarding Native Americans' legal status. Although Native American tribes are considered sovereign (independent or self-governing) entities under the terms of more than 400 treaties drafted before 1871, they are also subjected to many of the federal, state, and local laws that govern the lives of all U.S. citizens. It is often the case that laws set by the various levels of U.S. government conflict with rules established by tribal governments. When legal conflicts arise on reservations, the outcome is typically decided by the U.S. court system.

The relocation of Indians in the nineteenth century

During the 1800s U.S. lawmakers and military leaders were preoccupied with fulfilling the nation's Manifest Destiny (the belief that the United States had a God-given right to all the territory between the Atlantic and Pacific Oceans). One obstacle to Manifest Destiny was that much of the desired land was already taken, either by Mexicans or by Indians. Undeterred, U.S. officials set out to conquer the land by force. In the process they killed tens of thousands of Native Americans.

Large portions of what is now the southwestern United States were ceded by Mexico following the U.S.-Mexico War (see chapter 3, "The U.S. takes over Mexican land"). Native American tribes, which occupied large territories throughout the present-day United States, were defeated one at a time and forced to sign treaties in which they ceded their land. The conquered peoples were moved onto small, and often undesirable, parcels of land.

The Indian Removal Act and forcible westward migration

The first push westward of the newly independent United States was onto lands between the Appalachian Mountains and the Mississippi River, which were previously owned by Great Britain. As settlers made their way to the territory in present-day Ohio, Illinois, Indiana, Kentucky, Tennessee, Alabama, and Mississippi, they often came into violent conflict with the various tribes occupying those lands. In order to secure the region for white settlers, the U.S. government in the early 1800s began the forcible removal of Native American tribes to lands west of the Mississippi River (where they assumed few whites would want to live).

In 1830 President Andrew Jackson signed the Indian Removal Act, which called for the relocation of Native Americans living east of the Mississippi to a tract of land called "Indian Territory" (present-day Oklahoma). Native Americans resisted relocation, sometimes by violent means. In the end, however, the Native Americans were defeated and were forced to move. Almost every treaty signed between the United States and native tribes in the mid-1830s stipulated that the Indians would move to Indian Territory. In all, nearly 100,000 Indians were moved west of the Mississippi under the terms of the Indian Removal Act. The removal was nearly complete by the end of the 1830s.

The Trail of Tears

The relocation of dozens of Native American tribes to Indian Territory in the 1830s and 1840s meant that people were forced to march for hundreds of miles. Five eastern tribes—

Geronimo, a Chiricahua Apache, became famous for his fierce resistance to U.S. expansion into the southwestern territories. *Reproduced by permission of the Library of Congress.*

Cherokee, Chickasaw, Choctaw, Creek, and Seminole—made the 800-mile trip during the cold winter months, with inadequate clothing and food. This march, known as the "Trail of Tears," was extremely difficult, and many people died along the way.

The term "Trail of Tears" is sometimes applied specifically to the forced march of the Cherokees. The Cherokee Nation fought removal through the legal system and won in

The Constitutional Status of Native Americans

The Constitution of the United States, which took effect in 1789, defines Native Americans not as U.S. citizens but as citizens of sovereign (independent or self-governing) nations, or tribes. The Constitution regards Indian tribes as foreign entities with whom Congress can make treaties and regulate commerce. (Indian tribes are the only groups inside U.S. borders with whom the federal government has negotiated treaties.) It establishes that the federal government has precedence over state and local governments in regulating Indian affairs and names the Department of War (later renamed the Department of Defense) as the agency responsible for negotiating treaties with Indian tribes.

Native Americans are first referred to in the Constitution in Article 1, Section 2, regarding representation in the House of Representatives. This article states that Indians, who are not subject to taxation, are not to be counted in state populations.

Article 1, Section 8, declares that Congress has the exclusive power to "regulate commerce with foreign nations, and among the several states, and with the Indian tribes." This clause was intended to end the confusion caused by contradictory state and national laws governing Indian affairs. Furthermore, it defines Indian tribes as independent nations and stipulates that treaties negotiated with Indian tribes have the same legal standing as treaties made with foreign sovereign nations.

Article 6 states that "all treaties made, or which shall be made, under the authority of the United States, shall be the supreme law of the land." Native Americans have long interpreted this to mean that treaties, negotiated by Congress with the powers vested by the Constitution, are sacred and everlasting.

In 1871 the U.S. government ceased making treaties with Native Americans and declared that the U.S. Congress would thereafter be charged with crafting legislation to govern Native American affairs. The new relationship between the U.S. government and Indian tribes was defined as one of "trust"—in other words, the United States had a responsibility to act in the best interest of Native Americans and to honor Indian treaty rights.

the Supreme Court (*Worcester v. Georgia,* 1832). President Jackson, however, chose to disregard the court ruling and sent in troops to evict the Cherokees. More than 4,000 Cherokee Indians perished during the wintertime march.

The Long Walk of the Navajos

Forcible relocation was not limited to the eastern United States. As settlers pushed farther westward, they provoked violent conflicts with Native Americans living on desirable

The Trickery of Treaties

Native American tribes, greatly weakened by the combined effects of war with the white settlers and diseases brought to the continent by Europeans, were forced to sign treaties with the U.S. government. In those treaties the United States promised supplies and services in exchange for large tracts of Indian land. Between 1778 and 1871 more than 400 treaties were made between the United States and Indian nations. As a result of those treaties and subsequent agreements made through the mid-1900s, Native Americans lost 98 percent of their land.

There are many indications that the treaties made during that period were unfair and tricked native peoples into giving up their lands. Native Americans had a different understanding of law, politics, and treaties than did U.S. diplomats. To the natives, land was not something that could be given away, even through a treaty. For centuries Indian tribes had made treaties with one another in which they agreed to share

territory. It is reasonable to assume that in making treaties with the United States, Indians believed they were allowing the government to share, but not possess, their land.

Native Americans also regarded treaties as living documents that could change over time as circumstances changed. The natives did not regard a treaty as an agreement through which one could permanently cede one's land. Furthermore, Indian custom dictated that decisions regarding their land could only be made by the entire tribe, since the entire tribe collectively owned the land. It was unthinkable that one or two members of the group could sign a document that would give away the group's land.

In an attempt to rectify these past injustices, modern government policy is that treaties made with Native Americans are to be interpreted from the point of view of the Native Americans at the time the treaties were signed.

lands. In 1860 Navajo Indians attempted to retake a portion of their land that had been conquered by U.S. forces two years earlier. U.S. troops put down the Navajo resistance, and the tribe's fields, orchards, and livestock were destroyed. Facing starvation, the tribe accepted the order to vacate its lands.

In 1864 thousands of Navajos undertook the Long Walk—a miserable 400-mile march to the Bosque Redondo reservation near Fort Sumner, New Mexico. Along the route the Navajos had insufficient food and were mistreated by U.S. soldiers. One in ten marchers died en route. Some of those who were unable to continue were shot by soldiers; others were picked up by slave traders.

When the survivors arrived at their destination (which was already crowded with other conquered Indian groups), they found hard-packed desert soil and no water. The only visible wildlife was swarms of grasshoppers. There were no forests for miles. The Indians suffered from a lack of food, clothing, and fuel. Many succumbed to disease. In July 1968 the U.S. government allowed the Navajos to return to a reservation created on one-tenth of their original land.

Indian Appropriations Act ends treaty-making

By 1870 the U.S. conquest of Indian lands was virtually complete. Indians had been moved onto reservations and had grown dependent on U.S. government assistance for their survival. The time had come to redefine the nature of the relationship between the United States and American Indian tribes. Ratified in 1871, the Indian Appropriations Act ended the era of treaty-making. The governments of the United States and the Indian nations would no longer interact as two sovereign nations; the U.S. was thereafter considered the guardian (or parent) and the Indian people, its ward (or children).

Under the terms of the Indian Appropriations Act, Indian affairs would be legislated by Congress. The U.S. government claimed sweeping powers to interfere in tribal affairs, without the consent of tribal governments. These powers were in direct violation of the sovereignty and self-government clauses in virtually every treaty made with Native American nations.

While the United States had previously acquired Indian land through treaties, after 1871 it acquired land through sales agreements. The agreements were essentially the same as treaties except that the native tribes were no longer recognized as sovereign nations.

The Supreme Court, in deciding the 1886 case *United States v. Kagama*, upheld the constitutionality of the federal government's jurisdiction in Indian matters. In part, the Court decision read:

[T]hey [Native Americans] are spoken of as 'wards of the nation,' 'pupils,' as local dependent communities. In this spirit the United States has conducted relations to them from its organization to this time.... These Indian tribes *are* wards of the nation. They are communities *dependent* on the United States.... From their very weakness and helplessness, so largely due to the dealing of the Federal Government with them, and its treaties in which it has been promised, there arises the duty of protection, and with it the power. The power of the General Government over these remnants of a race once powerful, now weak and diminished in numbers, is necessary to their protection, as well as the safety of those among whom they dwell.

Allotment and the loss of Native American lands

In 1871 Native American reservations accounted for about one-fourth of all territory between the Mississippi River and the Rocky Mountains. By the early 1900s most of this land had been transferred to the U.S. government or to non-Indian U.S. citizens. The most effective weapon in the U.S. land-acquisition arsenal was allotment—the practice of dividing up reservation lands and parceling them out to individual Indians.

Allotment policy was promoted by land-hungry speculators, white liberal Indian-rights defenders (called reformers), and policymakers alike. The speculators believed, correctly, that allotment would provide them access to Indian lands. Reformers mistakenly believed that the granting of land titles to individual Native Americans was the best way to protect those lands from further appropriation by whites. And policymakers believed that individual ownership, plus the granting of American citizenship that accompanied land titles, would help teach Indians "American values" and would mold them into independent, productive citizens.

As it turned out, allotment was disastrous for Indian communities. Under the traditional system of communal land ownership, Indians had access to large tracts of land. On that vast land, native peoples could support themselves by hunting or grazing livestock. Limited to a small piece of land, the only choice was to farm, but many

What's In a Treaty?

Most of the treaties made between the United States and Indian tribes between 1778 and 1871 contained the following five elements:

1. Indians would give up their land and move onto reservations (land set aside by the United States government).

2. Tribes would remain independent, self-governing entities and would be protected from foreign invaders by the United States.

3. The U.S. government would provide Indians on reservations with food, medical services, schools, and other supplies and services.

4. Native people would have rights to the water and minerals as well as fishing and hunting rights on the reservations (and sometimes on the lands they previously occupied).

5. The U.S. government would have jurisdiction over matters (such as crime or trading) involving non-Indians who were either on reservations, or engaged in dealings with Indians on reservations.

of the land parcels were not suitable for farming. In order to pay for basic living expenses, many Indians quickly (and illegally) sold their land. The buyers were usually non-Indians.

Native Americans resented having this change of lifestyle forced upon them. Not only did allotment rob native peoples of their lands, but it undermined their culture. Whereas Indian tribes believed in collective ownership of land, allotment necessitated individual ownership. Allotment also struck a heavy blow against the authority of tribal governments, since a significant function of those bodies had been the oversight of reservation land.

The General Allotment Act

The practice of allotment began in the 1850s. Sixty Indian treaties made between 1853 and 1857 called for the allotment of tribal lands. Allotment achieved the status of national policy in 1887, with the passage of the General Allotment Act (also called the Dawes General Allotment Act after its sponsor, Senator Henry Dawes of Massachusetts). The act called for the distribution of 160 acres of reservation land to each head of household, and smaller pieces of land to other family members.

Upon receiving his or her allotment, an Indian would be made a U.S. citizen. To prevent individuals from selling off their allotments, the government put the land into a trust and ruled that it could not be sold for a period of twenty-five years (this stipulation was frequently overlooked). The Dawes Act was amended in 1891 to provide only 80 acres per tribal member and to allow the leasing of allotted land to mining, ranching, timber, and agricultural companies.

Only two senators—Henry Moore Teller of Colorado and John Tyler Morgan of Alabama—joined the chorus of American Indian voices opposing the passage of the General Allotment Act. "Now, divide up this land and you will in a few years deprive the Indians a resting place on the face of this continent," stated Senator Teller. He continued: "No man who has studied this question intelligently, and who has the Indian interest at heart, can talk about dividing this land.... It is in the interest of speculators; it is in the interest of the men who are clutching up this land, but not in the interest of the Indians at all.... Mr. President, what I complain of in connection with this Indian business is that practical common sense is not applied to it.... This is a bill that, in my judgment, ought to be entitled 'A bill to despoil the Indians of their lands and to make them vagabonds on the face of the earth,' because, in my view, that is the result of this kind of legislation."

At the time of the Dawes Act's passage, there were 300,000 Indians living on 155 million acres of reservation land. After the parcels had been doled out, more than 100 million acres of land remained (it was called "surplus land"). The surplus land was offered for sale and was quickly bought by non-Indian land developers. The proceeds from the sale of surplus land were supposed to go to the tribes; however, in many cases the tribes did not receive the money.

Because of their fierce resistance to allotment, Native Americans living in Indian Territory in Oklahoma, as well as the Senecas of New

York and the Sioux in Nebraska, were initially exempted from the General Allotment Act. With the passage of the Curtis Act in 1898, allotment was extended to Indian land in Oklahoma.

The land grab continues into the early 1900s

The appetite of white land speculators, real estate agents, merchants, and corrupt government officials for Indian land was insatiable. In the early 1900s the federal government decided that the General Allotment Act had not gone far enough. The U.S. Congress passed a series of laws aimed at extracting even more land from Native Americans.

In 1902 the federal government began the process of voiding the twenty-five year waiting period for the sale of land allotments. In 1906 the Secretary of the Interior was empowered to exempt from the waiting period adult Indians deemed competent. By 1924 nearly 30,000 Indians had received exemptions and sold lands totaling 27 million acres at deflated prices.

The passage of the Dead Indian Act in 1902 made it legal for Indians to sell land they had inherited from relatives who had died. Four years later the Alaska Allotment Act extended the allotment policy to native peoples living in Alaska. The allotment era ended in 1934, with the passage of the Indian Reorganization Act (see *"Meriam Report* calls for reforms"). By that time Native American land holdings totaled less than 50 million acres, half of which

In October 1888 Sioux leader Sitting Bull went to Washington, D.C. to negotiate a compromise between the government and the Sioux over the redistribution and sale of Indian land. *Reproduced by permission of the National Archives and Records Administration.*

was desert. This amount represented less than two percent of the Indians' pre-Columbus landholdings of three billion acres. Tens of thousands of Native Americans had been reduced to landless poverty.

Court upholds allotment policy, defines "plenary powers"

In 1903 Chief Lone Wolf of the Kiowa tribe claimed that allot-

Massacre at Wounded Knee

One of the worst slaughters of Native Americans by U.S. military forces occurred in 1890 at the Pine Ridge Reservation in South Dakota. The conflict began with the overzealous response of U.S. agents posted on the reservation. The agents, alarmed by the nature of an Indian religious ritual called the Ghost Dance, called for troops.

The Ghost Dance religious movement originated with the Paiute Indians in present-day Nevada, in the 1880s. The main tenet of this religion was that by performing the Ghost Dance, as well as by following the traditions of their ancestors, believers would receive protection from white soldiers' bullets. By some accounts, Ghost Dancers also believed they would bring on an apocalypse in which all whites would die and all deceased Indians would rise to live again. In 1890, members of the Lakota nation of North Dakota traveled to Nevada and learned about the Ghost Dance. They then returned to teach their people the Paiute ritual.

On December 15, 1890, members of the Indian police force (Native American law enforcement officials, trained in U.S. methods of policing) were directed by the U.S. government to arrest Sitting Bull, a Sioux spiritual and political leader believed to be a follower of the Ghost Dance movement. During the attempted arrest, a struggle broke out in which Sitting Bull and twelve of his Sioux supporters were killed. This incident aggravated already-high tensions on the reservation.

ment policies violated the 1867 Treaty of Medicine Lodge. The Medicine Lodge treaty stated that only with the approval of three-quarters of adult male Indians could land from the Kiowa-Comanche Reservation be sold. Nevertheless, the government had allotted pieces of the reservation to individuals and sold the "surplus" land without permission of tribal members. In deciding the *Lone Wolf v. Hitchcock* case, the Supreme Court cast aside treaty rights and ruled in favor of the government. The justices noted that "the power exists to abrogate [void] the provisions of an Indian treaty, though presumably such power will be exercised only when circumstances arise which not only justify the government in disregarding the stipulations of the treaty, but may demand, in the interest of the country and the Indians themselves, that it should do so."

The Court defined the authority of Congress to abrogate treaties as "plenary powers." Furthermore, it ruled that the courts were powerless to limit Congress' plenary powers. In the 1913 case *United States v. Sandoval* re-

On December 28, 1890, U.S. forces encountered a group of armed Sioux on the Pine Ridge Reservation and ordered them to drop their weapons. After disarming the Indians, the soldiers led them to the Indian settlement at Wounded Knee Creek. The next day, while the soldiers were searching the Indians for weapons, a scuffle began. U.S. forces opened fire on the Indians, killing more than 150 people (by some estimates, the number was as high as 370), including women and children. Twenty-five U.S. soldiers were also killed, many of them with bullets fired by other U.S. troops.

American Horse, a Sioux eyewitness to the event, recalled that "when the firing began, of course the people who were standing immediately around the young man who fired the first shot were killed right together, and then they turned their guns ... upon the women who were in the lodges standing there under a flag of truce.... Right near the flag of truce a mother was shot down with her infant; the child not knowing that its mother was dead was still nursing, and that especially was a very sad sight. The women as they were fleeing with their babies were killed together ... and the women who were heavy with child were also killed. All the Indians fled in these three directions, and after most all of them had been killed a cry was made that all those who were not killed or wounded should come out of their places of refuge, and as soon as they came in sight a number of soldiers surrounded them and butchered them there."

garding the Pueblo Indians of New Mexico, the Supreme Court revealed the racist underpinning of plenary powers. The Court wrote: "Always living in separate and isolated communities, adhering to primitive modes of life, largely influenced by superstition and fetishism, and chiefly governed according to crude customs inherited through their ancestors, [Pueblo Indians] are essentially a simple, uninformed and inferior people.... As a superior and civilized nation [the United States has both] the power and the duty of exercising a fostering care and protection over all dependent Indian communities within its borders."

The concept of plenary powers became a cornerstone of U.S. Indian policy in the early 1900s. "Plenary power" was repeatedly evoked as a justification for government invasion into virtually every aspect of Native Americans' lives. According to noted attorney and Native American rights advocate Alvin J. Zionitz, the doctrine of plenary power "means that Congress has the power to do virtually as it pleases with the Indian tribes. It is an extraordinary

Two Native American boys in their boarding school uniforms. The purpose of the boarding schools was to "civilize" Native American children and teach them Christian ways. *Reproduced by permission of the National Archives and Records Administration.*

doctrine for a democracy to espouse.... it justifies the imposition of controls over the lives and property of the tribes and their members. Plenary power thus subjects Indians to national powers outside ordinary constitutional limits."

Assimilation

The dawn of the twentieth century was one of the worst periods in the history of Native Americans.

Not only had much of their land been stolen and their population reduced to an all-time low of 237,000, but Indians were facing an attack on their culture by assimilationist policymakers. (Assimilation is the process of becoming like, or being absorbed into, the dominant culture.) In the case of Native Americans, assimilation meant the loss of traditional ways of life and the adoption of the values of white America. The underpinning of assimilation was summed up by Commissioner of Indian Affairs T. J. Morgan in 1889. Morgan stated that Indians must be made to "conform to the white man's ways, peaceably if they will, forcibly if they must."

A number of government policies from the late 1800s through the 1920s, implemented under the "plenary powers" provision, were aimed at the assimilation of native peoples. U.S. agents pressured tribal governments to adopt U.S.-style governing procedures and paid missionaries to convert tribal members to Christianity.

Perhaps the most invasive and destructive assimilationist policy was the removal of Indian children from their homes and the placement of those children in boarding schools. The purpose of the boarding schools was to "civilize" the children and teach them Christian ways. The children were forbidden to speak native languages, practice native religions, or wear native clothing. Children who violated the rules were subjected to harsh punishment that amounted to physical abuse.

The most common form of punishment was whipping, using a wide leather strap on a child's bare buttocks. Other forms of punishment were even more cruel and unusual. There are documented cases of children being suspended from overhead pipes by handcuffs; being made to kneel on sharp rocks for long periods of time; and being sprayed with cold water outdoors in very cold weather. There are thousands of cases of children "disappearing" from boarding schools. Many of these disappearances remain unsolved to this day.

Indians are made American citizens

Another way that assimilationists sought to "Americanize" Indians was to make them U.S. citizens. In 1924 Congress passed the Synder Act (see box), also called the American Indian Citizenship Act, which granted citizenship to all Native Americans. This measure was taken despite the protests of many Native American leaders who believed that the imposition of U.S. citizenship would undermine the authority of tribal governments.

"The Citizenship Act did pass in 1924 despite our strong opposition," stated Clinton Rickard, chief of the Tuscarora Indians. "By its provisions all Indians were automatically made United States citizens whether they wanted to or not. This was a violation of our sovereignty. Our citizenship was in our own nations. We had a great attachment to our style of government. We

 The Snyder Act of 1924

With the passage of the Snyder Act in 1924, American Indians became citizens of the United States. The Snyder Act was the culmination of a long campaign for American Indian citizenship by liberal reformers in Congress and assimilationists (people who sought to integrate Indians into mainstream society). The Snyder Act, named for its author, Congressman Homer P. Snyder of New York, guaranteed "that all noncitizen Indians born within the territorial limits of the United States be ... declared to be citizens of the United States: Provided, that the granting of such citizenship shall not in any manner impair or otherwise affect the right of an Indian to tribal or other property."

Along with the newly granted citizenship came the right to vote. In a situation paralleling that of African Americans, however, the legal voting rights of Native Americans did not translate to free access to the voting booth. Many states made it difficult, if not impossible, for Indians to vote by imposing literacy tests, poll taxes, and other restrictive practices (for more information on these restrictive practices, see chapter 1, "The right to vote revoked"). Some states, such as Wyoming, New Mexico, and Arizona, denied the Indian vote outright until the late 1940s.

wished to remain treaty Indians and reserve our ancient rights."

While Indian leaders, at the time the Synder Act was passed, feared that U.S. citizenship would necessitate the revocation of Indians' citizenship in their own tribes, that did not come to pass. Today Native Americans belonging to federally recognized tribes have dual citizenship—they are citizens of both the United States and their respective tribes.

Meriam Report calls for reforms

In 1926, amid growing concerns over the effects of allotment and assimilationist policies on native peoples, Commissioner of Indian Affairs Hubert Work called for an investigation into the matter. The job was assigned to a private research organization called the Institute for Government Research (later renamed the Brookings Institution). Social scientist Lewis B. Meriam coordinated the efforts of a team of anthropologists, educators, legal experts, economists, and health specialists in gathering information at ninety reservations over a seven-month period. In 1928 "The Problem of Indian Administration," better known as the *Meriam Report,* was published. The researchers' findings shocked the nation.

The *Meriam Report* painted a dismal picture of Native America. The report documented a nearly complete lack of health services and sanitation systems, crushing poverty, low rates of literacy, and no protected legal rights. Native Americans were found to have the shortest lifespans of any racial or ethnic group in the nation, and Indi-an infant mortality rates (the percentage of children who die during infancy) were more than double those of non-Indians. Large numbers of Native Americans suffered from malnutrition, and epidemics of measles, tuberculosis, pneumonia, and trachoma ravaged Indian nations. The report found that 96 percent of all Native Americans had incomes under $200 per year.

The *Meriam Report* severely criticized the government-run boarding schools for Indian children, calling them "grossly inadequate." The report stated that the schools were overcrowded, staff members were unqualified, and that the children received insufficient medical care and nutrition and were subjected to harsh discipline.

BIA implicated

The Bureau of Indian Affairs (BIA) was implicated in the report as the primary party responsible for the destruction of Native America. The BIA—a government agency charged with overseeing tribal lands, education, and other aspects of Native American life—was depicted as not only insensitive to the needs of Indians but also hostile toward native families and culture. The allotment system was named as the specific policy responsible for the impoverishment of Native Americans. Nearly half of all Indians interviewed by Meriam's team had lost their lands through allotment.

The authors of the *Meriam Report* made several recommendations. First, they called for an oversight department within the Bureau of Indian

Indian Policy Reformer John Collier

John Collier (1884–1968), the Roosevelt Administration's reformist Commissioner of Indian Affairs from 1933 to 1945, was a civil rights activist long before assuming his government post. Collier was born in Atlanta, Georgia, in 1884 and educated at Columbia University and the Colege de France. His first activist position, in 1907, was as secretary of the New York-based immigrants'-rights group The People's Institute. In 1919 Collier began a two-year stint as director of California's adult education program before state funding for the position was withdrawn. Collier's next move was to Taos, New Mexico, where he lived among the Pueblo Indians and became familiar with the injustices they faced, as well as their strong spirit of resistance.

While in Taos, Collier worked as a researcher for the Indian Welfare Committee of the General Federation of Women's Clubs. In 1923 Collier became a founding member the American Indian Defense Association (AIDA). AIDA fought for an end to allotment policies (the division of reservation lands and allotment of small parcels to individuals), the protection of Native American political and economic rights, and the preservation of native cultures. Collier directed AIDA in these efforts until his appointment as Commissioner of Indian Affairs in 1933. As Commissioner, Collier was able to carry out many of the reforms for which AIDA had lobbied.

During the World War II years (1939–1945), the nation's attention shifted away from Indian policies and other domestic matters, to foreign affairs. The Bureau of Indian Affairs' budget was cut; at the same time, provisions of the IRA came under attack by an increasing number of politicians. Frustrated by his office's growing ineffectiveness, Collier resigned as commissioner in 1945. Collier went on to teach at the City College of New York and Knox College in Galesburg, Illinois. He died in Talpa, New Mexico, at the age of eighty-two.

Affairs to keep an eye on existing programs and institute new programs; second, they called upon Congress to pour substantial funds into reservation hospitals, schools, and loan programs for tribal businesses. The *Meriam Report* recommended that the allotment program be completely revamped and that BIA offer high salaries in order to attract more qualified employees.

The "Indian New Deal"

In response to the *Meriam Report,* as well as pressures from native peoples and Indian rights organizations, government policies were completely revamped in the 1930s. The "Indian New Deal" was the name of the package of reforms instituted from 1933 to 1945, during the presidency of Franklin Delano Roosevelt (1882–1945). Roosevelt instituted an aggressive policy called the "New Deal," aimed at ending the Great Depression (the nation's worst economic crisis, lasting from 1929 through the late 1930s).

The New Deal consisted of hundreds of social programs, building projects, and economic initiatives. The cornerstones of the Indian New Deal were the abolition of the allotment program, the restoration and support of tribal governments, the end of compulsory attendance at boarding schools, and a respect for Indian cultures and traditions. The Indian New Deal's primary author and strongest proponent was Roosevelt's Commissioner of Indian Affairs, John Collier (1884–1968; see box).

The Indian Reorganization Act of 1934

The Indian Reorganization Act (also known as the Wheeler-Howard Act for its sponsors, Representative Edgar Howard of Nebraska and Senator Burton K. Wheeler of Montana), passed in 1934, was the legislative basis for the "Indian New Deal." The Indian Reorganization Act (IRA) put an end to allotment, returned "surplus" reservation lands to the tribes, recognized tribal governments, and recommended that Indian nations adopt their own constitutions. In addition, the IRA allotted $2 million for the purchase of additional lands for tribes, $10 million for loans to tribal corporations (associations of tribal members, created by law), and $250,000 per year for the organization of tribal govern-

ments. A fund of $250,000 annually was set up to provide scholarships to Native American students.

In the IRA the government—for the first time—officially defined Indians. The definition read:

> The term 'Indian' as used in this Act shall include all persons of Indian descent who are members of any recognized Indian tribe now under Federal jurisdiction, and all persons who are descendants of such members who were, on June 1, 1934, residing within the present boundaries of any Indian reservation, and shall further include all other persons of one-half or more Indian blood. For the purposes of [this Act] Eskimos and other aboriginal peoples of Alaska shall be considered Indians.

While the "Indian New Deal" raised Native American standards of living, improved the quality of health and education services available to Indians, and increased the reservations' land base (and protected that land from division or theft), it was not without its Native American critics. Some native people, wary of government programs, resented John Collier and the BIA for attempting to force reforms on them. Collier was particularly cited for overzealousness in his campaign for the adoption of tribal constitutions. (In the end, only 181 out of a total of 258 tribes accepted the provisions of the IRA, and only 92 tribes adopted constitutions.)

The IRA gave tribal governments very little say over how programs were administered or federal money was spent on reservations (that power remained with the BIA). Nonetheless, few would question that Native Americans fared better under the "Indian New Deal" than they had during the preceding era of allotment and assimilation.

Reform period ends during Cold War

The period of U.S. reformist policy toward Native Americans came to an early end as the Cold War (a period of tense relations between the former Soviet Union and the United States, lasting from around 1945 to 1990) got underway. The late 1940s and early 1950s were a time of rising racism, as well as anti-communism, in the United States. (Communism—a political and economic system based on community ownership of all property—was practiced in the former Soviet Union.)

Many white Americans in the late 1940s and early 1950s believed that the Native Americans were being given too much government assistance. Non-Indians also regarded the Native American tradition of collective ownership of tribal lands with suspicion. (They equated the natives' collectivism with Soviet-style communism.) And white developers resented their loss of access to native lands. A combination of all of these forces ushered in a new era of U.S. government policies that were harmful to Indians.

The era of termination and relocation

Indian policy in the early 1950s consisted of a two-pronged as-sault on Native American culture and identity: termination and relocation. Termination was both a legislative and a philosophical concept, at the core of which was the termination (ending) of the standing relationships, governed by treaties, between the United States and Indian tribes. Policymakers believed that by voiding Native American treaty rights, they could force Native Americans to assimilate (blend) into mainstream American society.

Relocation was the policy by which Native Americans were encouraged to move off reservations and into cities. Assimilationist advocates of relocation argued that by moving into urban areas, Native Americans would shed their tribal identities and customs and adopt the values of individualism and free enterprise. They argued that native peoples could find work in the industrial sector and send their children to public schools. As was the case with allotment, the policies of termination and relocation were dismal failures for the native population.

Termination policy

The policy of termination (originally called "liquidation") was first proposed by a House Select Committee in 1944. "Liquidation policy" was defined by the committee as "the cessation of all federal services and programs to the Indian reservations" and was being touted as a "final solution to the Indian problem." The terms "liquidation" and "final solution" were problematic because the same words were used by the German

Nazi Party during World War II (1939–1945) to describe their campaign of killing Jews and other groups deemed undesirable. Therefore, lawmakers changed the policy name to "termination."

The goal of termination policy was to solve the "Indian problem" in the United States by terminating the official relationship of "trust" between the U.S. government and the tribes ("trust" was the promise of the U.S. government to look out for the Indians' best interests). Native Americans would then be treated just like all other United States citizens, and would be free to realize the "American dream." Terminated tribes would also experience (as stated in the 1949 Report of the Committee on Indian Affairs of the Hoover Commission) "the ending of tax exemption and of privileged status for Indian-owned land and the payment of the taxes at the same rates as for other property in the areas."

House Concurrent Resolution 108

The program of termination was described in House Concurrent Resolution 108, passed in 1953 despite overwhelming opposition from Native Americans. The resolution read, "[I]t is the policy of Congress, as rapidly as possible, to make the Indians within the territorial limits of the United States subject to the same laws and entitled to the same privileges and responsibilities as are applicable to other citizens of the United States, to end their status as wards of the United States, to grant

them all the rights and prerogatives pertaining to American citizenship."

Resolution 108 described a process by which tribal status would be terminated immediately for all tribes in Texas, California, New York, and Florida. The tribal status of other Indian nations would be terminated gradually, on a case-by-case basis over a fifty-year period. Each tribe was to be evaluated to determine the appropriate date for its termination.

The resolution was the brainchild of Commissioner of Indian Affairs (as of 1950) Dillon S. Myer. Before joining the BIA, Myer had directed the War Relocation Authority—the body charged with overseeing the internment of thousands of Japanese Americans in concentration camps from 1942–1945 (for more information, see chapter 2, "The internment of Japanese Americans").

Between 1954 and 1958 Congress passed termination acts for a total of 109 tribes, including the Menominees, Klamaths, Paiutes, Alabamas, Coushattas, Utes, Wyandottes, Peorias, and Ottawas. More than 13,000 individuals were moved off reservations and lost their treaty rights as Native Americans. (Treaty rights are rights granted only to federally recognized Native American tribes, and are extended only to the members of those tribes living on federally recognized Indian reservations.)

About 3.3 million acres of Indian land was confiscated between 1948 and 1957. Much of the confiscated land was flooded as dams were

National Congress of American Indians Opposes Termination

One of the strongest forces opposing termination policies was the National Congress of American Indians (NCAI). The NCAI got its start in 1944, with support from then-Commissioner of Indian Affairs John Collier (see box). NCAI leaders D'Arcy McNickle, Ruth Muskrat Bronson, and Louis Bruce received their training in politics and leadership from Collier and his aides.

The original aims of the NCAI were the preservation of Native American culture and tribal self-government, as well as the attainment of voting rights for Native Americans in New Mexico, Arizona, and other states. In the early 1950s the NCAI switched its focus to the prevention of the passage of termination policies. To that end, the NCAI brought Indians from more than eighty tribes to Washington, for an eight-week-long protest in the halls of Congress in the winter of 1954.

While NCAI failed in its effort to forestall termination, the organization was instrumental in discrediting termination policies once they had been implemented, leading to termination's early demise. In the 1960s and 1970s the prominence of the NCAI declined as more radical Indian-rights groups such as the American Indian Movement and the National Indian Youth Council took center stage. As of 1996, however, NCAI still listed more than 200 tribes as member organizations.

built along the Colorado River, Missouri River, and other rivers; other Indian land was made into parks or used for a variety of development projects.

Public Law 280 shifts power from tribes to states

Public Law 280 was passed in 1953 as a companion policy to House Concurrent Resolution 108. Public Law 280 shifted jurisdiction over criminal and civil proceedings on reservations of terminated tribes from tribal governments to state governments in California, Minnesota, Nebraska, Oregon, and Wisconsin.

Public Law 280 was the first in a series of laws during the termination era aimed at diminishing tribal authority. Subsequent laws turned control over Indian health and education programs over to state governments. Public Law 280 was repealed with the passage of the American Indian Civil Rights Act in 1968 (for more information, see "Native American civil rights in the 1960s").

The end of termination

By the late 1950s the disastrous effects of termination were clear. Native Americans from terminated tribes had plunged into poverty, and

Lakota Times Columnist Comments on Relocation

Tim Giago, an Oglala Sioux and columnist for the *Lakota Times,* wrote a column on August 5, 1987, in which he discussed the impact of relocation on Native Americans. (The *Lakota Times* is an Indian newspaper based in Rapid City, South Dakota; Lakota is the traditional name for Sioux.) What follows is an excerpt from Giago's column, entitled "Notes from Indian Country":

> Indian reservations were much different in [the 1930s]. The people of the tribe lived and worked on their own land.
>
> This was long before the U.S. government decided that it would be extremely economical to build houses in clusters in town in an effort to save on plumbing, sewage and electrical costs. This was the beginning of instant ghettos on many Indian reservations.
>
> Tribal members were told that life would be much easier for them if they would move from their land and settle into the brand-new cluster housing projects.
>
> Indian people abandoned homes on their own land in droves. They sold their cattle, horses, and in the case of many Navajo families, their sheep, and moved to the cluster houses....
>
> Since there are few job opportunities on most reservations, by abandoning their land, and hence their livelihood, many tribal members gave up what little independence they had for nearly total dependence....
>
> Why did so many Indian people abandon their homes and independence and move into the cluster homes? When a person has nothing, or very little, and is told by a trusted source, the U.S. government, that life will be better for them if they move into town, into the new homes, what are they to believe?

many Indians subsisted on welfare. While health care had been free and housing and utilities subsidized on reservations, Native Americans who had moved to cities were suddenly forced to foot the entire bill for rent, heat, and doctor's bills. Non-Indian land speculators were the only group to profit from termination policies.

In 1958 Secretary of the Interior Fred Seaton announced his refusal to terminate any additional Indian tribes. Seaton made good on his word. By the time Seaton left his post in 1961, termination had fallen into disfavor in Washington, D.C. In 1970 the administration of President Richard M. Nixon (1913–1994) officially ended termination as government policy. Nonetheless, the debate over termination lingered on Capitol Hill until 1988 when Congress passed the Repeal of Termination Act. Under the terms of the act, Congress was forbidden from terminating any tribe without the express consent of that tribe.

Since the Nixon Administration's reversal of the termination policy, several terminated Indian nations have regained their tribal status. The first nation to do so, in 1973, was the Menominee tribe of Wisconsin. Other restored tribes include the Siletz, Klamath, and Grand Ronde tribes of Oregon; the Ottawa, Peoria, and Wyandotte tribes of Oklahoma; and certain bands of Paiutes in Utah.

Relocation brings Native Americans to cities

Relocation—the removal of Indians from reservations to urban areas—was another of the assimilationists' answers to the "Indian problem" in the late 1940s and early 1950s. The first step in the implementation of relocation policy came in 1947, when the Bureau of Indian Affairs (BIA) started up the Labor Recruitment and Welfare Program on the Navajo and Hopi reservations. The purpose of the Labor Recruitment and Welfare Program was to prepare tribal members to work in Denver, Los Angeles, Salt Lake City, and Phoenix. Two years later the BIA established job placement centers for Native Americans in several cities.

In 1952 the BIA stepped up efforts to relocate Native Americans to cities by providing assistance with moving expenses and finding housing. They also subsidized Indians' living expenses for their first thirty days after leaving the reservation. In 1956 Congress authorized funds for a job training program for relocated Native Americans; participants received financial support during the six-month training period.

Although relocation was in theory "voluntary," in many cases it was actually forced on native people. For example, 130 families were evicted from the Allegany Seneca reservation in western New York when the Kinzua Dam was built. The dam flooded 9,000 acres of farm land and destroyed the tribe's longhouse (a ceremonial center of traditional Indian life). The families were resettled in suburban-style housing clusters in the cities of Steamburg and Jimersontown. In another example, many Sioux families were forcibly relocated when 200,000 acres of reservation land in North and South Dakota were flooded during the construction of the Fort Randall, Big Bend, and Oahe dams.

As a result of relocation programs, the proportion of Indians living in cities jumped from less than 10 percent in 1930 to 45 percent in 1970 and to 66 percent in 1990. Cities in which the greatest numbers of Native Americans reside include Tulsa and Oklahoma City, Oklahoma; Tucson and Phoenix, Arizona; Albuquerque, New Mexico; Seattle, Washington; Minneapolis and St. Paul, Minnesota; San Diego, San Francisco, and Los Angeles, California; Dallas, Texas; Denver, Colorado; New York City; and Chicago, Illinois.

Despite BIA promises of assistance and a better life, relocated Indians were by and large disappointed with city living. They found they had given up the traditional lifestyles and sense of community they had known on the reservation for shabby housing, menial (and often seasonal) jobs, isolation from their communities, and culture shock. More than 10,000 of the relocated Native Americans eventually moved back to reservations. In the late 1960s the government slowed its relocation efforts.

Native American civil rights in the 1960s

In the pre-civil rights years, Native Americans were subjected to many of the same discriminatory practices and civil rights violations as African Americans, Latinos, and other people of color. The "separate but equal" doctrine kept Native Americans out of places of public accommodation, unjust measures such as literacy tests and poll taxes prevented Native Americans from voting, and racist policies and practices barred Native Americans from obtaining desirable housing and employment.

Native Americans benefitted from much of the civil rights legislation passed during the 1960s. Protections for Native Americans were included in the Voting Rights Act of 1965 (including bilingual ballots for individuals whose first language was not English), the Fair Housing Act of 1968, and the Equal Employment Opportunity measure contained in the Civil Rights Act of 1964. The promise of civil rights protection restored a measure of dignity and optimism to a

people still smarting from a decade of termination and relocation policies.

The American Indian Civil Rights Act of 1968

In 1968 Congress passed sweeping legislation to guarantee the civil rights of American Indians living on reservations. The Indian Civil Rights Act (ICRA)—also called the Indian Bill of Rights—extended to Indians virtually every right guaranteed other U.S. citizens under the U.S. Bill of Rights (the amendments to the Constitution). Indian nations, regarded as sovereign entities, had previously been responsible for handling their own internal affairs and were not protected under or responsible to the U.S. Constitution. The Indian Civil Rights Act simultaneously protected individual Native Americans and chipped away at the authority of tribal governments.

Congress was moved to enact this landmark legislation after hearing testimony from Native Americans who had been subjected to abuse by tribal authorities. (Some lawmakers, however, may have been motivated by a desire to erode Indian nations' right to self-governance.) Many Native Americans and Indian rights groups criticized the act for infringing upon the self-determination of their nations. The Indian Civil Rights Act confers civil rights on persons living in areas of tribal jurisdiction and gives the federal courts the power to enforce those rights.

There were four provisions that Congress, for fear of infringing too

Specific Guarantees of the ICRA

Section 202, the main provision of the Indian Civil Rights Act, guaranteed several specific rights. The section reads:

No Indian tribe in exercising powers of self-government shall: (1) make or enforce any law prohibiting the free exercise of religion, or abridging the freedom of speech, or of the press, or the right of the people peaceably to assemble and to petition for a redress of grievances; (2) violate the right of the people to be secure in their persons, houses, papers, and effects against unreasonable search and seizures, nor issue warrants, but upon probable cause, supported by oath or affirmation, and particularly describing the place to be searched and the person or thing to be seized; (3) subject any person for the same offense to be twice put in jeopardy; (4) compel any person in any criminal case to be a witness against himself; (5) take any private property for a public use without just compensation; (6) deny to any person in a criminal proceeding the right to a speedy and public trial, to be informed of the nature and cause of the accusation, to be confronted with the witnesses against him, to have compulsory process for obtaining witnesses in his favor, and at his own expense to have the assistance of counsel for his defense; (7) require excessive bail, impose excessive fines, inflict cruel and unusual punishments, and in no event impose for conviction of any one offense any penalty or punishment greater than imprisonment for a term of six months or a fine of $5,000, or both; (8) deny to any person within its jurisdiction the equal protection of its laws or deprive any person of liberty or property without due process of law; (9) pass any bill of attainder or ex post facto law; or (10) deny to any person accused of an offense punishable by imprisonment the right, upon request, to a trial by jury of not less than six persons.

deeply on tribal customs and modes of government, did not include in the Indian Civil Rights Act. First, the ICRA did not prohibit the government sponsorship of churches. This was because some tribes are theocracies. (A theocracy is a form of government based on the rules of a particular religion.) The other three provisions in the Bill of Rights not included in the IRCA were the right to legal counsel free of charge for poor people (many tribes would not have the resources to accommodate such a provision); the right to a jury trial in civil (as opposed to criminal) cases; and the requirement to convene a grand jury in criminal cases. (A grand jury, usually made up of twelve to thirty-three people, examines evidence to determine whether or not the evidence is sufficient for bringing a suspect to trial on criminal charges.)

The tribal court system was the branch of tribal government most profoundly affected by the ICRA. Prior to the act's passage, there had been no uniform procedures used in tribal courts. Each nation had developed its own methods of conflict resolution and criminal justice. After the passage of the ICRA, however, tribal courts were held to certain standards: they had to advise criminal defendants of their right to a jury trial; use clear and specific wording in their criminal laws; forbid the use of a single person as both judge and prosecutor; keep thorough records of all court proceedings; and uphold a defendant's right against self-incrimination (the act of giving evidence leading to one's own conviction).

"Red Power": The Native American rights movement

"Red Power" is the name used to describe the Native American rights movement of the 1960s and 1970s. American Indians from many tribes participated in campaigns to protest the injustices inflicted on their people by U.S. government policies, particularly the policies of termination (the ending of treaty rights) and relocation (the resettlement of Indians from reservations to cities).

Red Power was a response by Indian activists to the dismal state of Native America in the early 1960s. Indian people only lived, on average, forty years, and often died from alcoholism, malnutrition, or disease. Indi-

an infants died at a rate twice the national average. Unemployment was ten times that of the national average, and at least 50,000 Indian families lived in dilapidated shacks or castaway cars. The suicide rate for adolescents and teens was the highest in the nation, and alcoholism claimed the lives of Indians under age twenty-four at twenty-eight times the national average.

Red Power activists sought respect for tribal self-governance and sovereignty, civil rights for urban Indians, the return of Indian lands, and hunting and fishing rights protected by treaty. Similar to the African American "Black Power" movement (see chapter 1, "The radicalization of the movement"), the Native American "Red Power" movement had as its central tenets racial pride, self-determination (the control by a person or group of people over their own lives and systems of government), and the belief that the people themselves had the power to better their own conditions.

The Red Power movement was mainly comprised of young, militant activists, including some college students and streetwise youths. The activists used confrontational and sometimes violent and illegal tactics. Young activists undertook dramatic actions all across the nation, at places such as Alcatraz Island, Wounded Knee, Ellis Island, and Bureau of Indian Affairs (BIA) offices in several cities (including the headquarters in Washington, D.C.), to force change in a political system that they felt was unresponsive and inhumane.

The National Indian Youth Council

Many people trace the roots of the Red Power movement to a 1961 gathering called the American Indian Chicago Conference. The purpose of that meeting was to obtain Indian input regarding government policy-making for the Kennedy Administration. The meeting was organized by social scientists from the University of Chicago and attended by nearly 500 Indians from more than sixty-five tribes. At the meeting youthful Indian activists voiced frustration over the moderate, slow-moving strategy of the older tribal leaders of the National Congress of American Indians (NCAI; see box "National Congress of American Indians Opposes Termination").

A few months after the Chicago meeting, a group of young, mostly urban, Indians met in Gallup, New Mexico, to form the National Indian Youth Council (NIYC). The founding members were Herbert Blatchford (a Navajo graduate of the University of New Mexico), Clyde Warrior (a Ponca active in the civil rights movement in the South), Shirley Hill Witt (a Mohawk), Melvin Thom (a Nevada Paiute graduate student in civil engineering), and Mary Natani (a Winnebago).

The NIYC set up headquarters in Albuquerque, New Mexico. The group's members developed a platform calling for an end to racist U.S. policies toward Native Americans and demanding that Native Americans have a greater voice in the creation of

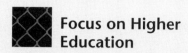 **Focus on Higher Education**

One of the aims of the Native American rights movement in the late 1960s was the establishment of greater opportunities for Indians to receive college educations and for the inclusion of Native American studies in educational curricula. The year 1968 saw the formation of the first tribal college, the Navajo Community College. More than twenty colleges were established on reservations over the following decade. Between 1968 and 1970, Native American studies programs were established at numerous colleges and universities.

Accompanying this educational push was a surge in the number of Indian newspapers and magazines. There were only eighteen reservation newspapers in 1963; that number surpassed 220 in 1978. Examples of Indian publications that enjoy wide circulation today include the *Lakota Times* (the official journal of the Lakota [Sioux] nation) and *Akwasasne Notes* (the official journal of the Mohawk nation).

policies affecting their own people, both on and off reservations.

Writing in *The Nations Within,* NIYC member and noted Native American historian Vine Deloria Jr. remarked that the message of the NIYC was that "Indians were no longer to bow their heads in humble obedience to the Bureau of Indian Affairs or the institutions of white soci-

The Campaign for Fishing Rights

From the mid-1960s through the early 1970s the Native American Youth Council led a series of demonstrations called "fish-ins" to draw attention to the right of Native Americans to fish, free from state interference. Disregarding the treaties that exempted Indians from fishing restrictions, state governments—especially in Washington and Wisconsin—had since the late nineteenth century been attempting to regulate Indian fishing. In particular, state officials were trying to prevent Native Americans from fishing with nets and from fishing outside of the established "fishing season."

At fish-in protests at the Quillayute and Nisqually Rivers, demonstrators purposely violated state fishing laws in order to assert their treaty rights. The fish-ins were inspired by the sit-ins of the African American civil rights movement, during which black students demanded service at "whites-only" lunch counters and bus terminals throughout the South in the early 1960s (for more information on sit-ins, see chapter 1, "Student sit-ins strike a blow at Jim Crow"). Hundreds of Indian activists were arrested during fish-ins in Washington state. Many activists were beaten by club-wielding police, and one person was shot by a white vigilante (a citizen who takes criminal justice matters into her or his own hands). The fish-ins came into the spotlight of the national media when actors Dick Gregory and Marlon Brando joined the demonstrations.

The fish-in movement ended in victory in 1974, when Native American fishing rights were upheld in a landmark court case entitled *United States v. Washington*. U.S. Judge George H. Boldt of the federal court for the District of Washington State wrote in his ruling: "Because the right of each Treaty Tribe to take anadromous [migrating from the ocean up a river to spawn; such as salmon] fish arises from a treaty with the United States, that right is preserved and protected under the supreme law of the land, does not depend on State law, is distinct from rights or privileges held by others, and may not be qualified by any action of the State."

Boldt's decision was upheld by the Supreme Court in 1979.

ety. The NIYC called upon Indians to look back at their own great cultural traditions and make decisions based on the values they had always represented." In *Custer Died for Your Sins,* Deloria characterized the NIYC as "the SNCC of Indian Affairs." (The Student Nonviolent Coordinating Committee, or SNCC, was an activist African American student civil rights group founded in 1960; for more information on the SNCC, see chapter 1.)

NIYC champions fishing rights, the environment During the 1960s the NIYC concentrated its energies on a cam-

Government representatives meet with Native American fishermen at their camp in Alaska to determine whether or not the area should be opened to petroleum development. Since the 1960s, Native American groups have championed both fishing rights and the environment.
Photo by David Germain. Reproduced by permission of AP/Wide World Photos.

paign for Native American hunting and fishing rights. To this end the group conducted numerous protests, many involving acts of civil disobedience (nonviolent action in which participants refuse to obey certain laws, with the purpose of challenging the fairness of those laws). The NIYC organized several "fish-ins" in Washington state (see box, "The Campaign for Fishing Rights"), where gaming and fishing oversight authorities were interfering with treaty rights that guaranteed Indians the right to hunt and fish.

The first "fish-in" was at the Quillayute River in 1964. At the Quillayute, activists fished in violation of state laws in order to assert their treaty rights. That same year, the NIYC staged a large protest march in the state capital of Olympia.

In the 1970s and 1980s the NIYC shifted its emphasis to environmental protection and voter registration. The NIYC pushed for the cleanup of sites of environmental contamination and worked to forestall develop-

The Alcatraz Proclamation

The following is an abridged version of the statement drafted by the Indians of All Tribes who occupied Alcatraz Island in 1969. While making a serious bid for the purchase of the island, the proclamation mocks (in its references to "Caucasians" and "Caucasian inhabitants") the way in which white authorities have historically belittled and betrayed the Indian people. Note the authors' reference to the forced "sale" of Manhattan Island to European colonists in 1626, as well as their offer to establish a "Bureau of Caucasian Affairs" to help "civilize" white people.

To the Great White Father and All *His* People—We, the native Americans, reclaim the land known as Alcatraz Island in the name of all American Indians by right of discovery.

We wish to be fair and honorable in our dealings with the Caucasian inhabitants of this land, and hereby offer the following treaty:

We will purchase said Alcatraz Island for twenty-four dollars (24) in glass beads and red cloth, a precedent set by the white man's purchase of a similar island about 300 years ago. We know that 24 dollars in trade goods for these 16 acres is more than was paid when Manhattan Island was sold, but we know that land values have risen over the years.... We will give to the inhabitants of this island a portion of the land for their own to be held in trust ... by the bureau of Caucasian Affairs to hold in perpetuity—for as long as the sun shall rise and the rivers go down to the sea. We will further guide the inhabitants in the proper way of living. We will offer them our religion, our education, our life-ways, in order to help them achieve our level of civilization

ment projects that threatened to upset the ecological balance on Indian lands. The NIYC also filed a number of lawsuits over practices that interfered with Native Americans' right to register and vote. The NIYC continues to oversee the Indian Voting Project, a project that encourages Native Americans to register to vote and to become involved in the political process.

Indians of All Tribes occupy Alcatraz Island

In 1969 members of the activist group Indians of All Tribes occupied Alcatraz Island, the former penal colony located in San Francisco Bay. Alcatraz prison, which had once housed such famous criminals as Al Capone and "Machine Gun" Kelley, was closed in 1962 after three inmates escaped. The Indian occupiers demanded that the island be returned to native peoples under the terms of the 1868 Sioux treaty called the Treaty of Fort Laramie. The treaty promised that abandoned federal properties on former Indian land would be returned to Indians.

The Indians of All Tribes group drew members from Sioux, Navajo, Cherokee, Mohawk, Puyallup, Yakima, and thus raise them and all their white brothers up from their savage and unhappy state. We offer this treaty in good faith and wish to be fair and honorable in our dealings with all white men.

We feel that this so-called Alcatraz Island is more than suitable for an Indian reservation, as determined by the white man's own standards. By this we mean that this place most resembles Indians reservations in that:

1. It is isolated from modern facilities, and without adequate means of transportation.

2. It has no fresh running water.

3. It has inadequate sanitation facilities.

4. There are no oil or mineral rights.

5. There is no industry and so unemployment is very great.

6. There are no health care facilities.

7. The soil is rocky and non-productive, and the land does not support game.

8. There are no educational facilities.

9. The population has always exceeded the land base.

10. The population has always been held as prisoners and kept dependent upon others.

Further, it would be fitting and symbolic that ships from all over the world, entering the Golden Gate, would first see Indian land, and thus be reminded of the true history of this nation. This tiny island would be a symbol of the great lands once ruled by free and noble Indians.

Hoopa, Omaha, and other tribes. Indians of All Tribes was characterized as a "Pan-Indian" organization, meaning that it emphasized the common concerns of all Native Americans and advocated that tribal differences be put aside for the purpose of creating a unified Native American political force.

The takeover begins The Alcatraz action began on November 9, 1969, when fourteen members of Indians of All Tribes slipped ashore under the cover of night. The Indians remained on Alcatraz for nineteen hours before they were forced to leave by armed U.S. officials from the Coast Guard and other agencies.

Eleven days later, on November 20, 1969, eighty-nine members of Indians of All Tribes occupied the island once again. The group, led by Mohawk activist Richard Oakes (1942–1972), included students from various California universities and residents from the San Francisco Bay area. This time the occupation lasted nineteen months. Groups of Native Americans—numbering between 15 and 1,000, but usually averaging around 100—took turns living on the island. Native peoples from all over the North and South America came to Alcatraz to participate in the occupation. Hundreds of Indians performed support functions off the island, such as raising money and gathering food, clothing, and other supplies.

Indians of All Tribes outlined plans for the island's conversion to a Native American spiritual, cultural, and educational center. The group also called attention to the inadequacies in health care and education available to Indians, and to ongoing assaults on Indian culture. While on the island, the protesters published a newsletter called *The Rock,* broadcast a radio program called "Radio Free Alcatraz," and held numerous press conferences and pow-wows. (A pow-wow is a traditional religious ceremony with dancing, drumming, and chanting.) Publicity efforts were coordinated by Santee Sioux activist John Trudell (1947–).

Federal officials attempted to pressure the Indians into leaving by blocking their supply boats. In the spring of 1970 officials cut off electricity and water to the island. On June 11, 1971, federal officials raided the island and forced the Indians to leave. Rather than ceding control of the island to the Indians, the government made Alcatraz part of the Golden Gate National Recreation Area.

The occupation of Alcatraz was a tremendous source of inspiration for Native American activists and today remains a symbolic rallying point for Indian self-determination.

The publicity generated by the Alcatraz action was instrumental in finally ending termination policy (see "The era of termination and relocation").

The American Indian Movement

The American Indian Movement (AIM), perhaps the best known of all Red Power groups, was founded in 1968 in Minneapolis, Minnesota. The original mission of AIM was to stop police brutality toward Native Americans in Minneapolis and other cities. (Like other people of color, Indians were frequently harassed and beaten by white police officers.) AIM also sought to draw attention to the poverty and lack of opportunity plaguing Indian communities in cities and on reservations. Soon after its founding, AIM broadened its mission to include demands of improved services to urban Indians; Native American control of the Bureau of Indian Affairs (BIA); and the return of all tribal lands to native peoples.

AIM modeled its organization on the Black Panthers, an African American self-defense and community improvement organization founded in Oakland, California, in 1966 (see chapter 1, "The Black Panther Party").

"This was the time of the antiwar movement, and signs of Red Power had begun to appear beside Black Power slogans across the country," wrote historian Rex Weyler, author of *Blood of the Land: The Government and*

Mohawk activist Richard Oakes (far left) led the Indians of All Tribes group in a nineteen-month occupation of Alcatraz Island. *Reproduced by permission of AP/Wide World Photos.*

Corporate War against the American Indian Movement. "But soon the Red Power graffiti changed to AIM.... AIM was an indigenous, land-based spiritual movement, a call to the Indian people to return to their sacred traditions and, at the same time, to stand firm against the tide of what they call European influence and dominance."

Under the direction of founders Dennis Banks, Russell Means, brothers Clyde and Vernon Bellecourt, Mary Jane Williams, George Mitchell, and others, and with the guidance of elder Pat Ballanger (considered the "Mother of the American Indian Movement"), AIM quickly established chapters in several cities with large Indian populations. In addition to creating "Indian patrols" to monitor police conduct, AIM members either initiated or supported numerous Indian actions around the nation between 1969 and 1978.

AIM participated in the Alcatraz Island occupation in 1969, fish-ins in the late 1960s and early 1970s, the occupation of Mount Rushmore in 1970 and 1971, a protest at Plymouth Rock in 1971, the Trail of Broken

Police Brutality and the AIM response

In an interview with Richard Ballad in July 1973, AIM activist and Chippewa Indian Vernon Bellecourt described the way Indian watchdog groups, called "AIM Patrols," kept an eye on police behavior:

> [The AIM Patrols] got a small grant from the Urban League of Minneapolis to put two-way radios in their cars and to get tape recorders and cameras. They would listen to the police calls, and when they heard there was going to be an arrest or that police were being dispatched to a certain community or bar, they'd show up with cameras and take pictures of the police using more than normal restraint on the people.

> They got evidence of beatings and of ripping people around with handcuffs too tight, ripping their wrists. It was very vicious. This sometimes becomes a way of life for the police. They just fall into it. They think that's the way Indians have to be treated. So AIM would show up and have attorneys ready. Often they would beat the police back to the station. They would have a bondsman there, and they'd start filing law suits against the police department.

Treaties caravan to Washington, D.C., and occupation of the BIA headquarters in 1972, the occupation of Wounded Knee on the Pine Ridge Reservation in 1973, and the "Longest Walk" in 1978.

Many of AIM's members were former prisoners, and the group favored the use of direct-action tactics.

For these reasons, AIM frequently found itself at odds with law enforcement authorities. Several AIM members were killed in the 1970s, either during firefights with law enforcement officials or under mysterious circumstances on reservations.

COINTELPRO infiltrates AIM AIM was targeted for infiltration and harassment by the Federal Bureau of Investigation (FBI), under its notorious Counter-intelligence Program (COINTELPRO). The alleged purpose of COINTELPRO was to combat domestic terrorism. In reality, COINTELPRO was used as a weapon against the anti-Vietnam War and civil rights movements and against militant organizations of people of color. By the end of the 1970s the FBI's tactics had greatly diminished AIM's effectiveness—just as the FBI has done to the Black Panthers (see chapter 1, "The Black Panther Party") and the Brown Berets (see box in chapter 3). AIM activist Dennis Banks told a *Rolling Stone* magazine interviewer in 1977, "All kinds of strange things have been happening. I suppose [AIM is] 99 percent infiltrated by now."

The occupation of Mount Rushmore

On September 18, 1970, about fifty Indians from AIM, the United Indians of America, the United Tribes of Alcatraz (a group established to coordinate ongoing demonstrations at the island), and other organizations undertook an occupation of Mount Rushmore National Memorial in the

Black Hills of South Dakota. The group was led by AIM activist and Oglala Sioux Russell Means, a Lakota Indian and doctoral candidate at the University of California-Berkeley named Lehman "Lee" Brightman, and a Santee Sioux and publicity coordinator during the occupation of Alcatraz Island named John Trudell. The men demanded that the United States honor its 1868 Treaty of Fort Laramie with the Sioux nation and return to the Sioux all the lands in South Dakota west of the Missouri River, including Mount Rushmore and the rest of the Black Hills.

Upon meeting at Mount Rushmore, the group first approached a concessions booth and destroyed a stack of postcards bearing a photograph of Indian bodies piled up following the 1890 Massacre at Wounded Knee. The activists yelled at the tourists: "Think of the Jews at Dachau and Auschwitz. If the park sold pictures of their remains, would you buy them?"

The Indians then took over the stage in the amphitheater usually used by park rangers to speak to tourists. Lee Brightman delivered a speech to a surprised audience about the true history of the four presidents whose faces were sculpted into the mountain. In his autobiography called *Where White Men Fear to Tread,* Means described the contents of Brightman's speech:

> Lee explained that George Washington had become famous as an Indian killer during the French and Indian War.... He had risen quickly through the militia ranks by butchering Indian communities and burning the homes.... Then Lee spoke of Thomas Jefferson, who more than once had proposed the annihilation of the Indian race to 'cleanse' the Americas.... It was ... Jefferson who wrote the Declaration of Independence, which as every American schoolchild should know, includes the phrase "the merciless Indian savages, whose known rule of warfare is an undistinguished destruction of all ages, sexes, and conditions."

> Next, Lee spoke about Abraham Lincoln who, two days before issuing the Emancipation Proclamation, signed an order to execute thirty-eight Indians for the so-called Great Sioux Uprising in Minnesota. Lincoln apparently didn't care that those men had been chosen at random, without a hearing, much less a trial....

> Finally, Lee spoke about Teddy Roosevelt, the biggest thief ever to occupy the White House. Roosevelt violated scores of treaties, and illegally nationalized more Indian land than any president, before or since. He called his booty 'national parks' and 'national forests' to cement the thefts into law.

As darkness crept over the mountain, the group of Indians made their way up the monument. They were quickly captured by Forest Service rangers and brought back down. The Indians, who outnumbered the rangers, managed to slip away one by one and climb back up the mountain. They set up camp in an open space behind the sculpture of Roosevelt's head. Supporters from nearby Rapid City brought food, water, and other supplies. The demonstration received national news coverage. Groups of Indians remained on Mount Rushmore until that December, when winter storms forced them off.

On June 6, 1971, a group of twenty-four Indian activists returned to the top of Mount Rushmore and again demanded the return of Sioux lands. Rather than permitting another long occupation, the rangers called in the National Guard to remove the demonstrators. The Indians, many of whom were roughed up by guardsmen on the trip down the mountain, were charged with trespassing. "In our defense," wrote Means in his autobiography, "we cited the 1868 treaty, which affirmed that the Black Hills were our holy land. We couldn't be trespassing on our own sacred mountain." The charges were dropped.

AIM's Thanksgiving Day action at Plymouth Rock

At the invitation of Wampanoag Indians living near Martha's Vineyard (close to the original Plymouth Colony), AIM members and other Indian activists traveled to the site of the first Pilgrims' landing on Thanksgiving Day in 1970. The Wampanoag nation had eventually been all but wiped out by the very settlers whom the tribe had helped survive for their first two years on this continent. The modern-day Wampanoag people wanted to spread their version of Thanksgiving—that the tradition originated as a feast in celebration of, and giving thanks for, the massacre of the Indians.

Indian activists kicked off their 1970 Thanksgiving Day protest with a march down the highway to a reconstructed pilgrim village called Plimoth Plantation. Beating drums and singing songs, the marchers entered the village dining hall and overturned tables, upsetting the feast. The protesters then headed for the harbor, where a reproduction of the *Mayflower* (the ship on which the original pilgrims came to America) was open to tourists. AIM members boarded the ship, evicted the tourists, took down the American flags, and destroyed displays depicting the pilgrims' version of Thanksgiving. After reaching an agreement with police who had gathered at the water's edge, the Indians left the ship with guarantees they would not be prosecuted.

During the night, John Trudell and a few compatriots snuck through the fence surrounding Plymouth Rock monument and covered the rock with red paint—symbolizing the blood of the Indians on the white people's hands.

Trail of Broken Treaties

The Red Power movement took its demands to Washington, D.C., in the fall of 1972 with the famous Trail of Broken Treaties protest. Organized by AIM leaders Dennis Banks and Russell Means, and fish-in leader Hank Adams, a caravan of trucks, cars, and buses departed from the West Coast that October. The vehicles headed east, stopping at reservations along the way to pick up more participants. Upon their arrival in Washington, D.C., the Trail of Broken

The Longest Walk was a five-month protest march that began on Alcatraz Island and ended in Washington, D.C. The 1978 walk commemorated the 1972 "Trail of Broken Treaties" caravan. *Reproduced by permission of UPI/Bettmann.*

Treaties group went to the Bureau of Indian Affairs and presented their sweeping list of demands called "The Twenty Points."

Foremost among the protesters' demands was the repeal of the Indian Appropriations Act of 1871, which had ended the Indians' treaty-making status. Other demands included restitution for all treaty violations; the return of 110 million acres of land to native peoples; the revocation of state government authority over Indian affairs; the repeal of termination laws; the reinstatement of government services to unrecognized Indian tribes in the eastern United States; the opportunity to address a joint session of Congress; and the establishment of an Office of Federal Indian Relations and Community Reconstruction in lieu of the Bureau of Indian Affairs.

When security guards tried to dislodge the Indians from BIA headquarters, the confrontation turned violent. The Native Americans kicked out the BIA officials and blockaded themselves in the building for six

Native Americans stand guard at the Sacred Heart Catholic church during AIM's 1973 Wounded Knee occupation. *Reproduced by permission of Corbis-Bettmann.*

days. During that time, the protesters destroyed files and equipment. They stated their terms for surrender as the granting of their demands and amnesty for all participants.

Negotiations between the government and the Indians led to a truce. The protesters agreed to leave the building, and the government agreed to consider the group's demands, exempt the protesters from prosecution, and provide $66,000 for the group's return trip. The government later rejected the Indians' demands.

The occupation of Wounded Knee

"It is better to die on your feet than to live on your knees" read the message on the paper nailed to the trading post at Wounded Knee in 1973. One of the most powerful and confrontational displays of Red Power occurred over a ten-week period beginning in late February 1973, at the village of Wounded Knee in the Pine Ridge Reservation in South Dakota. This action occurred at the historic site where more than 150 (by some estimates as many as 370) Native Americans were massacred by U.S. forces in 1890 (see box, "Massacre at Wounded Knee").

The occupation of Wounded Knee began as a quest by Oglala Sioux (or Lakota, the native name for "Sioux") traditionalists to oust their corrupt tribal government. (Traditionalists are adherents of Native American cultural practices and religions.) According to Native American scholar Vine Deloria Jr., writing in the *New York Times Magazine,* "the message of the traditionalists is simple. They demand a return to basic Indian philosophy, establishment of ancient methods of government by open council instead of elected officials, a revival of Indian religions and replacement of white laws with Indian customs; in

short, a complete return to the ways of the old people."

The Indian traditionalists regarded tribal chairman Richard Wilson—as well as his ruthless, BIA-financed police force, the Guardians of the Oglala Nation (commonly referred to as the "GOON squad")—as puppets of the BIA. Traditionalists believed that Wilson was compromising the interests of the Oglala Sioux people for his personal gain.

Traditionalists storm church, store On February 28, 1973, several hundred Oglala Sioux traditionalists stormed a church and general store in Wounded Knee and took hostages. They called upon AIM for assistance, and several AIM members answered the call. As representatives of national and international media flocked to the scene, the protesters took advantage of the opportunity to publicize the plight of Indians in America.

According to a *New York Times* article dated March 1, 1973, "the embattled Indians relayed demands to Washington that the Senate Foreign Relations Committee hold hearings on treaties made with the Indians, that the Senate start a 'full-scale investigation' of Government treatment of the Indians, and that another inquiry be started into 'all Sioux reservations in South Dakota.' Mr. Camp [Carter Camp, a spokesman for AIM] said: 'We will occupy this town until the Government sees fit to deal with the Indian people, particularly the Oglala Sioux tribe in South Dakota. We want a true Indian nation, not one made up of Bureau of Indian Affairs puppets.'"

Soon after the takeover, the Indian occupiers found themselves encircled by heavily armed agents of the FBI and BIA, as well as U.S. marshals and members of tribal and local police forces. The U.S. Army prepared for an invasion by dispatching to the scene seventeen armored personnel carriers, 130,000 rounds of ammunition for M-16 firearms, 41,000 rounds of ammunition for M-1 firearms, 24,000 flares, twelve grenade launchers, 600 cases of tear gas, 100 rounds of M-40 explosives, helicopters, and Phantom jets.

Standoff turns into siege The armed standoff lasted seventy-one days. During that time AIM leader Russell Means was sent to Washington, D.C., to try to strike a deal with the BIA, but was unsuccessful. Twice during the standoff firefights broke out, resulting in the deaths of two AIM members and one FBI agent.

Negotiations brought the siege to an end on May 8. While the action did not remove Wilson from government, it discredited his administration. In the 1974 tribal government elections, Russell Means challenged Wilson for the tribal chairmanship. Wilson declared victory in the election, however the U.S. Commission on Civil Rights found widespread fraud and charged that almost one-third of all votes cast appeared to have been in some way improper. Two years later, Wilson was unseated by Al Trimble, considered a political moderate.

Wounded Knee inspired and revitalized Red Power activists. The occupation of Wounded Knee was "the ultimate in a man's life," according to Dennis Banks in *Native American Testimony.* "Looking back, I really believed that the broken hoop was mended at Wounded Knee, and that the water was being given to the tree of life. Wounded Knee was an attempt to help an entire race survive."

The Pine Ridge Reservation after Wounded Knee

From 1972 to 1975, a series of more than 300 politically-motivated killings made the Pine Ridge Reservation the murder capital of the world. There were more killings per capita at Pine Ridge than in Detroit, Chicago, or even in Chile following the 1973 military coup. It was clear that AIM members had been especially targeted by Dick Wilson's GOON squads for revenge. From 1973 to 1975, sixty-nine AIM members were gunned down or died under mysterious circumstances. Another 350 people associated with AIM were wounded in shootings, stabbings, or beatings.

Gunfight leads to deaths It was amid this tension and fear that two FBI agents described by some observers as "John Wayne types" came to the Pine Ridge reservation on June 26, 1975, to arrest a Oglala Sioux Indian teenager named Jimmy Eagle. Eagle had been charged with armed robbery for allegedly stealing a white man's cowboy boots with a pocket knife. A gunfight broke out between the FBI agents and Indians, the details of which remain in dispute. In the end, however, the conflict claimed the lives of the two FBI agents and a twenty-four-year-old Indian man.

Outraged that two of its agents had been killed, the FBI began an all-out assault on the reservation. In an alleged search for the killers, the FBI dispatched assault teams armed with helicopters, fully automatic weapons, and tracking dogs. The teams broke into and vandalized homes, harassed residents, and trampled upon sacred ceremonial grounds.

Activists are charged Ten weeks after the shoot-out, the FBI charged three AIM activists—Leonard Peltier (1944–), Bob Robideau, and Dino Butler—with the two FBI agents' deaths. The FBI, however, was unable to produce hard evidence linking any of the three activists to the murders. Robideau and Butler were brought to trial one year after the killings and acquitted by all-white juries (the prosecution's two key witnesses both admitted that the FBI had bought their testimony). Peltier escaped to Canada rather than face a trial in South Dakota, where anti-Indian sentiment ran extremely high. Peltier fled, he later stated, because he "realized the possibility of getting a fair trial was very slim."

Peltier tried In February 1976 Peltier was arrested in Canada and soon after extradited (returned) to the United States. The Justice Department spared

In 1975 Native American activist Leonard Peltier was charged with the murder of two FBI agents at the Pine Ridge Reservation. Despite a lack of hard evidence linking him to the crime, Peltier was eventually found guilty and sentenced to two life terms. *Reproduced by permission of AP/Wide World Photos.*

no efforts in building a case against Peltier. One potential witness approached by the FBI was AIM activist Anna Mae Aquash. When Aquash claimed that she had no information about the killings, she was warned by an FBI agent that she would be "dead within a year." Indeed, Aquash was found shot to death on the Pine Ridge Reservation in February 1976 (her murder remains officially unsolved to this day). After approaching and harassing several other Pine Ridge residents, all of whom refused to cooperate, the FBI finally produced a woman named Myrtle Poor Bear to implicate Peltier. Poor Bear later claimed that she had given her statement under threat of bodily harm.

A controversial conviction Peltier was convicted of the murders of the FBI agents and handed two life sentences to be served consecutively (one after another). Peltier's trial was very controversial, and the evidence against him was limited and inconclusive. The *Los Angeles Times* reported that prosecutors in the case "shopped" for a judge, meaning that they sought out a judge for the case who was sympathetic to the prosecutors' position and who would likely convict Peltier. In his column of December 28, 1982, Jack Anderson wrote that even though "'shopping' for a friendly judge is an old, if not particularly honorable, practice in the American system of justice ... the FBI and federal prosecutors carried it to an unsavory extreme in the murder trial of American Indian activist Leonard Peltier."

Peltier is currently being held at Leavenworth Federal Prison in northeastern Kansas. His supporters and the governments of many nations around the world consider him a political prisoner of the United States, and continue to press for his release. In 1994 AIM activists and founders Dennis Banks and Mary Jane Wilson-Medrano led the Walk for Jus-

tice, calling for Peltier's release. Similar to the "Longest Walk" of 1978 (see box), the Walk for Justice began on Alcatraz Island on February 11 and ended in Washington, D.C., on July 15. Marchers gathered signatures in support of Peltier along the way.

Legislative victories of the 1970s, 1980s, and 1990s

By the mid-1970s the various demands of the Red Power movement had been whittled down to one essential call: self-determination. Self-determination can best be defined as the desire of Indians to control their own institutions—such as programs in health, education, and economic development—and their own destinies. Indian activists denounced assimilationist policies and pressures and advocated the preservation of Native American culture and values. They pressed for the return of sacred objects, cultural artifacts, and human remains held in museums.

Self-determinationists have made substantial legislative gains over the past three decades. Congress passed numerous acts expanding Native American rights in the areas of education, religious freedom, cultural artifacts and human remains, children's welfare, self-government, and tribal status. In addition, some tribes have seen the return of sacred lands, and others have been awarded monetary compensation (the majority of land claims filed by tribes, however, have been rejected).

AIM and the Pine Ridge Reservation on Film

Two movies about the activities of the American Indian Movement (AIM) on the Pine Ridge Reservation—one a documentary and the other a fictional portrayal—were released in 1992. *Incident at Oglala: The Leonard Peltier Story* and *Thunderheart*, both directed by Michael Apted, feature AIM members in their casts.

Incident at Oglala chronicles events on the Pine Ridge Reservation, beginning with AIM's 1973 occupation of Wounded Knee and ending with the campaign to free AIM activist Leonard Peltier. The film covers the events leading up to the 1975 shootout that claimed the lives of two FBI agents and one Indian. It critically examines the controversial trial of Peltier, as well as his con-

viction and sentencing to two consecutive life terms. Executive producer Robert Redford makes a convincing case that Peltier was framed. The footage includes interviews with AIM activists John Trudell, Dennis Banks, and Leonard Peltier.

Thunderheart touches on similar themes as *Incident at Oglala*. This drama was filmed on the Pine Ridge Reservation and stars Val Kilmer, Sam Shepard, and Graham Greene, and features appearances by John Trudell and Dennis Banks. The story revolves around an FBI agent (played by Kilmer) who is one-quarter Lakota Sioux. As the agent investigates a murder on the reservation, he comes to accept and embrace his Native American heritage.

The Indian Education Act of 1972

In the late 1960s Indian rights advocate Senator Edward Kennedy (1932–) commissioned a report on the status of Indian education in America. The report, published in 1969 by the Senate's Indian education subcommittee and entitled *Indian Education: A National Tragedy—A National Challenge* (also called the Kennedy Report) painted a grim picture of Indian education.

The report's authors found that the educational system was failing Native American students, as evi-

denced by very high dropout rates among Native American high-school and middle school students. In addition, very few Indian students were going on to college. The report asserted that racism, poverty, and misguided social policies such as termination (see "The era of termination and relocation") were all working against the academic achievement of Indian students. The report included several recommendations, including the addition of Native American history, culture, and languages in school curricula; and the consultation of tribal leaders and Indian parents in the establishment of school policies.

Congress included many of the Kennedy Report's recommendations in the Indian Education Act of 1972. The act required that public school districts with significant numbers of Indian students solicit input from tribes and parents; allocate funds for schools, colleges, and adult education programs on reservations; and provide funds for public schools, colleges, and tribes to develop Native American studies programs.

The Indian Education Act also established an Office of Indian Education within the Department of the Interior, to be staffed entirely by Native Americans and charged with implementing the Education Act. As a result of the establishment of tribal colleges, the number of Indians attending college was five times higher at the end of the 1970s than it was in the early 1960s.

The Indian Financing Act

In 1974 Congress responded to Native American rights groups' calls for self-determination in economic matters with the passage of the Indian Financing Act. This act was touted by its congressional sponsors as providing funds to tribal members, so that they could develop tribal economies. The Indian Finance Act's stated purpose was "to provide capital on a reimbursable basis to help develop and utilize Indian resources, both physical and human, to a point where the Indians will fully exercise responsibility for the utilization and management of their own resources and where they

will enjoy a standard of living from their own productive efforts comparable to that enjoyed by non-Indians in neighboring communities."

Most of the monies provided by the act were given or loaned to individual Indian entrepreneurs (businesspeople) for the start-up of new businesses. Contrary to the intentions of the act's authors, however, the influx of funds did not significantly improve the health of tribal economies.

"The act was applauded as a major step forward in financing reservation development," wrote Indian historian Vine Deloria Jr. and professor of political science Clifford Lytle in their book *The Nations Within,* "but it was more a cosmetic reordering of existing loan programs administered by the Bureau of Indian Affairs.... The secretary of the interior was authorized to pay interest subsidies and to guarantee or insure loans from private lenders."

The Indian Self-Determination and Education Assistance Act

The Indian Self-Determination and Education Assistance Act, passed in 1975, spelled the end of government officials' domination over reservation life by granting Indian tribes control over the administration of all government assistance programs. This act contained several provisions: tribal governments were empowered to negotiate with the BIA and other U.S. government departments over the terms of social welfare and education programs; tribal governments could oversee, restructure, or even reject social programs that did not meet tribal needs; tribal governments were eligible to receive grants for training their members in administrative procedures and financial management, as well as for the construction and operation of health clinics; and every school district with a sizable Native American student population was required to establish an Indian Parents Committee that would participate in decision making.

The introduction to the Indian Self-Determination and Education Assistance Act reads:

> The Congress hereby recognizes the obligation of the United States to respond to the strong expression of the Indian people for self-determination by assuring maximum Indian participation in the direction of educational as well as other Federal services to Indian communities so as to render such services more responsive to the needs and desires of those communities.
>
> The Congress declares its commitment to the maintenance of the Federal Government's unique and continuing relationship with and responsibility to the Indian people through the establishment of a meaningful Indian self-determination policy which will permit an orderly transition from Federal domination of programs for and services to Indians to effective and meaningful participation by the Indian people in the planning, conduct, and administration of those programs and services.

The Indian Self-Determination and Education Act has been characterized by some Native American scholars and activists as more fluff than substance, insofar as its provisions have little real effect on Indian affairs. "Although heralded by its congressional sponsors as a major development in Indian policy, the act was actually only a footnote to the original ideas of 'self-government' promulgated [promoted] by Commissioner John Collier four decades before," wrote Laurence M. Hauptman, professor of history at the State University of New York and expert on Indian affairs, in his essay "Congress, Plenary Power, and the American Indian, 1870 to 1992". Hauptman continued: "Although the 1975 act allowed and encouraged Indian contracting, in actuality it only formalized the tenuous relationships which had grown up in the 1960s when Indian tribes became sponsoring agencies of federal poverty programs."

The Indian Child Welfare Act

Long a source of bitterness among Native Americans toward the federal and state governments was the practice of taking of Indian children out of their communities. Between the years 1900 and 1926 federal government policy dictated that all Indian children be placed in boarding schools, where the children would be "civilized" and converted to Christianity. In the years that followed, large numbers (on some reservations, 25 to 35 percent) of Indian children were removed from homes deemed unfit by state welfare workers.

The authority of state courts to make decisions regarding Native American children was formally rescinded in 1979 with the passage of the Indian Child Welfare Act. This act granted responsibility for deciding the best interests of Indian children to the tribal courts. The act stated that whenever an Indian child was removed from his or her home, all efforts should be made to place that child in the care of a relative, a member of the child's tribe, or an Indian family, before placing that child with non-Indians. The legislation also provided funds for the improvement of family court systems and foster care programs on reservations.

In part, the Indian Child Welfare Act states that:

> there is no resource that is more vital to the continued existence and integrity of Indian tribes than their children and ... the United States has a direct interest, as trustee, in protecting Indian children who are members of or are eligible for membership in an Indian tribe ... it is the policy of this Nation to protect the best interests of Indian children and to promote the stability and security of Indian tribes and families by the establishment of minimum Federal standards for the removal of Indian children from their families and the placement of such children in foster or adoptive homes which will reflect the unique values of Indian culture, and by providing for assistance to Indian tribes in the operation of child and family service programs.

The American Indian Religious Freedom Act

Beginning in the early 1800s, American legislators outlawed many Native American religious traditions on reservations. The aim of the law-makers was to turn Indians away from their ancient customs so that they could more easily blend in with white Americans. While the most blatant attacks on Indian religious freedom were curtailed during the Indian New Deal of the 1930s (see "The 'Indian New Deal'"), more subtle forms of religious discrimination persisted into the modern era.

The most common infraction on Indians' religious rights in recent times has been the denial of access to sacred sites on federal lands—lands formerly belonging to Indian tribes. Most American Indian tribes attribute great religious significance to their ancestral homelands; in fact, many Indians believe that the Great Spirit (the equivalent of a god or creator) forever resides there.

Native Americans were finally granted, in word if not in deed, religious freedom in 1978. In that year Congress passed the American Indian Religious Freedom Act. The act opens with the line, "Henceforth it shall be the policy of the United States to protect and preserve for American Indians their inherent right of freedom to believe, express, and exercise the traditional religions of the American Indian, Eskimo, Aleut, and Native Hawaiians, including but not limited to access to sites, use and possession of sacred objects, and the freedom to worship through ceremonials and traditional rites."

A decade after the act's passage, however, its application failed an important test. In the 1988 *Lyng v.*

Young dancers perform at the Gathering of Nations pow wow in Albuquerque, New Mexico. This annual event—featuring more than 700 tribes—celebrates Native American traditions and culture. *Photo by Eric Draper. Reproduced by permission of AP/Wide World Photos.*

Northwest Indian Cemetery Protective Association case, the Supreme Court ruled that the U.S. Forest Service could construct a road through sacred Indian sites in the Six Rivers National Forest in northern California. The Court came to its conclusion despite its recognition that "the logging and road-building projects at issue in this case could have devastating effects on traditional Indian religious practices." The judges justified their decision by claiming there was no proof of intentional violation of Indian religious rights on the part of the Forest Ser-

vice—and therefore no violation of religious freedom had occurred.

The American Indian Religious Freedom Act was further weakened in 1990, when the Supreme Court refused to uphold Native Americans' right to consume peyote. Peyote (pronounced pay-OH-tee) is a type of cactus that has a hallucinogenic effect when eaten. Peyote ingestion is an important element of some Indian religious rites.

In *Employment Division, Department of Human Resources of Oregon et al.*

v. Smith, the Supreme Court validated the decision by the state of Oregon to fire (and deny unemployment benefits to) two Indian drug counselors and members of the Native American Church who had ingested peyote during a religious ritual. The justices ruled that peyote use could be prohibited under a state criminal statute.

The *Employment Division* ruling was overturned in 1994, when Congress passed the American Indian Religious Freedom Amendments. In part, this legislation stated that "notwithstanding any other provision of law, the use, possession, or transportation of peyote by an Indian for bona fide traditional ceremonial purposes in connection with the practice of a traditional Indian religion is lawful, and shall not be prohibited by the United States or any State. No Indian shall be penalized or discriminated against on the basis of such use, possession or transportation, including but not limited to, denial of otherwise applicable benefits under public assistance programs."

Sacred artifacts and human remains

One rallying point for Native American activists in the 1970s and early 1980s was the return of sacred artifacts and human skeletal remains that had been removed from reservation burial sites over the years by white traders and social scientists. Many of the items that had not been destroyed had ended up in government-funded and private museums, historical societies, and universities. The Smithsonian Institution had collected and stored Indian remains and artifacts since its inception in 1846; in the mid-1980s the Smithsonian housed the nation's largest single collection with more than 18,500 items. For this reason, the Smithsonian was the target of protests by Indian activists in the 1980s.

The federal government's first step toward the return of sacred objects came in 1989, with the passage of the National Museum of the American Indian Act. That act mandated that the Smithsonian return gravesite items to Indian tribes for reburial. It also directed the Smithsonian to establish a separate Museum of the American Indian.

In 1990 Congress passed the Native American Graves Protection and Repatriation Act (NAGPRA). This legislation mandated that sacred artifacts and human remains in the possession of all government-funded agencies be returned to their respective tribes. Specifically, federal agencies and federally funded institutions were ordered to catalogue their Indian skeletal remains and gravesite objects, identify the tribal affiliations of those items, and offer the return of those items to the appropriate tribes.

As stated in NAGPRA, the purpose of the legislation is to "protect Native American burial sites and the removal of human remains, funerary objects, sacred objects, and objects of cultural patrimony on Federal, Indian and Native Hawaiian lands. The Act

The Longest Walk

The Longest Walk was a protest march that began on Alcatraz Island (in remembrance of the 1969–1971 occupation; see "'Red Power': The Native American rights movement') on February 11, 1978, and ended five months later in Washington, D.C. Indians representing many different tribes participated in this action, commemorating the 1972 "Trail of Broken Treaties" caravan (see "Trail of Broken Treaties"). The marchers held educational workshops on issues facing Native Americans as they headed eastward across the nation.

The focus of the marchers' discontent was a series of "new termination" policies (legislation introduced, but not ratified, in the late 1970s by congressmen from the Pacific northwest) that once again threatened the treaty status of Indian tribes. Participants in the march also publicized the history of Native Americans' forced removal from their homelands and the problems that continued to plague Native American communities. They demanded civil rights, tribal self-rule, and the return of stolen lands.

The Longest Walk ended on July 25 with a demonstration at the Washington Monument, attended by tens of thousands of Indians and their supporters. Three days later, twenty-five Native American leaders met with Vice President Walter Mondale and Secretary of the Interior Cecil Andrus to discuss their concerns. One week later, Congress passed a nonbinding resolution calling for religious freedoms for Indians.

---

also sets up a process by which Federal agencies and museums receiving federal funds will inventory holdings of such remains and objects and work with appropriate Indian tribes and Native Hawaiian organizations to reach agreement on repatriation or other disposition of those remains and objects."

The current state of Native America

In the 1960s the federal government began to replace its network of repressive Indian policies with legislation aimed at restoring a measure of self-determination and prosperity to American Indian tribes. Yet U.S. policy still has a long way to go before it can be considered just and fair toward native peoples. Tribes continually fight for their treaty rights and religious freedoms, and are subject to ongoing attempts by the U.S. Congress to revoke their sovereign status.

As in the past, U.S.-Indian policies are largely crafted by white lawmakers on Capitol Hill. Native American activists claim that the entire basis of the relationship between the U.S. government and the Indian tribes must be changed from one of parent-child to one of equals in order for tribes to regain their treaty rights as sovereign nations.

The centuries of plunder, killings, and racist and misguided social policies have inflicted grave harm upon Native America. This harm is evidenced in many forms. Indians, for example, presently have the lowest levels of education and employment and the highest rates of poverty, alcoholism, and suicide of any group of people in the United States.

"Many of the problems faced by American Indian nations today stem from a pattern of congressional intrusions and manipulations over the past two centuries," wrote historian Laurence M. Hauptman in "Congress, Plenary Power, and the American Indian, 1870 to 1992." He added that "nearly every congressional change in Indian policy has been presented as a reform or a 'benefit' to Indians regardless of their wishes.... The doctrine of plenary power and the whole nature of the present federal-Indian relationship must be altered from one of paternalism and intervention to true self-government."

Indian standards of living, 1979–present

In 1979 a U.S. government report found that "Native Americans, on average, have the lowest per capita income, the highest unemployment rate, the lowest level of educational achievement, the shortest lives, the worst health and housing conditions, and the highest suicide rate in the United States. The poverty among Indian families is nearly three times greater than the rate for non-Indian families and Native people collectively rank at the bottom of every social and economic statistical indicator." In 1980 more than half of all Indians lived off reservations—most of them in cities. About 25 percent of urban Indians lived below the poverty line, and the dropout rate for urban Indian teenagers was 40 percent.

Unemployment for American Indian men in 1979 was 17 percent (compared to 6 percent for white men). Of the 83 percent of Indian men who worked in 1979, fewer than half had full-time jobs. And the majority of those with full-time jobs were not employed year-round, but had seasonal jobs in sectors such as construction, tourism, and agriculture.

Indians workers are disproportionately represented in low-paying, menial jobs. In 1980, 25 percent of white men worked in high-paying professions while only 15 percent of Indian men held similar jobs. One in four Indian women in 1980 worked as a motel maid, waitress, or other low-paying job.

In 1990 the U.S. Census Bureau documented the deplorable housing conditions on Indian reservations. The bureau's findings determined that nearly 18 percent of households were overcrowded (more than 1.5 persons

Hopi-Navajo Relocation at Big Mountain

In October 1996 President Bill Clinton signed into law the Navajo-Hopi Land Dispute Settlement Act of 1996. This act gave the Hopi tribal government—which is considered by many Hopi people to be corrupt and controlled by the U.S. government and large energy companies—authority over a large tract of reservation land in northern Arizona. The act empowered the Hopi tribal government to begin evicting Navajo (also known by their traditional name, Dineh) people living on that land after December 31, 1996.

The 1996 legislation is only the most recent milestone in a decades-long dispute on the area known as Big Mountain. In the 1970s vast coalfields were discovered beneath the desert land of the Hopi and Navajo reservations, especially beneath the sacred Hopi area called Black Mesa. The existence of coal captured the interest of Peabody Coal Company. Peabody persuaded the Hopi tribal government to lease Black Mesa and the surrounding lands and proceeded to turn the land into the world's largest strip mine. To make room for the mining operation, thousands of people (mostly Navajo, but also some Hopi) were forced to move.

There are several parties involved in the Big Mountain dispute, and the battle lines are somewhat ambiguous. The most obvious conflict pits Navajo and Hopi traditionalists and their supporters against Peabody Coal Company and their supporters (the Hopi tribal government, the Bureau of Indian Affairs, and the Department of the Interior). There is also a long-standing rivalry, however (the seriousness of which is debatable), between the Navajo and Hopi people who jointly occupy the coal-rich land. Regardless of any problems that may exist between them, the Navajo and Hopi people have managed to live together in relative peace for centuries.

Many Native Americans and their supporters believe that the Navajo-Hopi conflict has been used as an excuse by energy interests to move both groups of people away from the area, so that coal mining can proceed. Some Navajo people have refused to leave their ancestral homelands, in defiance of court orders. Big Mountain is widely regarded as the most recent example of the age-old policies of relocation of Native Americans and theft of Indian land.

per room). Less than half of all households were connected to public sewers and 18 percent of households lacked complete kitchens (a sink with running water, a stove, and a refrigerator). About 20 percent of reservation households lacked complete plumbing (hot and cold running water, a flush

Navajo Indians protest the forced relocation of tribal members from Big Mountain under the Land Dispute Settlement Act of 1996 (see box). *Reproduced by permission of UPI/Corbis-bettmann.*

toilet, and a bathtub or shower) and 53 percent had no telephone.

The 1990 Census Bureau report also contained the following statistics on Native Americans: 23.7 percent of families lived in poverty (compared to the U.S. national rate of 10.3 percent); a 14.4 percent unemployment rate for all adult Indians with an unemployment rate of 45 percent for reservation Indians; a suicide rate of 15 per 100,000 persons (compared to the U.S. national rate of 11.7 per 100,000); and a dropout rate of

35.5 percent (compared to the U.S. national rate of 28.8 percent).

In the 1995 "Report to White House Domestic Council on Native Americans," the National Urban Indian Policy Coalition established that "as a direct result of various federal policies including the Relocation and Assimilation programs of the 1950s-1960s designed to assimilate American Indians from reservations into urban populations, large populations of American Indians are now faced with formidable barriers ranging from non-access to Indian-specific programs and policies to exclusion from public policies and programs. The federal government's assimilation effort has failed. Urban Indians lead the unemployment and poverty rates; the high school dropout rates; and the disease, infant mortality and suicide rates."

In September 1998 President Clinton's Council of Economic Advisers found that conditions had not improved for the Indian population. "American Indians are among the most disadvantaged Americans according to many available indicators, such as poverty rate and median income," wrote the council in its report *Changing America: Indicators of Social and Economic Well-Being by Race and Hispanic Origin.*

Sources

Books

Champagne, Duane, and Michael A. Paré, eds. *Native North American Chronology.* Detroit: U•X•L, 1995.

Churchill, Ward and Jim Vander Wall. *Agents of Repression: The FBI's Secret Wars Against the Black Panther Party and the American Indian Movement.* Boston: South End Press, 1988.

Deloria, Vine Jr. *Behind the Trail of Broken Treaties: An Indian Declaration of Independence.* New York: Dell Publishing, 1974.

Deloria, Vine Jr. *Custer Died for Your Sins: An Indian Manifesto.* New York: Macmillan, 1969.

Deloria, Vine Jr. and Clifford M. Lytle. *The Nations Within: The Past and Future of American Indian Sovereignty.* New York: Pantheon Books, 1984.

Grossman, Mark. *The ABC-CLIO Companion to The Native American Rights Movement.* Santa Barbara, CA: ABC-CLIO, 1996.

Harvey, Karen D. and Lisa D. Harjo. *Indian Country: A History of Native People in America.* Golden, Colorado: North American Press, 1994.

Hauptman, Laurence M. "Congress, Plenary Power, and the American Indian, 1870 to 1992," in *Exiled from the Land of the Free: Democracy, Indian Nations, and the U.S. Constitution,* edited by Oren R. Lyons and John C. Mohawk. Santa Fe, NM: Clear Light Publishers, 1992.

Hurtado, Albert L. and Peter Iverson, eds. *Major Problems in American Indian History: Documents and Essays.* Lexington, MA: Heath, 1994.]

Josephy, Alvin M. Jr., ed. *Red Power: The American Indians' Fight for Freedom.* New York: McGraw-Hill Book Company, 1971.

Lazarus, Edward. *Black Hills White Justice: The Sioux Nation Versus the United States: 1775 to the Present.* New York: HarperCollins, 1991.

Matthiessen, Peter. *In the Spirit of Crazy Horse.* New York: Viking Press, 1980.

Means, Russell, and Marvin J. Wolf. *Where White Men Fear to Tread: The Autobiography of Russell Means.* New York: St. Martin's Press, 1995.

Nabakov, Peter, ed. *Native American Testimony: A Chronicle of Indian-White Relations from Prophecy to the Present, 1492–1992.* New York: Viking, 1991.

Nies, Judith. *Native American History: A Chronology of a Culture's Vast Achievements and Their Links to World Events.* New York: Ballantine Books, 1996.

Olson, James S. *Encyclopedia of American Indian Civil Rights.* Westport, CT: Greenwood Press, 1997.

Rose, Cynthia and Duane Champagne, eds. *Native North American Almanac.* Detroit: U•X•L, 1994.

Sigler, Jay A., ed. *Civil Rights in America: 1500 to the Present*. Detroit: Gale, 1998, pp. 219–39.

Weyler, Rex. *Blood of the Land: The Government and Corporate War against the American Indian Movement*. New York: Everest House, 1982.

Periodicals

Anderson, Jack. "FBI Shopped for Its Judge in Indian Case." *Washington Post*. December 28, 1982: C14.

"Armed Indians Seize Wounded Knee, Hold Hostages." *The New York Times*. March 1, 1973: 1, 16.

Bergman, Lowell and David Weir. "The Killing of Anna Mae Aquash." *Rolling Stone*. April 7, 1977: 51–55.

Deloria, Vine Jr. "This Country Was a Lot Better Off When the Indians Were Running It." *The New York Times Magazine*. March 8, 1970.

Giago, Tim. "Notes from Indian Country." *Lakota Times*. August 5, 1987.

Web Sites

Committee on Indian Affairs."Navajo-Hopi Land Dispute Settlement Act of 1996." September 9, 1996. [Online] Available http://www.wais.access.gpo.gov (last accessed October 23, 1998).

Council of Economic Advisers (for the President's Initiative on Race). "Changing America: Indicators of Social and Economic Well-Being by Race and Hispanic Origin." September 1998. Washington: Government Printing Office. [Online] Available http://www.whitehouse.gov/WH/EOP/CEA/html/publications.html (last accessed on March 22, 1999).

Dineh Alliance. "Overview of the Dineh [Navajo] Crisis." [Online] Available http://www.primenet.com/~dineh/overview.html (last accessed October 23, 1998).

Johnson, Bernice Powell. "Threatening Indian Rights." *Civil Rights Journal*. September 8, 1997. [Online] Available http://www.ucc.org/justice/crj/cr090897.htm (last accessed on April 1, 1999).

National Urban Indian Policy Coalition. *Report to White House Domestic Council on Native Americans*. April 10, 1995. [Online] Available http://www.codetalk.fed.us/counrep.html (last accessed on March 15, 1999).

Ross, Bob. "Topic: Native Americans." *Tampa Tribune Movie Critic*. October 9, 1996. [Online] Available http://www.tampa-trib.com/baylife/rent3067.htm (last accessed on March 15, 1999).

Workers World News Service. "Clinton Approves Big Mountain Evictions." October 31, 1996. [Online] Available http://www.workers.org/ww/bigmtn.html (last accessed on April 1, 1999).

Civil Rights of Selected Immigrant Groups

The myth of the American melting pot must give way to the American tossed salad, with each ingredient retaining its integrity while forming a delicious whole.

Irene Natividad, in her speech "Political and Cultural Diversity: America's Hope and America's Challenge"

This chapter examines the civil rights of selected ethnic groups: Irish Americans, Italian Americans, German Americans, Jewish Americans, and Arab Americans. While each of these groups has experienced discrimination at certain periods throughout their history, most have successfully entered the American social and economic mainstream. At present, Arab Americans and Jewish Americans face a greater degree of negative stereotyping and discrimination than any of the other groups.

As each new group of immigrants entered the United States, they encountered a certain degree of hostility from the residents already there. During economic downturns, for example, it was common for the most recent arrivals to be made scapegoats. They were often blamed for flooding the labor market and contributing to rising unemployment. The type of behavior in which the dominant group blames its economic woes on "outsiders" and demands their expulsion is called nativism. It is interesting to note that some groups who were victims of nativism later expressed nativist hostilities toward other ethnic groups. The Irish, for example, shunned by other European

During the 1800s, millions of Europeans came to the United States. Some immigrants arrived seeking economic opportunities, while others sought to escape poverty, overpopulation, and political oppression. *Reproduced by permission of the Library of Congress.*

groups on the East Coast in the 1840s, moved to the West Coast where they conducted their own nativist campaign against Chinese workers.

The reasons for immigration to the United States, historically and at present, can be placed into two broad categories: an attraction to America's promise of opportunity and freedom; and a necessity to leave one's homeland. Immigrants in the latter category have left their homelands to escape poverty, overpopulation, political strife, warfare, or religious persecution.

During the 1800s, when the population of Europe doubled from 200 million to 400 million, millions of Europeans left their overpopulated homelands for American shores. The nineteenth century was also the time of the Industrial Revolution (the surge in technological and economic development that began in Great Britain around 1750 and spread throughout Europe and eventually to the United States). As a result of industrialization, the dominant means of production shifted from the farm to the factory. Many European farmers and artisans displaced by the Industrial Revolution chose to seek their fortunes in the New World. Waves of European immigration also occurred during World War I (1914–1918) and World War II (1939–1945).

Irish Americans

Irish immigration to the United States began in the 1840s, when the potato crop—the main food staple of the Irish—was destroyed by disease. With many people dying of starvation, hundreds of thousands of Irish people decided to voyage to America. By the end of the decade, there were 1.7 million Irish people in America, a number greater than the population of Ireland.

America was considered a land of plenty for many Irish people. Irish immigrants, who were predominantly Catholic, hoped to find jobs, land, and freedom of religion. Instead, they found that money, jobs, and materials, as well as religious tolerance, were in short supply. Most of the Irish immigrants settled in overcrowded and dirty slums in Boston, New York, and Philadelphia. For many immigrants, housing conditions in the New World were even worse than those they had left behind. The Irish immigrants also found that New England's majority Protestant population was virulently anti-Catholic.

Discrimination against Irish Americans

Because they were largely poor, illiterate, and Catholic, the Irish be-

came outcasts in the New World. They were offered work as domestic servants, ditch diggers, and other types of manual laborers. Many store owners placed signs in their windows reading "No Irish Need Apply," making even menial jobs hard to obtain.

Journalists fanned the flames of anti-Irish sentiment by portraying Irish people as drunken, lazy, stupid, and violent. The stereotypical Irishman, called a "Paddy" (a bastardization of the common Irish name "Patrick") was a buffoon with a large nose, wearing a top hat and carrying a whiskey bottle. Anti-Irish sentiment boiled over during a two day period in 1844, when rioters in Philadelphia killed thirteen Irish immigrants and burned down two Catholic churches. Two years later, a third Irish Catholic church was burned in Philadelphia.

The Know Nothing Party Protestant New Englanders formed nativist organizations to oppose the presence of Catholics in America. The Order of the Star Spangled Banner was one such nativist organization, formed in 1843. By 1849 that organization was renamed the Know Nothing Party because its members, when asked about their activities, responded "I Know Nothing." The Know Nothing Party advocated anti-Catholicism and recommended that immigration and naturalization, particularly for poor people, be restricted.

The Know Nothing Party steadily grew more powerful, and by 1854 it controlled forty-three seats in the U.S. House of Representatives. In Massachusetts members of the Know Nothing Party held the governorship plus a majority of seats in both houses of legislature. The Massachusetts government harassed the Irish population by conducting mass investigations of Catholic schools and convents. At the same time, in Baltimore an anti-Catholic group called the "Plug-Uglies" used guns to keep Irish voters away from polling places.

In 1856 Millard Fillmore (1800–1874) was the unsuccessful presidential candidate for the Know Nothing Party. (Fillmore had previously served as president under the Whig Party from 1850 to 1853.) That a mainstream politician would run for president under the Know Nothing banner demonstrates how acceptable ethnic and religious intolerance was at the time.

Had the Know Nothing Party still existed in 1875 (it disbanded in late 1856), it would have had an ally in the White House. President Ulysses S. Grant was known for making anti-Catholic comments, such as: "If we are to have another contest in the near future of our national existence, I predict that the dividing line will not be Mason and Dixon's, but between [Protestant] patriotism and intelligence on one side, and [Catholic] superstition, ambition, and ignorance on the other." (Named for the surveyors who mapped it from 1763 to 1767, the Mason-Dixon line was a boundary area between Pennsylvania and Virginia. This "line" also marked the divi-

sion between states in the North and states in the South.)

Kennedy's election

Prejudice against Irish Americans gradually diminished beginning in the 1860s. A century later, in 1961, voters elected John F. Kennedy (1917–1963)—an Irish American and a Catholic—to the presidency. During his campaign, Kennedy was forced to address his ethnic and religious heritage. "I believe in an America," Kennedy was quoted as saying in *The Making of the President 1960,* "where the separation of church and state is absolute—where no Catholic prelate would tell the President (should he be a Catholic) how to act and no Protestant minister would tell his parishioners for whom to vote .... I am not the Catholic candidate for President. I am the Democratic Party's candidate for President, who happens also to be a Catholic."

Italian Americans

Immigrants from Italy, especially from southern Italy, first began coming to the United States in large numbers in the 1870s. This mass exodus began after the unification of Italy in 1870 (prior to that year, Italy had been a collection of small states). Economic conditions in the south, which historically had been poor, took a turn for the worse after unification. Wealthy landowners, government officials, and the Catholic church tightened their hold on the region's resources. Although the federal government taxed

The Molly Maguires

Facing a lack of opportunity in American cities, many Irish immigrants sought employment in the countryside. A popular destination for Irish immigrants was the coalfields of northeastern Pennsylvania. Irish Americans worked underground, in dangerous conditions and for meager pay, alongside immigrants of other ethnicities. Above ground in the company towns, however, the miners' housing was segregated by ethnicity.

As a means of protection, Irish laborers banded together in fraternal organizations that had their roots in Ireland. Primary among these organizations was the Ancient Order of Hibernians (AOH). The miners also brought with them from Ireland the tradition of militant labor organizing.

In Ireland a secret organization called the Molly Maguires (named for a tenants-rights activist) was believed to have been responsible for numerous acts of sabotage against landlords and employers in the 1840s. In the 1870s a band of Irish immigrant coalminers in Pennsylvania resurrected the mantle of the Molly Maguires. The coalminers' secret organization, which was believed to have used the AOH as a front group, was suspected of planning and carrying out the killings of two coal mine bosses, one in 1871 and the other in 1875.

The coal mine owners hired a private detective agency to infiltrate and gather information on the AOH. At a series of trials during the years 1875 to 1877, in which the private detective's testimony was the main evidence presented, ten members of the AOH were found guilty of the coal bosses' murders and sentenced to death by hanging. Since that time, the "Molly Maguire" trials (as they came to be known) have come under close critical scrutiny. Evidence indicates that the ten convicted individuals were framed by coal mine owners and their detectives. Judge John P. Lavelle of Carbon County, Pennsylvania (the county in which the Molly Maguire trials took place), addressed the trials by noting that "a private corporation initiated the investigation through a private detective agency. A private police force arrested the alleged defenders, and private attorneys for the coal companies prosecuted them. The state provided only the courtrooom and the gallows."

In 1970 Paramount released a dramatized account of the Molly Maguires's story starring Sean Connery and Richard Harris.

all of Italy, it only spent tax dollars on northern Italy. At the same time, overpopulation and poor weather led to food shortages throughout the south.

Five million people, or one-third of all inhabitants of southern Italy, left their homeland between 1870 and 1914. Most of these immigrants traveled to the United States or Canada. In the United States, Italian immigrants formed communities in New York City; Boston, Massachusetts; Providence, Rhode Island; and in various cities in New Jersey and Pennsylvania. By 1910 there were more Italians living in New York City than in Rome.

Italian immigration to the United States slowed in 1917 because of changes in immigration policy that restricted the entry of eastern and southern Europeans. Italians were not again free to immigrate to the United States in large numbers until after World War II (1939–1945).

Discrimination against Italian Americans

The experience of Italian immigrants in America strongly resembles the experience of Irish immigrants in America. Like the Irish immigrants, Italian immigrants were largely poor and illiterate, and predominantly Catholic. And like the Irish immigrants, Italian immigrants found their housing options limited to dirty, overcrowded tenements and their employment options limited to menial labor.

In addition to facing religious discrimination, Italian immigrants in the United States faced discrimination over their perceived association with the Mafia. (The Mafia is a secret crime organization that originated in Sicily.) As a result, Italians were often stereotyped as short-tempered and prone to impassioned violence.

Nativists and anti-Catholics attempted to dissuade Italian immigration through acts of harassment and assault. The worst display of anti-Italian violence took place in 1891 in New Orleans. An angry mob killed eleven Italians, creating an international scandal. The eleven victims had been suspected, but acquitted, of murdering a city official.

Another case of anti-Italian violence took place in 1895 in Colorado, when residents killed six Italians suspected of involvement in a saloonkeeper's death. The following year, a mob in Louisiana broke into a jail and killed three Italian prisoners.

German Americans

The first German immigrants came to the New World in 1683 at the invitation of William Penn (1644–1718), the Quaker governor of Pennsylvania. The German settlers founded a village outside of Philadelphia, called Germantown. By 1776, the year of American independence, there were 225,000 people of German descent in the United States. While Germans comprised just 6 percent of the U.S. population, they represented the largest group of non-English speaking immigrants and comprised one-third of the population of Pennsylvania.

Eighteenth-century German immigrants came to the New World for a variety of reasons. Many came to escape warfare, poverty, religious persecution, and political intolerance in their homeland. The Germans, whose

The Case of Sacco and Vanzetti

The murder convictions, and subsequent executions, of Italian immigrants Nicola Sacco and Bartolomo Vanzetti reflect the anti-Italian sentiment that was widespread around the turn of the century. Sacco, a shoemaker, and Vanzetti, a fish peddler, had immigrated to the United States from Italy in 1908. Both men were anarchists-dissidents who favored a political system based on voluntary cooperation instead of centralized government rule. (Anarchists believe that governmental rules and regulations interfere with personal liberties.) In the early 1900s (as is the case today), anarchism was an unpopular position because it was considered by most people to be radical and extreme.

Sacco and Vanzetti were accused of the April 15, 1920, burglary-murders of a shoe factory paymaster and his guard. The accused men, however, proclaimed their innocence. During the trial that followed, very little evidence was brought to bear against Sacco and Vanzetti. Nevertheless, on July 14, 1921, both men were found guilty in Massachusetts Superior Court and sentenced to death.

The trial, conviction, and sentencing of Sacco and Vanzetti remains a source of great controversy. During the trial, the accused men's political views were frequently brought up by the prosecutor. It seemed to many people that Sacco and Vanzetti were convicted on the basis of their political beliefs rather than on evidence relating to the crime.

In 1925, while Sacco and Vanzetti were awaiting execution, a convicted murderer named Celestino Madeiros confessed to committing the crime for which Sacco and Vanzetti had been convicted. Despite this compelling new evidence, the state Supreme Court refused to reopen the case.

Sacco and Vanzetti were executed on August 23, 1927. That same day there were protests around the world, and demonstrators exploded bombs in New York City and Philadelphia. While legal opinion presently remains divided on the guilt or innocence of Sacco and Vanzetti, there is a general agreement that the two men did not receive a fair trial. In 1977 Governor Michael Dukakis of Massachusetts cleared the names of Sacco and Vanzetti, claiming that the two men had been tried unjustly.

nationality in their native tongue is expressed by the term *Deutsche,* were mistakenly called the "Pennsylvania Dutch" by other colonists in the New World.

The period of greatest German immigration began in 1820. Between the years 1820 and 1860, 1.5 million Germans came to the United States. During the 1880s, the peak decade of

German immigration, another 1.5 million Germans came to the United States. Most of the nineteenth-century German immigrants settled in the midwestern towns of Chicago, Illinois; Cincinnati, Ohio; Milwaukee, Wisconsin; and St. Louis, Missouri. Although not as poor as the Irish who came during the same time period, many of the German immigrants had fled economic hardship at home. Others immigrated for political reasons. The political refugees, most of whom were well educated and idealistic, set sail for America with the hopes of establishing democratic, peaceful communities.

Germans continued immigrating to America in large numbers through the twentieth century. Between 1820 and 1960, more than 6.7 million Germans moved to the United States, a larger number than any other immigrant group during that time. According to U.S. Census Bureau statistics, as of 1986 more Americans traced their roots to Germany than to any other nation. About 44 million people, or 18 percent of the population, claimed to have German ancestors.

Early expressions of anti-German sentiment

In the eighteenth and nineteenth centuries, most German immigrants settled together in towns where they spoke their native language and wore their native clothing. There was little attempt to assimilate (blend in with other communities). Because of their "differentness," German immi-

grants were commonly the targets of discrimination.

German immigrants arriving in the latter half of the 1800s experienced conditions similar to Irish and Italian immigrants. They often lived in cramped quarters in tenements. Those people who could find employment had to work long hours (up to sixteen hours a day) for low wages.

In cities with large German populations, nativist politicians went to great lengths to keep German Americans and people of other ethnicities from voting. Officials were known to secretly change polling places on the eve of an election, close polling places before the end of the workday, intimidate voters, and stuff ballot boxes with fraudulent ballots. "We are fully justified in saying that the holiest institution of the American people," noted the German-language newspaper *Verbote* in 1880, "the right to vote, has been desecrated and become a miserable farce and a lie."

Anti-German organizations A growing cultural and political awareness took root among German Americans in the late 1800s, following the 1871 unification of Germany. Anti-German organizations, such as the Immigration Restriction League and the American Protective Association, sprang up in response. These groups advocated limitations on German immigration, the requirement of all children in public schools to speak English, and a ban on alcohol. In fact, the campaign to ban alcohol—the Prohibition movement—was motivated in part by a desire to

The Haymarket Riot

In an effort to improve their working conditions—especially to secure an eight-hour workday—German immigrants in Chicago joined with other workers to form labor unions. In 1886 people of German descent constituted one-third of the membership of all labor organizations in Chicago. Over time, the German workers gained a reputation for being militant, uncompromising unionists.

Police frequently disrupted union meetings and harassed union members. They employed violence against striking workers and escorted strikebreakers (people hired to replace striking workers; called "scabs" by the strikers) into the workplace. Hostilities between union members and overzealous police escalated throughout the 1880s and came to a head in 1886.

On May 3, 1886, striking workers at Chicago's McCormick Harvesting Machine Company attempted to prevent strikebreakers from entering the plant. Police, acting to protect the scabs, killed one striker and injured several others. In response, unionists called a protest against police brutality for the following day in Haymarket Square.

The Haymarket rally proceeded without incident until a line of police officers attempted to break up the demonstration. A person whose identity remains unknown to this day threw a dynamite bomb at the approaching police. The bomb killed seven officers and wounded about sixty others. The police then fired at random into the crowd, and a riot ensued.

Eight union leaders were eventually convicted on charges of conspiracy to commit murder. At the trial, no evidence was presented linking the suspects with the bomb. Four of the convicted unionists, three of whom were German American, were hanged on November 11, 1887. A fifth defendant died in prison (the death was ruled a suicide). The surviving three Haymarket defendants were pardoned by the governor of Illinois in 1893.

harm German-American brewery owners. (Prohibition was a period that lasted from 1920 to 1933, during which federal law banned the manufacture or sale of alcohol.)

In 1890, when the militaristic kaiser Wilhelm took over as president of Germany, anti-German sentiment intensified in the United States. Many Americans feared that Wilhelm was bent on conquering the world by force and that German Americans were his representatives in the New World. In 1894 President Theodore Roosevelt (1858–1919) denounced German Americans, as well as Irish Americans, as unpatriotic.

German Americans face hostility during World War I

German Americans were treated with suspicion during World War I (1914–1918), in which the United States sided with Great Britain, France, and Russia against Germany, Austria-Hungary, Turkey, and Bulgaria. (The United States did not become militarily involved in the war until April 6, 1917.) There was a common fear that German Americans would engage in acts of sabotage out of secret sympathy for the German government.

In the fall of 1915 President Woodrow Wilson (1856–1924) delivered a series of speeches questioning the loyalty of German Americans. "There are citizens of the United States," stated Wilson in his 1915 State of the Union address, "who have poured the poison of disloyalty into the very arteries of our national life; who have sought to bring the authority and good name of our government into contempt." Wilson proclaimed that traitorous Americans "must be crushed out."

German Americans were under constant pressure to prove their loyalty to the United States. To ease the fears of their fellow Americans, many German Americans gave up their membership in German organizations, ceased speaking in German outside of their homes, stopped attending churches with predominantly German American congregations, and even changed their German surnames. Members of the German American Alliance chose to dissolve their organization and donate their funds to the American Red Cross. Thousands of German American men joined the U.S. armed forces. These actions, however, did little to alleviate public hostility. No act, it seemed, would convince the American public of German Americans' loyalty.

Telegram intensifies negative sentiment Anti-German sentiment in the United States intensified in 1917, when the British Navy intercepted a telegram from the German government to the Mexican government. In the message the German government offered to help the Mexicans retake Texas, Arizona, and New Mexico from the United States. (The United States had conquered those lands and others during the U.S.-Mexico War of 1846–1848; for more information, see chapter 3). The American public was outraged at Germany's overture of hostility against the United States.

In the wake of this development, German American-owned stores were boycotted, and German language newspapers were forced to submit English translations for censorship by the postmaster before they could be mailed. German Americans were pressured to buy Liberty Bonds (used by the Treasury Department to finance the U.S. armed forces), were jailed for making "disloyal" comments, and were forced to kiss the American flag in public displays. Music by German composers was banned, German textbooks were removed from the shelves, and German language classes were discontinued in schools.

An immigrant neighborhood in New York City. In many large cities, immigrants found that their housing options were limited to dirty, overcrowded tenements. *Reproduced by permission of the Library of Congress.*

There were many cases of vandalism against German American homes, businesses, and schools. German Americans were also targeted for violence—they were beaten, tarred and feathered, and even killed. (Tarring and feathering involves covering a person with tar, then feathers, as a form of humiliation and punishment.) In one incident a coal miner from Maryville, Illinois, named Paul Prager was singled out by his coworkers. The miners accused Prager of being a German spy. They made him sing patriotic American songs and kiss the flag in a public plaza before hanging him. As a result of incidents such as this, the cohesiveness of German American communities and cultural pride of German Americans never regained their pre-World War I status.

German Americans during World War II

Although Germany and the United States were once again on opposite sides during World War II, German Americans were not subjected to the same hostile treatment as during World War I. For years before the racist dictator Adolf Hitler (1889–1945) came to power, most German American organizations had vocally denounced Hitler's policies. When the United States entered the war in 1941, German Americans were quick to pledge loyalty to the war effort. (The United States was drawn into the war after the Japanese bombing of Pearl Harbor, Hawaii, on December 7, 1941.)

By 1941 a large proportion of German Americans were American-born (this was due to a lull in German immigration in the post-World War I years). These German Americans spoke English and had assimilated (or blended) into American society to a far greater extent than previous generations.

About 150,000 German citizens, mainly Jews, immigrated to the United States from 1933 to 1945 (the years preceding and during World War II). Most of these individuals were well-educated political and religious refugees, fleeing the regime of Adolf Hitler and his Nazi Party.

Among the World War II German immigrants were important scientists and intellectuals, including mathematician and physicist Albert Einstein (1879–1955) and Hans Bethe (1906–). In fact, German émigré scientists played an important role in the Manhattan Project, the secret U.S. government program to create nuclear weapons during World War II. The exodus of scientists, teachers, artists, and philosophers is sometimes referred to as Germany's "brain drain."

Jewish Americans

The first large Jewish settlement in the New World was not in North America, but in South America. In the early 1600s many Jews lived in the Dutch colony of Brazil. In 1654, when Portuguese invaders expelled the Jews from Brazil, a group of twenty-three Jews traveled to New Amsterdam (later renamed New York). By 1776 the number of Jews in New York had grown to 2,000. Jews in the United States and in other parts of the world were heartened by the guarantees of religious freedom included in the Constitution of the newly formed United States.

Jews first immigrated to America in significant numbers just prior to the Civil War (1861–1865). Between the years 1830 and 1860, in response to growing repression against Jews in Germany, about 144,000 German Jews came to the New World. (Many of these Jewish immigrants became active in the movement to abolish, or eliminate, slavery in the United States.) The major period of Jewish immigration to the United States began twenty years later, in response to a wave of anti-Jewish violence in Eastern Europe. Between the years 1881 and 1925, 3.5 million Jews immigrated to America.

In the 1920s the number of Jews immigrating to the United States dropped sharply. This reduction was due to the passage of laws that greatly restricted immigration from Eastern European nations. Jewish immigration picked up in two subsequent periods: from 1933 to 1945 and in the 1970s and 1980s. In the former period (the years prior to and during World War II), 150,000 Jews from Germany escaped the increasingly repressive Nazi Party (see box "U.S. Turns Its Back on Jews during World War II"). In the latter period, some 250,000 Jews fled religious persecution in the former Soviet Union.

Today, the United States is home to the world's largest Jewish population. Jews number about 6 million and account for about 3 percent of the U.S. population. Despite their humble beginnings, Jews in the United States have achieved a great measure of economic, social, and political success. One reason for this success has been the great emphasis the Jewish American community places on education. At present, about 80 percent of Jews in America have had some college education and about 40 percent hold advanced degrees. The proportion of Jews who graduate from college is higher than that of any other ethnic or racial group in America.

A brief history of the Jews

The Jewish people have a very long history as refugees. Approximately 4,000 years ago, the ancestors of the Jews, called the Hebrews, lived as nomads in the Middle Eastern desert region known as Canaan (the location of present-day Israel and Palestine). Around the year 1700 B.C., the Hebrews migrated to Egypt to escape famine in their homeland and were enslaved by the Egyptian pharaoh in about 1280 B.C.

The Hebrew slaves were led to freedom by the prophet Moses in the year 1225 B.C. and returned to their former homeland in Canaan. It was during their journey to freedom that the Hebrews established the tenets of Judaism and identified themselves as Jews. The A.D. 135 invasion of Palestine by the Roman army gave rise to the Jewish *Diaspora,* or "dispersal" of the Jewish people throughout Europe and the Middle East.

Antisemitism Wherever they went, Jewish refugees experienced a certain degree of antisemitism (a Semite is a descendant of any of the ancient tribes of southwestern Asia; anti-

Bodies are prepared for identification in a makeshift morgue after the Triangle Shirtwaist Company fire. This deadly sweatshop blaze led to a movement for workplace safety and child labor laws, as well as improved factory fire codes (see box). *Reproduced by permission of the Library of Congress.*

semitism is discrimination against Jews specifically). As a rule, Jews in Europe were not free to enter most professions or trades. One profession left open to Jews—largely because it was frowned upon by the Catholic church—was banking and money-lending. With other people refusing to fill such a role, Jewish immigrants, desperate to make a living, stepped in.

In every country inhabited by the Jews, there were periods of tolerance and periods of repression. Jews were expelled from England in 1290, from France in 1394, and from Spain in 1492. Antisemitism reached a frenzied pitch during the Spanish Inquisition (the period of religious persecution by the Catholic church lasting from 1480 to 1834, during which hundreds of thousands of Jews were burned at the stake or imprisoned). Most of the Jewish refugees fled to Poland, where their rights were protected.

In the late 1700s and early 1800s the political winds in Europe shifted again. While Western European nations guaranteed Jews civil rights and liberties, repression intensified in Eastern Europe. In a region on the Polish/Russian border called the Pale of Settlement, where half of the world's Jewish population resided in the mid-to-late 1800s, Jews were forced to live in segregated areas called ghettoes. In the ghettoes the Jews faced poverty and were vulnerable to massacres by Russian soldiers. Beginning in 1880, millions of Jews headed for America to escape the terrible conditions of the Pale.

In the New World, Jews were relatively free to practice their religion and to choose their occupations. They found it possible to maintain their communities and traditions, even while assimilating into the larger American society.

Conditions of Jewish immigrants in America

For Eastern European Jewish immigrants around the turn of the twentieth century, life in the New World began in the slums and sweatshops of New York City, Boston, Chicago, Philadelphia, Cleveland, St. Louis, and Baltimore. The largest American Jewish immigrant community was located on the Lower East Side of New York City. On the Lower East Side, people lived in dark, dirty, and overcrowded apartments. Working conditions were no better.

Sweatshops Jewish immigrants, many of whom had worked as tailors before

The Triangle Shirtwaist Company Fire

The terrible working conditions of garment industry employees in New York City were made shockingly clear to the nation on March 25, 1911. On that date, a fire at the Triangle Shirtwaist Company claimed the lives of 146 workers. Most of the victims were young Jewish or Italian immigrant women and girls.

The fire began on the eighth floor of the building and rapidly spread to the top two floors. Workers were trapped inside the burning rooms by doors that had been locked to prevent theft. The fire escape quickly became overloaded and collapsed. The firefighters' ladders, which only extended six stories, were of no use. Left with no other option, many workers leapt to their death from windows eight, nine, or ten stories up.

People throughout the United States were outraged by the incident. One hundred thousand people memorialized the dead workers with a march down Broadway. The tragedy sparked a movement for workplace safety laws, factory fire codes, and child labor laws.

coming to America, found work in garment sweatshops (large processing companies that hired workers to sew garments, such as dress shirts). The sweatshops were hot, stuffy, and dirty. Workers had to toil twelve-to-fifteen hours per day, seven days a week, for meager wages. The Jewish immigrants accepted those conditions because they were desperate for any kind of work. Their goal was to save enough money to pay the passage of family members still living in Europe to America. Another reason Jews were attracted to garment work was that most of the garment company owners were themselves Jewish.

Tensions steadily increased between the Jewish sweatshop owners and their Jewish employees. A shared religion was not enough to compel the owners—primarily German Jews whose families had been in America for two or three generations—to treat their workers fairly. It did not take long for the workers, many of whom had been active in social reform movements in Europe, to form labor unions and assert their rights in the workplace. Many of the Jewish union leaders were socialists (they believed that the means of production should not be controlled by owners, but by the community as a whole).

Unions are formed In the late 1880s and 1890s Jewish workers formed the United Hebrew Trades in New York, the Jewish Workers Educational Society in Chicago, and the Jewish Federation of Labor in Philadelphia. Unionists held a number of work stoppages during that period, leading to some improvements in working conditions. In 1900 Jewish American activists, with the help of newly arrived Jewish immigrants from Russia, formed the International Ladies Garment Workers Union (ILGWU).

In 1909 and 1910 some 30,000 ILGWU workers participated in strikes against the New York City garment industry. After a bitter struggle, workers won a 50-hour work week, better wages, and an agreement from employers that union members would receive preferential treatment in hiring.

Discrimination against Jewish Americans

Jews have faced discrimination since their arrival in America. Although this discrimination pales in comparison with the repression and genocide the Jews suffered historically in Europe and the Middle East, antisemitism in America continues to be a serious problem. One of the first publicized cases of antisemitic violence occurred in 1913, when a Jewish immigrant named Leo Frank was accused and convicted of a murder he did not commit. Frank was originally sentenced to death, but a judge commuted his sentence to life imprisonment. An angry mob, chanting "Hang the Jew," burst into the jail and lynched (executed by hanging) Frank in August 1915.

Similar to racial minorities, Jews were commonly forbidden entrance to golf courses, resorts, and many places of public accommodation. In the early twentieth century, signs reading "No dogs, No Jews" were posted at many resorts. In the 1920s the Ku Klux Klan (KKK) campaigned against Jews. The KKK organized boycotts of Jewish-owned stores and burned crosses in front of synagogues. At the same time, automobile-production pioneer

Henry Ford (1863–1947) fanned the flames of antisemitism in the pages of his newspaper, the *Dearborn Independent*. Ford maintained that Jews secretly controlled the world's wealth and were responsible for most of the world's problems. He claimed that Jews were engaged in "criminal" banking activities and did not know the meaning of "honest" manual labor.

Prior to the civil rights legislation of the 1960s, many colleges set quotas on the number of Jewish students they would accept. Similarly, corporations limited the number of Jewish employees they would hire. The practices of Realtors and landlords upheld patterns of housing segregation; Jews, like African Americans, were restricted to living in certain neighborhoods (see chapter 1, "Housing discrimination").

Concurrent with the rise to power of the Nazi Party in Germany in the 1930s, pro-Nazi groups such as the German American Bund increased their activity in the United States. During World War II, the Bund held Nazi marches and rallies in an attempt to intimidate Jewish Americans. In the 1980s and 1990s the United States experienced a resurgence of antisemitic groups, as well as an increase in antisemitic vandalism, such as the spray painting of swastikas (the symbol of the Nazi party in Germany) on synagogues. In 1997 the Federal Bureau of Investigation's statistics on hate crimes indicated that there were 1,087 violent crimes (assault or vandalism) directed at Jewish people and institutions.

 The U.S. Turns Its Back on Jews during World War II

World War II (1939–1945) was perhaps the saddest chapter in Jewish history. The German Nazi forces, under the command of Adolf Hitler, killed over 6 million Jews—nearly half the Jewish population of Europe—in concentration camps. (The Nazis killed an additional 6 to 10 million Gypsies, homosexuals, socialists, and other people deemed "defective".) Even after President Franklin D. Roosevelt and congressional leaders had been made aware of the situation, they refused to relax immigration quotas and take in additional Eastern European Jews. Had the United States accepted Jewish refugees during World War II, hundreds of thousands of people might have escaped the horrors of Nazi concentration camps.

In November 1998 the Anti-Defamation League of B'nai Brith (an organization that protects the rights of Jewish people in the United States and throughout the world) sponsored a survey entitled "Anti-Semitism and Prejudice in America." The survey, which measured attitudes toward the American Jewish community, found that 12 percent of all Americans hold views about Jews that are "unquestionably antisemitic." That figure was down from 20 percent in 1992 and 29 percent in 1964. The survey also found that the percentage of Americans who accept anti-Jewish stereotypes has steadily declined between 1964 and 1998.

Jewish Americans' own history of repression has made them sympathetic to the civil rights struggles of other people. This fact was evidenced by the prominent role played by Jewish Americans in the African American civil rights movement. From 1930 to 1966 Jewish Americans headed up the National Association for the Advancement of Colored People. Jewish American activists were present in large numbers at civil rights marches in the South between 1960 and 1965. Martin Luther King Jr. once stated that the contribution of Jewish Americans to the civil rights struggle was "so great" that it was "impossible to record."

Arab Americans

Arab Americans trace their ancestry to any of the following twenty-one northern African or western Asian nations, collectively known as the Arab World: Lebanon, occupied Palestine, Syria, Egypt, Morocco, Tunisia, Algeria, Libya, Sudan, Jordan, Iraq, Bahrain, Qatar, Oman, Saudi Arabia, Kuwait, United Arab Emirates, Djibouti, Somolia, Mauritania, and Yemen. Approximately two-thirds of all Arab Americans come from Lebanon, Syria, and Palestine. These nations share Arabic as a common language. While the majority of Arab people are followers of Islam, a sizable minority practice Christianity.

There are presently about three million people of Arab descent living in the United States. According to the American-Arab Anti-Discrimination Committee in Washington, D.C., the exact count is difficult to determine because there is no category for "Arab American" on the U.S. Census. About 60 percent of Arab Americans classify themselves as "Caucasian"; the remaining 40 percent check the box for "other," writing in "Arab American" or their specific nationality. About half of all Arab Americans are descendants of immigrants who arrived in the country between 1880 and 1940. The other half are immigrants, or descendants of immigrants, who arrived after 1945.

The first wave of Arab immigrants to the United States, arriving between the late 1800s and 1924, were from Greater Syria (an area that includes present-day Syria, Lebanon, Jordan, and Palestine). The Syrian immigrants came to America seeking economic opportunity. They worked as peddlers throughout the United States. By 1914 most of the Syrian peddlers had graduated to store owners. They rapidly assimilated (blended) into the U.S. middle class.

Beginning in 1916, the most popular destination for Syrian immigrants was Dearborn, Michigan. In Dearborn, many Syrian immigrants could find well-paying jobs at the Ford Motor Company. To this day, Dearborn is home to the largest Arab American community in the United States.

Syrian immigration slowed to a trickle in 1924, following the passage of the Johnson-Reed Immigration Act.

Negative Stereotypes of Arabs in the Movies

The negative stereotyping of Arabs in American movies, a decades-old problem, took on a new viciousness in the 1990s. In a series of films, Arab characters were portrayed as evil, incompetent, and obnoxious. Many were depicted as terrorists bent on destroying the United States. It is difficult to name a single recent American film that portrays Arab characters in a positive manner, or even as ordinary citizens.

The 1994 movie *True Lies,* for example, features Arnold Schwarzenegger as an all-American hero who conquers a group of evil Arabs. The Arab bad guys, characterized by the protagonist as "raving psychotics," unsuccessfully attempt to unleash nuclear weapons on the United States. The Arabs' failure to carry out their mission is due to both their own incompetence and to Schwarzenegger's heroics. In a number of scenes, the bumbling Arabs are killed in ways designed to evoke laughter from the audience. Not a single American dies in the film.

Father of the Bride II, released in 1995, features a cruel Arab American character named Mr. Habib. Habib—who is shifty, obnoxious, and mean to his wife—embodies the typical negative Arab American stereotype. In the story, Habib buys a house from a man named George Banks and then makes plans to bulldoze it. A horrified Banks, for whom the house holds many memories, convinces Habib to sell him back the house only after Habib extorts $100,000 from him.

The year 1997 saw the release of two more films with anti-Arab themes or characters: *G.I. Jane* and *Operation Condor. G.I. Jane* is the story of a woman, played by Demi Moore, who kills Arabs as part of her mission with a group of Navy Seals. In *Operation Condor,* Jackie Chan battles evil and irrational Arabs as he attempts to recover a chest of gold hidden by the Nazis at the end of World War II. Americans were presented with more negative images of Arabs in 1998, in the film *The Siege.* In this action movie, Bruce Willis and Denzel Washington thwart a plan by Arab-Muslim terrorists to bomb New York City.

"We fear the consequences of such negative images on the Arab American and Muslim communities," stated American-Arab Anti-Discrimination Committee President Hala Maksoud regarding *The Siege.* "When a community is vilified through a slew of negative stereotypes, innocent people suffer. In a society which prides itself on cultural mosaic, Arab American and Muslim children deserve to feel proud of who they are and where they come from."

This legislation restricted the number of Syrian immigrants allowed to enter the United States to 100 people annually.

The second wave of Arab immigration began in 1948. In that year the state of Israel was created, and several small Arab nations (which had previously been colonized by European powers) were granted independence. Most of these second-wave immigrants, particularly those from Syria and Lebanon, came to the United States seeking higher education. Many Palestinians came to the United States to escape political and military instability in their former homeland. Among the second-wave immigrants were a large number of doctors, lawyers, engineers, and other professionals.

Another large influx of Arab immigrants began in the mid-1960s, following the passage of the Immigration Act of 1965. This legislation abolished the system of national quotas, thereby opening the doors to thousands of immigrants from non-European countries. Arab immigration accelerated after the Six-Day War of 1967, in which Israel defeated Syria, Egypt, and Jordan, and occupied Palestinian lands. The majority of the immigrants since the mid-1960s have come from Lebanon, Syria, Palestine, and Egypt.

Discrimination against Arab Americans

Arab Americans are perhaps the only minority group in the United States against whom the general population sanctions discrimination. In the 1990s, an era in which there has been little tolerance for racial slurs against African Americans, Hispanic Americans, Asian Americans, or Native Americans, people still laugh at references to "A-rabs," "camel jockeys," and "towel heads"—all derogatory labels for Arab Americans. As author and professor emeritus of communications Jack G. Shaheen wrote in a February 29, 1988, *Newsweek* article entitled "The Media's Image of Arabs," "The Arab remains American culture's favorite whipping boy."

Over the past few decades, bigotry and discrimination against Arab Americans has intensified every time there is a conflict involving the United States and Arabs or Arab nations. For example, Arab American rights activist Alex Odeh was killed by a bomb wired to his office door after the 1985 Palestinian hijacking of the *Achille Lauro* ocean liner. Several incidents of harassment and violence against Arab Americans were reported in 1986, following the United States bombing of Libya, and in 1993, following the bombing of the World Trade Center.

In 1995, when right-wing militia members bombed the federal building in Oklahoma City, killing 169 people and injuring more than 500 others, television news commentators incorrectly speculated that the bombing was the work of Arab terrorists. The American-Arab Anti-Discrimination Committee received notice of 325 hate crimes committed against Arabs or Muslims in the three-day period following that bombing.

The Attempt to Deport the L.A. Eight

On January 26, 1986, Immigration and Naturalization Service (INS) agents arrested seven Palestinian men, as well as the Kenyan wife of one of the men, in the Los Angeles area. (One of the men was arrested at gunpoint while taking his chemistry final at Chaffee Community College in Rancho Cucamonga.) The eight immigrants were held in isolation at Terminal Island Prison for ten days and threatened with deportation. Their crime was distributing pro-Palestinian literature.

The INS accused the eight detainees with "fostering the actions of a terrorist group" (in this case, the Palestine Liberation Organization, or PLO) and advocating "world communism." The eight immigrants were singled out for prosecution under a little-used statute of the McCarran-Walter Immigration and Naturalization Act of 1952 that calls for the deportation of any non-citizen engaged in "subversive activity" (for more information on the McCarran-Walter Immigration and Naturalization Act, see chapter 2, "Immigration policies after World War II").

Lawyers for the "L.A. Eight" claimed that their clients were arrested for activity that is protected by the First Amendment. This argument convinced a district court judge to issue an injunction stopping the deportations. Government attorneys argued that First Amendment rights do not extend to noncitizens, a position that was rejected by numerous courts. The government has not yet appealed its case to the Supreme Court, however, the threat of deportation still hangs over the L.A. Eight.

In 1996 the government adopted a new strategy to facilitate the deportation of undesirable aliens. Congress passed a law prohibiting district court judges from issuing injunctions against federal directives. Had this law been in effect when the L.A. Eight were arrested, their case would have ended up in an INS court (as opposed to district court). Since constitutional issues (such as free speech) cannot be brought up in INS courts, the L.A. Eight would have had little ground on which to fight their deportations.

In late 1998 attorneys for the American-Arab Anti-Discrimination Committee appealed the constitutionality of the 1996 law before the Supreme Court. The Court's decision will seriously affect the rights of not just Arab immigrants, but of all immigrants in the United States. If this law is upheld, it will have a profoundly chilling effect on the liberties of immigrants from the Arab world or from any nation that is out of favor with the United States.

The scapegoating of Arab Americans reached a peak during the 1991 Gulf War. The American-Arab Anti-Discrimination Committee reported 119 hate crimes (violent crimes motivated by bias) against Arab Americans in that year. Arab Americans were beaten in New York City; Chicago, Illinois; Houston, Texas; Gaithersburg, Maryland; and Toledo, Ohio. The lives of several Arab Americans were threatened in San Francisco; Dearborn, Michigan; and Charlestown, Massachusetts. One of the victims of the Gaithersburg beating, an Iranian American (by definition not an Arab since Iran is not part of the Arab world), received a fractured skull and remains partially paralyzed.

An Arab American who was interviewed by an Albuquerque newspaper during the Gulf War received about 100 threatening phone calls after the interview was published. Throughout the United States, Arab Americans reported cases of verbal abuse and vandalism to their homes and cars. There were several incidents of vandalism against mosques, Arab American community centers, and Arab American-owned businesses.

Sources

Books

Archdeacon, Thomas J. *Becoming American: An Ethnic History.* New York: The Free Press, 1993.

Belth, Nathan C. *A Promise to Keep: A Narrative of the American Encounter with Anti-Semitism.* New York: Times Books, 1979.

Bernardo, Stephanie. *The Ethnic Almanac.* Garden City, NY: Dolphin Books, 1981.

Dinnerstein, Leonard. *Antisemitism in America.* New York: Oxford University Press, 1994.

Dinnerstein, Leonard, and David M. Reimers. *Ethnic Americans: A History of Immigration and Assimilation.* New York: Dodd, Mead & Company, 1975.

Dinnerstein, Leonard, Roger L. Nichols, and David M. Reimers. *Natives and Strangers: Blacks, Indians, and Immigrants in America,* 2nd ed. New York: Oxford University Press, 1990.

Galicich, Anne. *The German Americans.* New York: Chelsea House, 1989.

Muggamin, Howard. *The Jewish Americans.* New York: Chelsea House, 1988.

Naff, Alixa. *The Arab Americans.* New York: Chelsea House, 1988.

Portes, Alejandro and Rubén G. Rumbaut. *Immigrant America: A Portrait.* Berkeley: University of California Press, 1996.

Sigler, Jay A., ed. *Civil Rights in America: 1500 to the Present.* Detroit: Gale, 1998, pp. 241–57.

Witkoski, Michael. *Italian Americans.* Vero Beach, FL: Rourke Corporation, Inc., 1991.

Periodicals

Engelbert, Phillis. "Limiting Debate: McCarthyism in the '80s." *AGENDA: Ann Arbor's Alternative Newsmonthly.* May, 1987: 2, 7.

King, Coretta Scott. "Arab American Bashing Can't be Tolerated." *The Detroit Free Press.* September 10, 1990.

Natividad, Irene. "Political and Cultural Diversity: America's Hope and America's Challenge." Reprinted in *Asian American Policy Review.* spring, 1991: 91–97.

Shaheen, Jack G. "The Media's Image of Arabs." *Newsweek.* February 29, 1988.

Web Sites

American-Arab Anti-Discrimination Committee. [Online] Available http://www.adc.org/ (last accessed March 31, 1999).

American-Arab Anti-Discrimination Committee. "Anti-Arab Stereotypes in 'Father of the Bride II' Are No Laughing Matter." [Online] Available http://www.adc.org/adc/ActionAlerts/1996/04-Jan-96.html (last accessed March 31, 1999).

American-Arab Anti-Discrimination Committee. "Protest *Operation Condor*." [Online] Available http://wwwcafearabica.com/action/actopcond9.html (last accessed on April 16, 1999).

Anti-Defamation League of B'nai Brith. [Online] Available http://www.adl.org/ (last accessed March 31, 1999).

Ghomeshi, Jean. "Arnie Re-Wins War in Persian Gulf." *Toronto Star.* [Online] Available http://www.fruvous.com/news/94jiants.html/ (last accessed April 1, 1999).

Heyer, Marigrace. "Memory of the Molly Maguires Kept Alive." *Coalcracker Magazine.* [Online] Available http://www.tnonline.com/Coalcracker/mollies.html (last accessed March 28, 1999).

Hower, John. "Ethnic Lines Divided Coal Fields." [Online] Available http://www.leba.net/~jhower/Valley/Mollies1.html (last accessed March 27, 1999).

Hower, John. "Rough Conditions Existed in Coal Fields." [Online] Available http://www.leba.net/~jhower/Valley/Mollies2.html (last accessed March 31, 1999).

Hower, John. "Undercover Agent Infiltrated Mollies." [Online] Available http://www.leba.net/~jhower/Valley/Mollies 3.html (last accessed March 31, 1999).

Ibrahim, Haitham. "Disney's Crusade against Arabs." *ArabiaLiving.* [Online] available http://www.arab.com/content/living/crus9.15.97.html (last accessed on April 27, 1999).

Other

"Haymarket Riot," "Sacco-Vanzetti Case," and "Triangle Shirtwaist Company Fire." *Encyclopaedia Britannica CD 97.* Chicago: Encyclopaedia Britannica, Inc., 1997.

Nawash, Kamal (American-Arab Anti-Discrimination Committee Chief Legal Counsel). Telephone interview. January 8, 1999.

Civil Rights of Selected Nonethnic Groups

This chapter is about the civil rights of certain groups of Americans defined by characteristics other than race or ethnicity: women, lesbians and gay men, and people with disabilities. The members of these groups are vulnerable to unfair treatment by government and private entities. It is therefore necessary to take extra steps to ensure that their basic rights are guaranteed. Similar to racial minorities, the history of these nonethnic groups in America is largely about the denial of civil rights and the struggle for equality. And like members of racial minorities, members of these nonethnic groups continue to fight for their civil rights and their full acceptance into society.

The civil rights of women

At the time of America's founding, women were generally regarded as physically and intellectually inferior to men. Valued mainly for their ability to bear children, women were considered the property of, or extensions of, their husbands or fathers. Women were not even mentioned in the

Constitution. They did not have the right to own property, to vote, or to use birth control. Workplace rights for women were defined very differently than they are today, since a woman's earnings—with very rare exception—legally belonged to her father, guardian, or husband.

The status of women in society has advanced considerably since that time, largely because of the efforts of the women's rights movement. Women gained the right to own property in 1848; the right to vote in 1920; the right to serve on juries in 1972; the right to end unwanted pregnancies in 1973; and the right to work, free of sexual harassment, in 1980. In 1900 only 19 percent of college graduates were female; by 1984 that percentage had increased to nearly 50. Today women constitute more than half of all college students.

The goals of the women's movement have changed drastically since the movement's inception. Now that most basic rights are guaranteed to women (at least on paper), women's rights advocates have turned to other pressing issues, such as ending sexual assault and other forms of violence against women; developing nonsexist curricula and pressing for equal funding for girls' athletics in public schools; advocating for pay equal to that earned by men; breaking through the "glass ceiling" that keeps women from holding top positions in private and public agencies; and protecting a woman's right to abortion. (The "glass ceiling" is an invisible barrier that

Together with Ernestine Rose and Paulina Wright Davis, Elizabeth Cady Stanton campaigned for the passage of legislation guaranteeing women the right to own property. *Reproduced by permission of the National Archives and Records Administration.*

keeps women—and other minority groups—from reaching the upper levels of employment.)

The fight for property rights

Prior to the mid-1800s, women in the United States could not own property. All items in a woman's possession, from her clothes to her savings, were legally owned by her nearest male relative. It was even illegal for

A cartoon representing the first women's rights convention in Seneca Falls, New York.
Reproduced by permission of Corbis-Bettmann.

women to have their own bank accounts. These restrictions forced women to be dependent on brothers, husbands, or fathers, even when these men were abusive or incompetent.

The Married Women's Property Act
The lack of women's property rights was the primary focus of the first women's movement in America. Women's groups had previously campaigned on behalf of other issues, such as the abolition (elimination) of slavery, but few had worked on behalf of women's rights. Ernestine Rose

(1810–1892), Elizabeth Cady Stanton (1815–1902), and Paulina Wright Davis campaigned tirelessly for twelve years in the state of New York for the passage of legislation guaranteeing women the right to own property. The women's efforts met with success in 1848, when the New York legislature passed the "Act for the More Effectual Protection of the Property of Married Women," commonly referred to as the "Married Women's Property Act."

The Married Women's Property Act gave women living in New York state the right to own property and to retain that property once they got married or became widowed. The legislation also granted married women the right to make decisions regarding the use or sale of their property. Unfortunately, the act did not give women the right to enter into business contracts or have equal custody of children in divorce cases. It was not until 1860 that the New York legislature passed the "Act Concerning the Rights and Liabilities of Husband and Wife," which granted comprehensive rights to married women. This legislation became the model for similar acts in twenty-nine other states.

The campaign for suffrage

The leaders of the women's property rights movement next turned their attention to women's suffrage (the right to vote in public elections). To kick off the suffrage campaign in 1848, Lucretia Mott (1793–1880) and Elizabeth Cady Stanton organized a women's rights convention at Seneca Falls, New York. At the convention (whose attendees included several men), the women laid the groundwork for a voting rights campaign that would eventually attract more than two million women and last three-quarters of a century. During the meeting, Stanton composed and read her "Declaration of Sentiments," a document based on the Declaration of Independence that defined the suffrage movement's goals and resolutions.

The NAWSA In 1869, just prior to the ratification of the Fifteenth Amend-

In 1869 Susan B. Anthony cofounded the NWSA with Elizabeth Cady Stanton. *Reproduced by permission of the Library of Congress.*

ment (which granted black men the right to vote), a split developed among the participants in the women's suffrage movement. Some women felt that too much attention had been paid to the abolition of slavery and the right of black men to vote, at the expense of women's suffrage. Other women felt that it was important to secure the rights of black men and that women would eventually win the right to vote. That year saw the formation of two women's suffrage organizations: the more militant National Woman

Portraits of Two Suffragists

Lucy Stone (1818–1893) was widely regarded as the suffrage movement's best public speaker. Stone, cofounder of the American Woman Suffrage Association (AWSA), believed in the use of civil disobedience (the refusal to comply with laws one feels are unjust) to further her goal. To that end, in 1858 Stone refused to pay property taxes on the grounds that she was denied the right to vote. Stone was arrested for this action and her property was auctioned off to pay her taxes. She also attracted controversy for her refusal to take her husband's name after marriage (Stone and her husband Harry Blackwell defined themselves as "equal partners"). Stone established the Woman Suffrage Association in New Jersey and published the *Women's Journal* (a suffrage newspaper) from 1870 to 1917.

Another charismatic leader of the suffrage movement was Alice Paul (1885–1977). Paul graduated from Swarthmore College in 1905 with degrees in social work and sociology. She continued her studies at a Quaker training school in England from 1907 to 1909. While abroad, Paul met British suffragettes who taught her political organizing tactics. On her return to the

Alice Paul. *Reproduced by permission of the Library of Congress.*

United States, Paul organized a group called the Congressional Union and dedicated herself to the suffrage movement. Paul helped stage a large suffrage parade through the streets of Washington, D.C., in 1913 on the eve of the presidential inauguration of Woodrow Wilson. Her group employed a range of tactics from lobbying members of Congress, to picketing the White House, to staging hunger strikes.

Suffrage Association (NWSA) and the more moderate American Woman Suffrage Association (AWSA).

The NWSA was founded by Susan B. Anthony (1820–1906), considered the movement's best organiz-er, and Stanton, considered the movement's leading philosopher and writer. The NWSA did not admit men, criticized churches for their sexist teachings, and even published articles about "free love" in its newsletter. The AWSA, which admitted men and took

NAWSA leader Carrie Chapman Catt heads a suffrage parade in New York City. *Reproduced by permission of AP/Wide World Photos.*

less radical positions than the NWSA, was founded by noted orator Lucy Stone (1818–1893) and author Julia Ward Howe (1819–1910). In 1890 the two organizations merged into the National American Woman Suffrage Association (NAWSA). Susan B. Anthony was named its president.

In 1900 NAWSA member Carrie Chapman Catt (1859–1947) succeeded Anthony to the helm of the organization. Chapman (like Anthony before her) campaigned for the passage of women's suffrage legislation in individual states as part of the overall strategy of securing national legislation. Around the same time, Harriet Stanton Blatch (1856–1940), daughter of Elizabeth Cady Stanton, founded the Equality League of Self-Supporting Women, which later became the Women's Political Union. The Equality League sponsored its first suffrage parade in New York City in 1910.

The Nineteenth Amendment The women's suffrage movement succeeded in getting a voting rights bill before Congress in 1878, only to have it rejected. It was not until 1920—after

The Equal Rights Amendment

To this day, the rights of women are not explicitly defined in the Constitution. While there are presently numerous laws protecting the rights of women, there is no one piece of sweeping legislation that grants equality to women in all aspects of life. The Equal Rights Amendment (ERA), the proposed constitutional amendment guaranteeing women's rights, was officially defeated in 1972.

The idea of an equal rights amendment was first brought before Congress in 1916. The amendment was drafted and proposed by the suffragist National Women's Party, under the leadership of Alice Paul (see box, "Portraits of Two Suffragists"). For six decades after the defeat of the original ERA, Paul continued to work for its passage. Paul, along with many other women's rights activists, managed to bring a weaker version of the original ERA before Congress in 1972.

Congress passed the bill and sent it along to the states for ratification (three-fourths of all states must ratify constitutional amendments). While two-thirds of the states ratified the amendment, campaigns by conservative organizations prevented its ratification in the other states.

As it was proposed in 1972, the Equal Rights Amendment read:

Section 1. Equality of rights under the law shall not be denied by the United States or any state on account of sex.

Section 2. The Congress shall have the power to enforce, by appropriate legislation, the provisions of this article.

Section 3. This amendment shall take effect two years after the date of ratification.

countless pickets in front of the White House, the arrest of many suffragists, and hunger strikes—that the bill was brought back up as a constitutional amendment. This time the bill passed Congress and received ratification from the necessary thirty-six states (ratification by three-fourths of all states is necessary for the adoption of any constitutional amendment).

Women in the United States were granted the right to vote in 1920,

with the passage of the Nineteenth Amendment. By the time the Nineteenth Amendment was ratified, a majority of states had already granted women the right to vote (in elections at all levels of government). The first state to grant women suffrage, in 1870, was Wyoming, followed by Utah, Colorado, Idaho, Arizona, Kansas, Oregon, Montana, and Nevada.

In its entirety, the Nineteenth Amendment reads:

Betty Friedan (second from left) leads a march in support of the Equal Rights Amendment. First proposed by Alice Paul in 1916, the amendment was officially defeated in 1972 (see box). *Reproduced by permission of AP/Wide World Photos.*

The right of citizens of the United States to vote shall not be denied or abridged by the United States or by any State on account of sex. Congress shall have power to enforce this article by appropriate legislation.

The fight for equality in employment

The definition of women's rights in the workplace has continually changed over the years, as women have gradually entered the workforce. Women first went to work outside the home in large numbers at the turn of the twentieth century, in occupations such as office worker, switchboard operator, nurse, teacher, factory worker, and laundry worker. During both World War I (1914–1918) and World War II (1939–1945), thousands of women took jobs that had been vacated by men sent to war, in arms production plants and other factories. During this period, women were offered less desirable jobs than the remaining men and were paid less than men even when performing identical duties.

Charlotte Perkins Gilman was one of the first writers to address the problems facing working women. *Reproduced by permission of the Library of Congress.*

When the war ended, most women lost their production jobs to returning soldiers. Women were then relegated to the handful of jobs considered suitable for women: secretaries, teachers, waitresses, nurses, maids, sales clerks, and sweatshop workers. (A sweatshop is a factory where workers labor under poor conditions for low wages.) These jobs, however, paid poorly and had little room for advancement. Women were even barred by law from working at some occupations, such as bartender and lawyer.

Women who performed identical work as men, such as teachers, received less pay than their male counterparts. And several states had laws restricting the hours during which women were permitted to work.

Kennedy supports the rights of female workers Beginning in the late 1950s, women's groups spoke out against injustices in the workplace and fought for legislation to end job-related discrimination. In many states women convinced lawmakers to amend minimum wage laws to apply to women, as well as men, and to eliminate laws restricting women's work hours.

President John F. Kennedy (1917–1963) responded to women's advocates in 1961 by forming the President's Commission on the Status of Women (CSW). He named Eleanor Roosevelt (1884–1962; women's rights proponent and wife of the late President Franklin D. Roosevelt [1882–1945]) as the commission's leader. The commission made many recommendations, including that the federal government practice nondiscrimination in the hiring of its employees and hire women to policy-making positions, that Congress pass an equal-pay-for-equal-work law, and that the federal government offer paid maternity leave to women workers.

The Equal Pay Act of 1963 Two years later Kennedy signed into law the Equal Pay Act of 1963. This act, the first law against sex discrimination in employment, required that employers pay women the same as men for performing equal work. It also demanded gender equality in health insurance, vacation time, and other benefits. The law applied to people in all occupations except teaching and executive, administrative, and professional positions. The act was amended in 1972 to cover those classes omitted in the 1963 law.

Today, women still lag behind men in pay, benefits, and promotions. A typical working woman earns only about 74 cents for every dollar earned by a man. In addition, an invisible but very real "glass ceiling" often keeps women out of top leadership positions in most private firms and government agencies.

The Civil Rights Act extends protections The Civil Rights Act (CRA) of 1964, hailed as the most expansive civil rights policy in American history, outlawed a variety of types of discrimination based on race, color, gender, religion, and national origin. The act was introduced by President John F. Kennedy (1917–1963) in June 1963 and signed into law in July 1964 by President Lyndon B. Johnson (1908–1973). While the primary beneficiaries of the CRA were African Americans, women also benefitted from the act's antidiscrimination measures. (For more information on the Civil Rights Act of 1964, see box in chapter 1.)

Title VII of the CRA prohibited workplace discrimination against minorities and women in terms of hiring, firing, promoting, pay, and other aspects of employment. The legislation called for the formation of the Equal Employment Opportunity Commission (EEOC) to enforce antidiscrimination measures in job hiring and promotion. The EEOC was charged with drafting regulations, investigating claims of discrimination, attempting to settle complaints, and, where necessary, filing lawsuits on behalf of vic-

 ## Title VII of the 1964 Civil Rights Act

In 1964 Congress passed the Civil Rights Act, which outlawed a variety of types of discrimination based on race, color, gender, religion, and national origin. The act's Title VII, the main provisions of which read as follows, barred discrimination in employment:

It shall be an unlawful employment practice for an employer:

1. to fail or refuse to hire or to discharge any individual, or otherwise to discriminate against any individual with respect to his compensation, terms, conditions, or privileges of employment, because of such individual's race, color, religion, sex or national origin, or

2. to limit, segregate, or classify his employees or applicants for employment in any way which would deprive or tend to deprive any individual of employment opportunities or otherwise adversely affect his status as an employee, because of such individual's race, color, religion, sex or national origin.

The Educational Equity Act

In the 1970s women's rights activists recognized that in order for females in the United States to attain rights equal to those of males, the effort must start with the nation's youth. Activists shone the spotlight on public schools, where boys and girls were treated unequally in a number of areas. For example, boys were counseled to take academic classes (especially math and science) that would prepare them for vocations or professional careers, while girls were counseled to take home economics, art classes, and non-rigorous academics. The opportunities for boys to play sports were many; the opportunities for girls to play sports were few.

In order to rectify this imbalance, in 1974 women's rights activists convinced Congress to pass the Educational Equity Act. The Educational Equity Act mandated that public schools develop nonsexist curricula (meaning that they had to do away with negative stereotypes of girls and portray boys and girls as having equal capabilities); provide nondiscriminatory academic and career counseling services; and provide equal opportunities to boys and girls in sports. The act also stated that any school, business, or organization receiving federal money could not exclude girls or women.

tims. In 1972 Congress passed the Equal Employment Opportunity Act. This act empowered the EEOC to file suit on behalf of aggrieved workers against employers in federal court.

Affirmative action In the early 1970s the rights of women (and racial minorities) in the workplace, as well as in institutions of higher learning, were advanced with the adoption of affirmative action. Affirmative action is a set of directives that gives preferential treatment to women and minorities—groups that have been traditionally discriminated against—in hiring and admissions policies. Under affirmative action programs, employers found to have discriminated in the past have had to increase their proportion of minority and female employees, while colleges and universities guilty of past discrimination have had to increase their proportion of minority and female students.

As it was originally enacted in 1969, affirmative action only applied to government agencies and companies under contract to work for the government; in 1972 it was amended to cover companies in the private sector. (For more information on affirmative action, see chapter 1, "Gains and losses in the modern era".)

Sexual harassment Sexual harassment is defined as any activity that makes a female worker feel physically unsafe or creates a workplace atmosphere that is hostile or intimidating to women. (While victims of sexual harassment include some men, the vast majority of victims are women.) Activities that can constitute sexual harassment include: unwanted touching or sexual advances; sexist jokes; obscene gestures; asking about a person's sex life; displaying sexually explicit or demeaning photographs or other objects; or making sexually explicit or offensive comments to or about an employee. Sexual harassment may also be defined as the threat, implicit or explicit, that if a woman employee does not respond to the sexual advances of a male superior, she will lose her job or promotion.

In a 1988 study of federal employees, 42 percent of women and 15 percent of men claimed to have been victims of sexual harassment within the preceding two years. Among the types of activities victims reported suffering were touching, sexual remarks, leers and suggestive looks, pressure for dates, pressure for sexual favors, and rape.

Most cases of sexual harassment are brought before the Equal Employment Opportunity Commission (EEOC), which in 1980 identified sexual harassment as a form of sex discrimination. The EEOC defined sexual harassment as "unwelcome sexual advances, requests for sexual favors ... [and when] submission to such conduct is made either explicitly or implicitly a term or condition of an individual's employment." In a 1986 ruling, the Supreme Court upheld the legitimacy of EEOC's position regarding sexual harassment.

Sexual harassment suits are argued in federal or state court. Both the perpetrator of sexual harassment and the employer may be held liable for damages. The system designed to stop sexual harassment, however, is far from perfect. The investigation of a sexual harassment claim sometimes takes years; during that time, it is common for the woman who filed the claim to face retribution by male co-workers or supervisors.

Reproductive rights

Many women today, especially those who have come of age after 1973, take for granted the relative ease with which they can obtain birth control or an abortion (the termination of an unwanted pregnancy by removing the fetus from the uterus, usually within the first twelve weeks of pregnancy). For much of America's history, not only has abortion been illegal, but women have been prohibited from obtaining the information and means to prevent pregnancy.

The right to control one's own reproduction has made a tremendous difference in women's lives. The power to postpone or forego having children gives women the freedom to finish school, establish a career, or accomplish other goals. Since birth control and abortion have become available, women have chosen to have fewer children, on average, than they did in the past.

The Comstock Law In 1873 Congress made it illegal for doctors to discuss birth control with their patients with the passage of the Comstock Law. The Comstock Law was named for its sponsor, Anthony Comstock, a political reformer and antipornography crusader. Comstock asserted that contra-

Margaret Sanger: Birth Control Pioneer

"No woman can call herself free who does not own and control her own body. No woman can call herself free until she can choose conscientiously whether she will or will not be a mother," wrote birth control educator Margaret Sanger (1883–1866) in her 1920 book *Woman and the New Race.* Sanger, widely considered the founder of the birth control movement in the United States, worked as a nurse in the ghettoes of New York City in the early 1900s. She saw first-hand the consequences of the nation's archaic birth control laws: large numbers of women dying from self-induced or illegally obtained abortions; high rates of death among infants and mothers; and impoverished mothers being burdened with more mouths than they could feed. Sanger believed that much of the problem would be alleviated if women were able to control their own reproduction.

In 1914 Sanger established the National Birth Control League. That same year, she was charged with obscenity under the Comstock Law (see "Reproductive rights") for distributing pamphlets advocating the legalization of birth control. Two years later the charge was dismissed. Sanger then opened a birth control clinic in New York City. In 1917 the police closed down Sanger's clinic, calling it a public nuisance. Sanger was arrested and spent twenty days in jail.

Undeterred by the prospect of more jail time, Sanger continued her crusade. She founded the American Birth Control League in 1921, which worked for the legalization of birth control. In 1942 the Planned Parenthood Federation of American was formed from a merger of the American Birth Control League and other organizations.

ception, like pornography, was immoral. According to the law, doctors could only prescribe birth control in cases where they were concerned about the spread of disease.

The birth control pill In 1936 the Comstock Law was amended to legalize birth control in all instances. A breakthrough in birth control came in 1960, when the Food and Drug Administration approved the birth con-

trol pill for use. The arrival of the pill was greeted with controversy. While women's rights advocates hailed it as empowering women to limit the size of their families, the pill's opponents claimed that effective contraception would usher in an era of immorality.

Several states passed laws banning the dispensation of the pill. In 1965 the Supreme Court struck down the constitutionality of those laws. In the case *Griswold v. Connecticut,* the court ruled that contraception was a matter of personal privacy and that no state could ban the prescription, sale, or use of contraceptives.

Roe v. Wade Through the 1960s the movement to legalize abortion gained momentum. The National Organization of Women (NOW) joined the cause in 1967, making the "right of women to control their reproductive lives" part of the group's "Women's Bill of Rights." The members of Planned Parenthood, Church Women United, and other groups swelled the ranks of the pro-choice forces. (Pro-choice is a label applied to people who support a woman's right to choose between carrying a pregnancy to term or having an abortion.) Abortion was made legal in New York state and Hawaii in 1970.

In 1973 the landmark *Roe v. Wade* class action ruling made abortion legal throughout the United States. (A class action suit is a case brought on behalf of a group. Jane Roe was the alias, or false name, used by a pregnant single woman named Norma McCorvey who sought to have an abortion. Henry Wade was the district attorney of Dallas, Texas.) At the time, the state of Texas outlawed abortion except in cases where continuing the pregnancy endangered the mother's life. A three-judge panel of the Fifth Circuit Court in Dallas ruled in favor of Roe, overturning the Texas law; in response, Wade appealed the ruling to the Supreme Court.

The Supreme Court upheld the lower court's decision, noting that state of Texas did not have the authority to compel a woman to carry her fetus to term. "The right of privacy, whether it be founded in the Fourteenth Amendment's concept of personal liberty and restrictions on state action ... or ... in the Ninth Amendment's reservations of rights to the people," wrote Justice Harry Blackmun for the majority of the justices, "is broad enough to encompass a woman's decision to terminate her pregnancy."

By overturning Texas's restrictive abortion law, the Court also nullified the anti-abortion laws of other states. In its decision, the Court established abortion regulations using a trimester framework. During the first trimester (three months) of pregnancy, the state cannot interfere with pregnancy termination. In the second trimester (second three months) of pregnancy, states can regulate abortion only to protect a woman's health. Because the fetus may be viable (able to live outside a woman's womb) during the final trimester (last three months) of pregnancy, states may prohibit abortion unless the woman's health is at stake.

Abortion rights under attack The battle over abortion began immediately after the *Roe v. Wade* decision, and abortion rights remain a heated issue today. Anti-abortion forces have as their goal the repeal of *Roe*. Forces supporting a woman's right to have an abortion have as their goal the restoration of full access to abortion in all states.

Shocked by the *Roe v. Wade* decision of 1973, anti-abortion forces quickly mobilized to reverse the tide. The year after the *Roe* decision, conservative senators Jesse Helms and James Buckley sponsored an unsuccessful constitutional amendment to ban abortion. The anti-abortion National Right to Life movement, together with the Catholic church, began working to turn popular sentiment against abortion.

In the mid-1980s anti-abortion demonstrators began holding frequent demonstrations in front of clinics where abortions are performed. There have been many acts of vandalism committed at clinics, as well as violence directed toward clinic personnel. Three doctors who performed abortions, plus one volunteer, two receptionists, and one security guard, have been killed at abortion clinics in the United States since 1993. In this same time period there have been sixteen attempted murders of abortion doctors and 400 cases of stalking.

The powerful anti-abortion lobby has convinced several states to pass restrictions on abortions, such as forbidding government-sponsored health programs from paying for abortions for poor women; establishing a waiting period, during which a woman must view pictures of fetuses before having an abortion; requiring that minors have permission from a parent or guardian to obtain an abortion; and limiting the stage of a pregnancy (such as to the second trimester, or twenty-four weeks) during which a woman may have an abortion.

For its part, the pro-choice movement has been working to protect the right of women to have abortions. Pro-choice activists engage in the defense of clinics and health care personnel. Organizations such as Planned Parenthood and the National Organization of Women (NOW) are waging public relations and legal campaigns to keep the majority of the public in favor of legalized abortion. On January 22, 1999, for example, the Capital City NOW chapter staged a reproductive rights rally in front of the Supreme Court on the aniversary of the *Roe v. Wade* decision.

Workplace rights of pregnant women and new mothers

While the most visible battles regarding women's reproductive rights have been over the prevention or termination of pregnancy, the women's movement has also advocated for the rights of pregnant women and mothers. Throughout history, women workers have faced discrimination based on their pregnancy status and their choice to become mothers. Until fairly recently, many pregnant workers felt pressure to quit their jobs as soon as their pregnancy began to show and to stay home after their child was born. In some job fields, a pregnancy "time-off" period was mandatory. For example, until the late 1960s, many school boards legislated that pregnant teachers had to leave their jobs and would not let them resume teaching for a certain number of months after giving birth.

Over the last two decades more women have decided to work longer during pregnancy and to return to work after childbirth. Employer policies, however, have often made that choice difficult. While most companies had policies by which workers could take a certain number of days off for illness or disability, pregnancy and pregnancy-related difficulties were not considered legitimate uses of sick days. In addition, there was no allowance for recovery time after a woman gave birth. Consequently, pregnant women and new mothers often found themselves replaced during the time they were away from work.

The Pregnancy Discrimination Act In 1978 Congress sought to remedy this problem by passing the Pregnancy Discrimination Act. This policy outlawed discrimination against pregnant workers and mandated that sick leave or short-term disability leave be offered to pregnant workers. It also guaranteed women who took time off during pregnancy that they would not lose their job, status, or pay. Many employers, subsequently, devised policies granting women six to eight weeks of paid leave following childbirth.

The Family and Medical Leave Act In 1993 Congress passed the Family and Medical Leave Act to assist new parents and people with family health crises. The act mandates that private companies with more than fifty employees, the federal government, and public sector employers, must permit workers

 Children's Rights

Prior to the mid-nineteenth century, it was common for children to be treated as property. During the Industrial Revolution (the surge in technological and economic development that began in Great Britain around 1750 and spread throughout Europe and eventually to the United States), many children were used as cheap labor in factories, in mines, and on farms. Beginning in the early years of the twentieth century, U.S. lawmakers began to seriously examine the child labor issue. In 1912, Congress established the Children's Bureau to oversee child labor. Several laws passed between 1916 and 1920 attempted to further define working children's rights; most of these laws, however, were struck down after heavy lobbying by groups such as the American Farm Bureau Federation and the Catholic church.

The Fair Labor Standards Act of 1938 established nationwide standards for the minimum wage, overtime pay, and children's employment. In 1962 the Social Security Act defined a wide range of child welfare services and protections. Several recent court decisions have addressed other personal rights issues, such as children's right to privacy and freedom of speech.

to take up to twelve weeks each year of unpaid leave following the arrival of a child, or to deal with personal illness or the illness of a family member. It also states that an employee's job must be held for her or him until the employee returns to work.

Violence against women

At the forefront of the agenda of many women's rights groups today is the issue of violence against women. At least 2.5 million American women each year are victims of rape, battering, or stalking. More than two-thirds of violent incidents against women are committed by someone the woman knows.

Domestic violence Domestic violence is the physical or verbal assault of one adult member of a household by another. It often involves the repeated physical assault (battering) of a wife or girlfriend by a husband or live-in boyfriend. Domestic violence is the number one cause of injury for women between the ages of fifteen and forty-four in the United States. Between 21 and 34 percent of all women in the United States are victimized by domestic violence. Each year in the United States, about 1,500 women are killed by a husband or boyfriend (this figure represents more than one-half of homicides against women yearly).

The term "domestic violence" is relatively new to Americans' vocabulary. Prior to 1970 the law paid little attention to what occurred between adults in private homes. The prevailing attitude was that "a man's home is his castle" and that if a woman agreed to marry or live with a man, she had no right to complain about how she was treated. Beginning in the 1970s women's rights advocates worked diligently to change that perception.

Since 1970 state and local governments have passed a series of laws making it a crime to commit acts of violence in one's home. Police forces have been retrained in how to respond to calls involving domestic violence. Many states passed laws requiring hospital workers to report evidence of battering to the police. Women's rights advocates in many cities have established shelters for women (and their children) fleeing situations of domestic violence.

Sexual assault Sexual assault is a violent crime in which the perpetrator (most often a male) forcibly has sex with the victim (most often a woman) or forcibly touches the victim in a sexual way. Historically, the seriousness of rape was diminished by the belief that rape was a crime of passion. It was thought that the victim must have somehow encouraged the attack and that the rapist, caught up in the heat of the moment, was powerless to stop himself. Only recently has it been recognized that rape is a crime of violence. The true intent of the rapist is to injure, exert power over, and humiliate the victim.

The statistics on rape in the United States are frightening. More than 683,000 rapes are committed each year (118 of every 100,000 women are victims) and one in eight women will be a victim of sexual as-

Miranda Rights

Originally created to protect the poor and innocent, the practice of "reading the defendant his rights" has become standard in police departments across the country. These rights—spelled out in the so-called "Miranda Warning"— are familiar to most Americans from their use in television police shows. A "Mirandized" suspect has the right to remain silent; to consult with an attorney before and during questioning; to have a lawyer appointed if she or he cannot afford one; to stop answering questions at any time; and to consult with an attorney during the questioning process.

The protections outlined in the Miranda Warning have their basis in the 1963 Ernesto Miranda trial and appeal. At the age of twenty-three, Miranda, an eighth-grade dropout with a criminal record, was arrested for kidnapping and raping an eighteen-year-old movie theater attendant. Despite the fact that the victim could not positively identify him as her attacker, Miranda signed a confession after two hours of questioning by the police. (At no time during the questioning, however, was Miranda advised of his right to consult with an attorney.) The confession was later introduced into evidence at Miranda's trial. On July 27, 1963, Miranda was convicted and sentenced to two concurrent terms of twenty-to-thirty years' imprisonment.

Miranda's case was eventually appealed to the Supreme Court on the grounds that his confession was improperly obtained. On June 13, 1966, Chief Justice Earl Warren delivered the Court's opinion, which established clear guidelines for suspects in police custody. Warren wrote that "unless [the Court is] shown other procedures which are at least as effective in apprising accused persons of their right to silence and in assuring a continuous opportunity to exercise it, the following safeguards must be observed."

In 1968 Congress passed a federal law (in legal circles referred to as "3501") that allows suspect statements to be used even if Miranda violations are present, as long as a federal judge is convinced that the statements were produced voluntarily. This legislation came under close scrutiny on February 9, 1999, when the 4th U.S. Circuit Court of Appeals held that 3501 took precedence over the Supreme Court's Miranda interpretation. While the Circuit Court's decision only applies to the five states under its jurisdiction—Maryland, Virginia, West Virginia, North Carolina, and South Carolina—the implications of the ruling are more far-reaching. Many legal experts fear that law enforcement officials will use the ruling as an excuse to get around the Miranda protections. The Justice Department—which has long held that 3501 is unconstitutional—is expected to appeal the decision.

sault during her lifetime. Eighty percent of all women raped know their attacker. Nearly one-third of all survivors of rape suffer from psychological disorders after the attack, and rape survivors are thirteen times more likely than the general population to develop addictions to alcohol.

One form of sexual assault that has received much attention in recent years is date rape. (Date rape is the rape of a woman by a man— or, in rare cases, a man by a woman—with whom she has a social, or dating, relationship.) Recent statistics show that one of four women in college falls victim to rape; a large portion of these attacks are date rapes. Concern has recently surfaced about so-called "date rape drugs," such as GHB (a colorless, odorless substance often dissolved in liquid), that can render a recipient weak—even unconscious—and unable to fend off an attack.

Despite recent reforms in the legal system and educational campaigns on sexual assault, the prosecution and conviction rate of rapists continues to be low. Rape is a difficult crime to prove because, in most cases, there are no witnesses. It is a matter of one person's word against another's. The trial is an undeniably difficult experience for any survivor of rape. The rape victim must confront her attacker and relive the crime as she describes it to a courtroom full of strangers. It is therefore not surprising that 84 percent of rape survivors never report the crime to the police. Most of the women who do not report the crime

fear that they will be blamed for having instigated the rape themselves.

Since the 1970s the women's movement has done much to educate the public about the nature of rape and to assist survivors of rape. Activists have worked for the passage of rape shield laws which prevent defense attorneys from bringing up information about the accuser's past boyfriends and behaviors in an attempt to discredit her. Women's rights advocates in many cities have established crisis hotlines on which they provide counseling for rape victims. Activists have also pushed for sensitivity training for police officers, teaching the officers to be supportive of rape victims who are reporting the crime.

Stalking Stalking is defined as the persistent, unwanted following of one person by another. Stalkers and victims may be of either gender, although the majority of victims are women. The stalker may harass his victim by showing up at her home or place of work; calling her on the telephone; sending her letters, e-mail messages, or presents; threatening her; or forcibly entering her home. These behaviors sometimes escalate into abduction, assault, or murder. The stalker may simply annoy his victim, may make her feel emotionally and physically threatened, or may make her fear for her life.

Some stalkers are ex-spouses or partners seeking to win back or harass their former mates. Other stalkers are casual acquaintances or strangers to their victims. An estimated 200,000

Lesbians and gay men march in New York City's annual Gay Pride Parade. *Reproduced by permission of Archive Photos.*

people are currently being stalked, and statistics indicate that one in twenty women will be stalked at some point during her lifetime. California passed the nation's first antistalking law in 1991. Forty-eight states had passed antistalking laws by January 1, 1994.

The civil rights of lesbians and gay men

In the 1960s lesbians and gay men in America began to openly assert their sexual identities and fight for their rights. In 1975 the American Psychiatric Association advanced the cause of gay rights with its finding that homosexuality (sexual desire or behavior exhibited between persons of the same sex) is a not mental disorder. Since that time, a handful of scientific studies documenting the biological underpinnings of homosexuality—in genes, brain structure, and inner ear function—have strengthened the notion that homosexuality is a physiological condition rather than a "chosen" lifestyle.

The traditional view of homosexuality as sinful and that lesbians and gay men are deviants needing to be "cured" has become less prevalent in recent years. An October 1998 *Time Magazine*/CNN poll found that 64 percent of people interviewed are accepting of homosexuals while 33 percent are not (those percentages were 35 and 59, respectively, in 1978). Forty-eight percent of respondents in the recent poll believe that homosexual relationships are morally wrong, while 43 percent feel that homosexuality is not a moral issue (those percentages were 53 and 38, respectively, in 1978).

Today there is a growing acceptance of openly gay individuals as family members, coworkers, and characters on television shows. That acceptance, however, is by no means universal. While some states and localities have passed statutes defending the civil rights of lesbians and gay men, other states and localities have passed statutes denying those rights. The federal government is ambivalent on the matter. President Bill Clinton has spoken before gay rights advocacy organizations and has invited gay activists to meetings at the White House. Clinton also signed an Executive Order banning discrimination against gay federal employees. Yet in 1996 Clinton approved a piece of legislation, the Defense of Marriage Act, that effectively denies homosexuals the right to marry (see "The question of gay marriage").

In contrast to the growing acceptance of homosexuality in American society, hate crimes against lesbians and gay men are on the rise. In 1997, according to statistics reported by the Federal Bureau of Information, there were 1,102 incidents of anti-gay violence nationwide. Any perceptions that it is "safe" to be homosexual in America were shattered by the brutal beating and murder of Matthew Shepard, a gay man in Laramie, Wyoming, in October 1998 (see "A death in Wyoming").

The Stonewall Rebellion

The beginnings of the gay liberation movement in the United States can be traced to June 27, 1969. On that night police raided the Stonewall, a gay bar in Greenwich Village, New York City. Unlike previous police raids in which bar patrons had fled as quickly as possible to avoid being arrested and identified in the newspaper as homosexual, the patrons that night fought back. After pelting the police with bricks and any other objects they could find, bar patrons took to the streets. Upon hearing of the happenings in Greenwich Village, lesbians and gay men from all parts of the city joined the demonstration. The marching and shouting continued all through that night and into the next day and night.

Out of the Stonewall Rebellion (as the incident came to be known) the Gay Liberation Front was formed. Gay Liberation Front chapters quickly sprang up in cities throughout the nation, including Iowa City; Los Angeles; Bangor, Maine; and many other places.

The evolution of gay activism

The gay rights movement took root at a time of political and cultural upheaval in the United States. While the Vietnam War (1954–1975) was being waged thousands of miles away, a war for democracy and civil rights was being waged in the streets of America. It was in this spirit of profound social change that gay activists of the late 1960s and early 1970s adopted the slogan "Gay Is Good."

The activists challenged the assertion that homosexuality was "abnormal." They came out of the closet and into the streets, no longer willing to hide their sexual identities.

Over the years the gay rights movement, in many respects, has become more mainstream. Talk of sexual freedom has been replaced by the language of antidiscrimination bills. Gay rights groups have become focused on changing laws and policies that deny them protections and prevent them from gaining full acceptance into society.

Gay and lesbian rights organizations

One of the earliest major organizations to grow out of the gay liberation movement was the National Gay and Lesbian Task Force (NGLTF). Founded in 1973, the Washington, D.C.-based NGLTF was the most prominent national gay rights organization through the late 1980s. Although the NGLTF has lost influence to other gay rights organizations in recent years, the 35,000-member-group continues to work for the passage of gay rights legislation at the federal, state, and local levels.

The Human Rights Campaign Fund Reflecting the national trend toward conservatism in the 1990s, the most influential national organization working for the civil rights of lesbians and gay men today is the Human Rights Campaign Fund (HRCF). Headquartered in Washington, D.C., and with a current

Members of Act-Up stage a "die in" in New York City on June 24, 1994. The group sought increased funding for AIDS research. *Reproduced by permission of Reuters/Mike Sagar/Archive Photos.*

membership of 250,000, the HRCF's agenda reflects the values and concerns of middle-class lesbians and gay men. The HRCF has a strong lobby on Capitol Hill that works for the passage of gay rights legislation. The HRCF also assists its constituents in efforts to pass local statutes and operates a political action committee that raises money for the campaigns of gay-friendly congressional candidates.

More than any other gay rights organization in history, the HRCF has entered the mainstream of political activity in Washington, D.C. Attesting to this fact is that President Bill Clinton was the keynote speaker at the HRCF's annual black-tie, fundraising dinner in 1997; Vice President Al Gore was the keynote speaker at the 1998 fundraiser.

Act-Up and Queer Nation The AIDS epidemic has also influenced the agenda of the gay rights movement. (AIDS, which stands for acquired immunodeficiency syndrome, is a disease caused by infection with human immunodeficiency virus [HIV]. HIV works by seriously weakening the victim's immune system, leaving the body unequipped to fight off a wide range of illnesses.) Since the late 1980s, groups of mostly young, militant activists have loudly demanded increased funding for AIDS research and the preservation of the rights of people with AIDS, as well as an end to anti-gay violence and discrimination. Two of the largest groups in this area of gay activism are ACT-UP (which stands for AIDS Coalition to Unleash Power) and Queer Nation. Both groups use street theater and civil disobedience (the refusal to comply with laws one feels are unjust) to draw attention to their cause.

Antidiscrimination laws protecting lesbians and gay men

An unsuccessful federal statute that would have banned discrimination against lesbians and gay men was first proposed to Congress by New York Representative Bella Abzug in 1974. Although the Gay and Lesbian

Civil Rights Bill has been brought before several subsequent sessions of Congress, it has never passed. In addition, the Employment Non-Discrimination Act (ENDA), a federal law that would have banned discrimination against gays in employment, lost by one vote in the Senate in 1997.

Ten states and dozens of cities presently have antidiscrimination measures that protect the rights of lesbians and gay men in housing, employment, and other areas. As gay rights activists recently learned, however, gains at the state and local levels can be lost. In February 1998, for example, Maine residents voted to overturn their 1997 state law protecting lesbians and gay men from discrimination in employment, housing, credit, and public accommodations.

Gay rights activists attribute the Maine loss to a massive "get out the vote" drive by the Christian Civic League of Maine and the Christian Coalition. In the wake of the Bill Clinton-Monica Lewinsky sex scandal, conservative forces convinced their constituents that voting against Maine's gay rights law was a way to stem the tide of America's moral decay. Energized by their victory in Maine, anti-gay groups declared they would next work to repeal gay rights laws in Vermont and Wisconsin.

Court sends mixed messages on gay rights

In 1996 the Supreme Court appeared to take the side of gay rights

 Anti-Gay Forces

A powerful anti-gay lobby in the United States works to counter the gains of the gay rights movement. Anti-gay groups, such as the Family Research Council and the Christian Coalition, seek to preserve the stereotypes of gay men and lesbians as social deviants and sinners. The anti-gay lobby opposes all legislation that would protect the rights of homosexuals. The groups also promote "treatment programs" that claim to "cure" people of homosexuality, much like twelve-step programs for alcoholics. (In December 1998 the American Psychiatric Association denounced treatment programs aimed at changing homosexuals into heterosexuals as harmful to gays. The organization asserted that a person's sexual orientation is determined at birth.)

Among the most outspoken opponents of gay rights on Capitol Hill is the Senate Majority Leader, Republican Trent Lott. In a June 1998 taping of "The Armstrong Williams Show," Lott stated he considers homosexuality a sin. "You should try to show them," said Lott, in reference to gay men and lesbians, "a way to deal with that problem, just like alcohol ... or sex addiction ... or kleptomaniacs."

when it threw out an amendment to the Colorado state constitution. The Colorado amendment was to have prohibited the passage of any law, at the state or local level, that would protect lesbians and gay men from discrimination. In the case *Romer v. Evans*, the Supreme Court ruled that the amendment was unfair because it rendered lesbians and gay men "unequal to everyone else." By singling out homosexuals, it denied them equal protection of the laws as guaranteed by the Fourteenth Amendment to the Constitution.

In 1993 Cincinnati voters approved a charter amendment that, similar to the Colorado state amendment, denied discrimination protection to gay men and lesbians. Lawyers for gay rights activists in 1994 convinced a local judge to stop implementation of the charter amendment. That decision was later reversed by the Sixth District Court of Appeals and then taken before the Supreme Court. In October 1998 the Supreme Court seemingly contradicted its position in the Colorado case by backing the Court of Appeals and letting the Cincinnati statute stand.

The Sixth District Court of Appeals, in upholding the Cincinnati statute, had pointed to differences between the Colorado and Cincinnati cases. While the Colorado statute had suppressed the will of local governments and citizens by prohibiting them from passing certain types of legislation, the Cincinnati statute was, in the words of the court, a "direct expression of the local community will." Members of the Supreme Court emphasized that their ruling was not a judgment on gay rights in general or an endorsement of the Cincinnati statute.

The question of gay marriage

For many gay rights activists, the right to same-sex marriage represents the ultimate acceptance of homosexual relationships. If allowed to marry, same-sex couples would enjoy the same benefits as opposite-sex couples —namely, official recognition of their union, tax breaks, and legal rights regarding inheritance and children.

Presently, no state in the union allows gay marriages, and thirty states have statutes against gay marriage. In 1996 President Clinton signed into law the Defense of Marriage Act (DOMA). The DOMA stipulates that the federal government will only recognize marital unions between opposite-sex couples. The act also gives individual states the authority not to honor gay marriages licensed in other states. An October 1998 *Time Magazine*/CNN poll revealed that popular sentiment runs against gay marriage, with 29 percent of respondents supporting such a practice and 64 percent opposing it.

Hawaii and Alaska grapple with gay marriage In the mid-1990s it appeared possible that Hawaii and Alaska would become the first two states in the union to allow gay marriages. Voter referenda held in 1998 in both states, however, put the issue to rest.

In 1993 the Hawaii state supreme court upheld the right of gay couples to wed. The court found that the state had no constitutional power to deny any group of citizens the right to marry. In response to this ruling, gay and lesbian couples began planning weddings in Hawaii. For their part, Hawaiian lawmakers began drafting a ballot proposal that, if passed, would allow them to amend the state constitution to ban homosexual marriages. On November 3, 1998, Hawaiian voters soundly supported the referendum, thereby dealing a severe blow to the gay marriage movement.

November 3, 1998, was also the date on which Alaska voters decided to ban same-sex marriages in their state. The Alaska initiative was drafted in response to a superior court judge's ruling in favor of two gay men. The judge claimed that the two men had a fundamental right to marry and the state had no compelling reason to interfere with that right. With the passage of the Alaskan ballot measure, however, the state constitution was amended to define marriage as the union of one man and one woman.

At present, gay and lesbian activists have set their sights on Vermont. The state supreme court heard arguments from three same-sex couples wishing to marry in late 1998. If the court's ruling affirms the right of gay people to marry, it is likely that Vermont will face a referendum similar to those in Alaska and Hawaii.

Domestic partnership ordinances

Many states and localities have avoided the question of gay marriage by establishing domestic partnership ordinances. Under such ordinances, gay and lesbian couples who register as "domestic partners" are granted certain privileges automatically extended to married couples. In Hawaii, for example, same-sex and other unmarried couples are entitled to inheritance rights and spousal medical benefits. In many cities, public employees with registered domestic partnerships have the same rights to sick leave, bereavement leave, and health insurance as married employees. In the private sector, several employers—such as Levi Strauss, the American Civil Liberties Union (ACLU), and the *Village Voice*—allow domestic partners of employees to enjoy the same health and other benefits available to spouses of married employees.

Gays in the military

Prior to 1993 gay men and lesbians were prohibited from serving in the U.S. armed forces. The policy of all branches of the military was that any soldier suspected of being homosexual could be deemed unfit and discharged. In his 1992 presidential campaign, Bill Clinton won the endorsement of gay rights advocates by promising he would overturn the military's ban on gays. When Clinton won the presidency and tried to change the military's policy, however, he faced a great deal of opposition from military personnel. On July 19, 1993, a compromise policy on gays in the military was adopted; it is commonly known as "Don't Ask, Don't Tell."

The Secretary of Defense's "Policy on Homosexual Conduct in the Armed Forces" states that no individual may be expelled from the

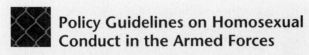

Policy Guidelines on Homosexual Conduct in the Armed Forces

The Secretary of Defense summarized the "Policy Guidelines on Homosexual Conduct in the Armed Forces" in a memo dated July 19, 1993. The guidelines read:

Accession Policy: Applicants for military service will no longer be asked or required to reveal if they are homosexual or bisexual, but applicants will be informed of the conduct that is proscribed for members of the armed forces, including homosexual conduct.

Discharge Policy: Sexual orientation will not be a bar to service unless manifested by homosexual conduct. The military will discharge members who engage in homosexual conduct, which is defined as a homosexual act, a statement that the member is homosexual or bisexual, or a marriage or attempted marriage to someone of the same gender.

Investigations Policy: No investigations or inquiries will be conducted solely to determine a service member's sexual orientation. Commanders will initiate inquiries or investigations when there is credible information that a basis for discharge or disciplinary action exists. Sexual orientation, absent credible information that a crime has been committed, will not be the subject of a criminal investigation. An allegation or statement by another that a service member is a homosexual, alone, is not grounds for either a criminal investigation or a commander's inquiry.

armed forces on suspicion of homosexuality. A gay man or lesbian may live a closeted existence in the armed forces; if a soldier engages in homosexual activity or reveals that he or she is gay, however, that soldier is subject to dismissal. Legal challenges to the "Don't ask, Don't Tell" policy have been filed in New York and San Francisco.

In January 1999, a report released by the Defense Department indicated that in the years since the implementation of the "Don't Ask, Don't Tell" policy, the number of gay men and lesbians discharged from the armed services has risen steadily.

There were nearly twice the number of discharges in 1998 as there were in 1992—the year before the new policy took effect.

Anti-gay violence and hate crimes legislation

Large numbers of gay men, and a smaller number of lesbians, are singled out for violent attacks every year in the United States. The prevalence of anti-gay attacks, also called "gay bashing," should come as no surprise. The anti-gay sentiments expressed by influential lawmakers and religious leaders reinforces the anti-gay attitudes held by many Americans and, arguably, sanctions physical assaults on gays. The doctrine that gay men and lesbians "deserve what they get" is upheld in the criminal justice system, where there is a history of leniency in the sentencing of individuals convicted of anti-gay crimes.

A death in Wyoming While most incidents of gay-bashing go unreported or unnoticed, there have been a number of attacks over the last two decades that have received national attention. One of the most recent, and perhaps the most brutal, incidents was the beating death of Matthew Shepard in Laramie, Wyoming, in October 1998. Shepard, a twenty-one-year-old gay student at the University of Wyoming, was beaten unconscious by two men—Russell Henderson and Aaron McKinney—he met in a bar. The assailants, both high school dropouts from Laramie, then tied Shepard to a fence-post in near-freezing temperatures and left him; Shepard died five days after the attack.

Henderson and McKinney were charged in late 1998. Henderson was scheduled to go on trial for Shephard's murder in April 1999. He avoided a jury trial, however, by pleading guilty. As a result of his plea agreement, Henderson was sentenced to two consecutive life terms in prison. McKinney was scheduled to go on trial in August 1999. Four months after Shephard's death, Wyoming lawmakers defeated two bills that would have imposed stiffer fines for crimes motivated by prejudice.

Anti-gay violence made headlines again in February 1999. Two men known for their racist and anti-homosexual views beat and burned to death Billy Jack Gaither, a thirty-nine-year-old textile worker, in Sylacauga, Alabama.

The murders of Harvey Milk and George Moscone Twenty years before the murder of Matthew Shepard, there was another high-profile, anti-gay killing—the murder of Harvey Milk. Milk, a member of the San Francisco Board of Supervisors (city council), was gunned down by another member of the Board of Supervisors named Dan White. White shot Milk and Mayor George Moscone (Moscone was not gay, but was a supporter of Milk) in their city hall offices in 1978. White was convicted of voluntary manslaughter in the two killings and sentenced to just seven years in prison.

Gay men and lesbians rioted in the streets of San Francisco on the night of White's conviction, to protest the lack of justice for his crimes. White was released after serving just five years of his sentence. He committed suicide in 1985.

The Hate Crimes Statistics Act In 1990 Congress passed the Hate Crimes Statistics Act. This legislation directed the Department of Justice to collect and report statistics on crimes in which the perpetrator was motivated by the victim's race, religion, national origin, or sexual orientation. Although the bill passed the Senate by a vote of 92 to 4, it was not without its detractors. Conservative Republican senator Jesse Helms of North Carolina characterized the legislation as part of a conspiracy by "the radical elements of the homosexual movement." The Hate Crimes Statistic Act was the first federal anti-discrimination statute to include lesbians and gay men.

The Hate Crimes Prevention Act In the wake of the October 1998 murder of Matthew Shepard, Congress faced renewed pressure to pass the Hate Crimes Prevention Act (HCPA). If approved, the HCPA would become the first piece of federal legislation to specifically outlaw crimes motivated by hatred toward homosexuals. The HCPA would amend current federal law—which permits federal prosecution of a hate crime based on religion, national origin, or color—to include real or perceived sexual orientation, gender, and disability.

Thirty-nine states and the District of Columbia presently have hate-crimes statutes similar to the existing federal statute. Twenty-one states and the District of Columbia include sexual orientation as a protected category in their hate-crimes laws.

Hate crimes laws provide additional penalties for criminals whose actions are motivated by bias. If the HCPA is approved, the FBI would be able to investigate and prosecute violent hate crimes against gays, lesbians, and bisexuals. Federal hate crimes protection for lesbians and gay men is needed, noted Attorney General Janet Reno on CNN's "Late Edition" in October 1998, to "have a forum in which justice can be done if it is not done in the state court." An October 1998 *Time Magazine*/CNN poll found that 76 percent of respondents favor federal legislation protecting gay men and lesbians from hate crimes while 19 percent oppose such legislation.

The civil rights of persons with disabilities

There are currently more than 49 million people with disabilities in the United States. The legal definition of disability is any physical or mental condition that restricts one or more of an individual's major life activities. Examples of disabilities are hearing impairment, vision impairment, disuse of one or more limbs, mental illness, and HIV-positive status. (HIV, which stands for human immunodeficiency virus, is the agent that causes AIDS—acquired immunodeficiency syndrome.)

Prior to the 1990s the word "handicap" was used interchangeably with the word "disability." "Disability" is the most commonly accepted terminology today, both because it is the word chosen by disabled people to describe themselves and because it is scientifically more accurate than the term "handicap."

The fine distinction between "disability" and "handicap" has been delineated by the World Health Organization's International Classification of Impairments, Disabilities, and Handicaps (ICIDH). The ICIDH defines disability as the restriction or lack of ability to perform an activity considered part of the range of normal human behaviors. A handicap, conversely, is defined as a condition that prevents or limits the leading of a normal life. The term "handicap" may also have its roots in the days of old, when individuals with disabilities held out caps and asked for handouts.

The exceedingly bad record of civil rights for people with disabilities took a turn for the better in 1990. The Americans with Disabilities Act (see "The Americans with Disabilities Act"), passed in that year, outlaws a broad range of discriminations against people with disabilities in both the public and private sectors. These legislative protections, combined with new technologies that aid people with disabilities in performing a variety of functions, mean that people with disabilities have a greater opportunity than ever before to fully participate in American society.

Discrimination against people with disabilities

People with disabilities have faced, and continue to face, discrimination on a number of fronts. Some forms of discrimination are blatant and intentional, such as the segregation of people with disabilities in schools (in "special education programs") and housing (in institutions),

 Protecting the Rights of Older Americans

Over the past several decades, groups dedicated to protecting and expanding the rights of older Americans have become more visible and more powerful. Two of the most active organizations are the American Association of Retired Persons (AARP) and the Gray Panthers. The AARP was founded in 1958 by retired educator Dr. Ethel Percy Andrus. With a current membership of over 30 million, the AARP focuses on four primary areas: information and education; community service; legislative, judicial, and consumer advocacy; and member services. Under the motto "To Serve, Not to be Served," the AARP has successfully lobbied for improved health care, pension reform, and legislation against age discrimination.

The "intergenerational" Gray Panther organization was founded in 1970 by social activist Maggie Kuhn. "We are the risk takers; we are the innovators; we are the developers of new models. We are trying on the future for size—that is our role," Kuhn once wrote. Today, Panther members are active in more than fifty local networks on issues such as family security, housing, the environment, and campaign reform. Gray Panther programs have led to the end of forced retirement at age sixty-five; the exposure of nursing home abuses; and the advancement of universal health care.

result of indifference toward the needs of physically disabled people, such as the inaccessibility of buses, trains, buildings, and other types of public transportation or accommodations.

While discrimination against people with disabilities bears many resemblances to discrimination against racial minorities, there is at least one important difference: prior to 1990 there was no sweeping federal legislation protecting the civil rights of people with disabilities; racial minorities received their civil rights protections in 1964.

Centuries of accumulated unfair treatment toward people with disabilities has taken a serious toll. People with disabilities lag behind the general population in terms of income, level of educational attainment, and employment rates. The general public's lack of understanding of disabilities results in an underestimation of the capabilities of individuals with disabilities.

A 1986 poll by Lou Harris and Associates, entitled "Bringing Disabled Americans into the Mainstream," concluded that "by almost any definition, Americans with disabilities are uniquely underprivileged and disadvantaged. They are much poorer, much less well educated and have much less social life, have fewer amenities and have a lower level of self-satisfaction than other Americans."

A group of disabled protestors march on Washington to demand passage of the Americans with Disabilities Act. The act was passed in 1990. *Reproduced by permission of UPI/Corbis-Bettmann.*

and the exclusion of people with disabilities from many types of employment. Discrimination also comes as a

Federal legislation

Numerous federal and state statutes were passed between the late

Disabled Woman Testifies about Discrimination

The Senate Committee on Labor and Human Resources held hearings between September 27, 1988, and June 22, 1989, to determine the need for federal legislation protecting the civil rights of people with disabilities. On August 2, 1989, the committee voted unanimously in favor of the passage of the Americans with Disabilities Act (the act passed the following year). Judith Heumann, of the World Institute of Disability, was one of many witnesses to testify before the Senate committee on September 27, 1988. Heumann testified:

> When I was five my mother proudly pushed my wheelchair to our local public school, where I was promptly refused admission because the principal ruled that I was a fire hazard. I was forced to go into home instruction, receiving one hour of education twice a week for three-and-a-half years.

> As a teenager, I could not travel with my friends on the bus because it was not accessible. At my graduation from high school, the principal attempted to prevent me from accepting an award in a ceremony on stage simply because I was in a wheelchair.

> When I was nineteen, the house mother of my college dormitory refused me admission into the dorm because I was in a wheelchair and needed assistance. When I was twenty-one years old, I was denied an elementary school teaching credential because of "paralysis of both lower extremities sequelae of poliomyelitis." At the time, I did not know what sequelae meant. I went to the dictionary and looked it up and found out that it was "because of." So it was obviously because of my disability that I was discriminated against....

> In 1981, an attempt was made to forcibly remove me and another disabled friend from an auction house because we were "disgusting to look at." In 1983, a manager at a movie theater attempted to keep my disabled friend and myself out of his theater because we could not transfer out of our wheelchairs.

1960s and the late 1980s, outlawing various forms of discrimination against people with disabilities. This web of legislation, however, was not complete. It left people with disabilities unprotected in many areas (such as discrimination by private-sector employers). It was not until the passage of the Americans with Disabilities Act in 1990 that people with disabilities were awarded comprehensive civil rights protection by the federal government.

The Architectural Barriers Act The first piece of significant federal legislation regarding people with disabilities, passed in 1968, was the Architectural Barriers Act (ABA). The ABA stipulated that buildings financed or leased by the federal government had to be handicapped-accessible. This rule applied to buildings open to the general public and buildings in which disabled persons could be employed or housed. The act required that renova-

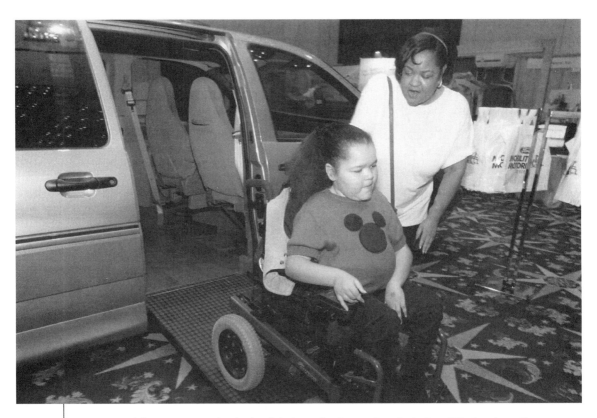

A young girl tests a motorized wheelchair at the Pennsylvania Assisted Technology Expo. Several state and federal statutes—in conjunction with the Americans with Disabilities Act— provide comprehensive civil rights protections to persons with disabilities. *Photo by Paul Vathis. Reproduced by permission of AP/Wide World Photos.*

tions be made to any such building that was not already accessible to people with disabilities.

The Rehabilitation Act of 1973 The Rehabilitation Act of 1973 prohibited any agency receiving federal funds from exercising, in matters of employment, discrimination against people with mental or physical disabilities. The act also provided people with disabilities legal access to all government-funded services and facilities.

The Rehabilitation Act is considered the forerunner to the Americans with Disabilities Act (ADA) of 1990. The ADA expanded the requirements regarding employment and accessibility to include the private sector.

The Individuals with Disabilities Education Act The Education for All Handicapped Children Act, passed in 1975 and later renamed the Individuals with Disabilities Education Act (IDEA), proclaimed that disabled children had the same rights as nondisabled children to a free and appropriate public education. Under the IDEA, the federal government awards grants to state and local education boards for the provision of high-quality education programs and individualized assistance, where required, for disabled children.

The Comprehensive Employment and Training Act

The early 1970s saw the implementation of several federal and state programs in job training and employment for people with disabilities. The Comprehensive Employment and Training Act of 1973 was the first federal legislation to give local governments a large role in the training and placement of disabled workers. The program reached its peak in 1980, when there were one million people with disabilities employed in the public sector. It was largely phased out in the early 1980s.

The Fair Housing Amendments Act

In 1988 the Fair Housing Amendments Act (FHAA) prohibited discrimination against people with disabilities in the sale or rental of housing. The FHAA added people with disabilities to the list of groups protected by the Fair Housing Act (Title VIII of the Civil Rights Act of 1968). The Fair Housing Act outlawed discrimination in the sale or rental of private housing based on race, sex, religion, or national origin (for more information on the Fair Housing Act, see box in chapter 1).

The FHAA required landlords to make changes in their policies and services (such as permitting a seeing-eye dog to live in an apartment building that has a policy against pets), where necessary, to accommodate disabled tenants. The act also gave disabled tenants the right to make structural modifications to their place of residence, to enhance its usability.

The Americans with Disabilities Act

The Americans with Disabilities Act (ADA), signed into law on July 26, 1990, is a wide-ranging set of guarantees of equal treatment for people with disabilities. It prohibits discrimination against people with disabilities in the areas of employment, government-run programs and services, public accommodations (such as hotels, restaurants, and movie theaters), and telecommunications. The purpose of the ADA is to ban all forms of discrimination against people with disabilities and thereby increase the economic and social opportunities available to people with disabilities.

The term "disability" is defined in the ADA as: A. a physical or mental impairment that substantially limits one or more of the major life activities of such individual; B. a record of such an impairment; or C. being regarded as having such an impairment." (Category B includes individuals who have recovered from a physical or mental illness; category C includes individuals who may or may not have a disability, but who suffer from other people's perceptions of them as having a disability, such as mental illness or HIV-positive status.)

Any person who falls within the boundaries of the above definition is granted protections by the ADA.

Areas of ADA coverage The ADA is divided into five sections, called titles. Title I covers employment and applies to all employers with fifteen or more employees. It prohibits discrimination against people with disabilities in hiring, promotions, wages, and benefits. Title I also stipulates that businesses must accommodate the needs of their workers with disabilities. For example, an employer must rearrange workplaces, modify equipment, or rewrite job descriptions where necessary.

Title II permits unrestricted access to all services and activities offered by state and local governments, including public transportation systems. This title requires that modifications be made to public buses, trains, and subways to make them accessible to people with physical disabilities. All new buses and trains on fixed routes must be outfitted with wheelchair lifts and other features that allow disabled riders to board and safely ride the vehicles.

Title III specifies that existing facilities of public accommodation be modified (if achievable without undue expense or difficulty), and new facilities be constructed so that they are accessible to people with disabilities. This rule means that restaurants, grocery stores, banks, libraries, hotels, retail stores, movie theaters, parks, schools, and other facilities used by the general public must be equipped with wheelchair ramps (where steps pose a barrier) and automatic doors. New buildings that are three stories or taller must have elevators. Shopping malls, professional buildings, and health care facilities with fewer than three stories must also have elevators.

Title IV outlines the requirements of telephone companies to provide non-voice services for the approximately 30 million Americans with hearing or speech impairments. Specifically, telephone companies must provide the requisite telecommunication relay services to permit communication via telephone lines using a telecommunication device for deaf persons (TDD).

Title V contains miscellaneous provisions, such as definitions, explanations, exemptions, and an authorization of the awarding of attorney's fees to any individual or group who wins a case under the ADA.

In April 1999 the ADA came under intensive review during a Supreme Court appeals session covering four disability-rights cases. At issue were two items: the coverage limits of Title II as interpreted by individual states, and the definition of what constitutes a disability under the law.

Sources

Books and Pamphlets

Americans with Disabilities Act of 1990. Alexandria, VA: National Mental Health Association, 1991.

Department of Education, Office for Civil Rights. *The Rights of Individuals with*

Handicaps Under Federal Law. Washington, D.C.: GPO, 1989.

Frost-Knappman, Elizabeth, Edward W. Knappman, and Lisa Paddock, eds. *Courtroom Drama.* Volume 1. Detroit: U•X•L, 1998, pp. 89–96.

Ginsburg, Ruth Bader. "Sex Discrimination," in *Civil Rights and Equality,* edited by Leonard W. Levy, Kenneth L. Karst, and Dennis J. Mahoney. New York: MacMillan, 1989.

Harrison, Maureen and Steve Gilbert, eds. *The Americans with Disabilities Act Handbook.* Beverly Hills, CA: Excellent Books, 1992.

McElroy, Lorie. *Women's Voices.* Vol. 2. Detroit: U•X•L, 1997.

Mill, John Stuart. *Essays On Equality, Law, and Education.* Toronto, Ontario: University of Toronto Press, 1984.

Nau, Charles J. *The ADA and HIV: What Employers Need to Know Now.* Washington, D.C.: National Leadership Coalition on AIDS, 1990.

Newton, David E. *Gay and Lesbian Rights: A Reference Handbook.* Santa Barbara, CA: ABC-CLIO, 1994.

President's Committee on Employment of People with Disabilities. *Americans with Disabilities Act in Brief.* Washington, D.C.: GPO, 1992.

Rhode, Deborah L. "Nineteenth Amendment," in *Civil Rights and Equality,* edited by Leonard W. Levy, Kenneth L. Karst, and Dennis J. Mahoney. New York: MacMillan, 1989.

Sinclair, Barbara. *The Women's Movement: Political, Social, and Economic Issues.* New York: Harper & Row, 1975.

Sanger, Margaret. *Woman and the New Race.* New York: Maxwell Reprint Company, 1969.

Sigler, Jay A., ed. *Civil Rights in America: 1500 to the Present.* Detroit: Gale, 1998, pp. 259–96.

Snodgrass, Mary Ellen, ed. *Celebrating Women's History: A Women's History Month Resource Book.* Detroit: Gale, 1996.

Thompson-Hoffman, Susan, and Inez Fitzgerald Storck, eds. *Disability in the United States: A Portrait From National Data.* New York: Springer Publishing Company, 1991.

U.S. Equal Employment Opportunity Commission. *The Americans with Disabilities Act: Questions and Answers.* Washington, D.C.: GPO, 1992.

West, Jane, ed. *Implementing the Americans with Disabilities Act.* Cambridge, MA: Blackwell Publishers, Inc., 1996.

Periodicals

Bruni, Frank. "A Battlefield Shifts." *The New York Times.* March 8, 1998: 36.

Carlson, Margaret. "Laws of the Last Resort." *Time.* October 26, 1998: 40.

Cloud, John. "For Better or Worse: In Hawaii, a Showdown Over Marriage Tests the Limits of Gay Activism." *Time.* October 26, 1998: 43–44.

Cohen, Jodi S. "Cops Give Warning on GHB." *Detroit News.* March 21, 1999: 3D.

Epstein, Aaron. "His Roe Opinion Set Off a Firestorm of Debate" (Harry Blackmun obituary). *Detroit Free Press.* March 5, 1999: 1A, 9A.

"FBI: Race is Top Hate-Crime Motive." *The Ann Arbor News.* January 22, 1999: A7.

Greenhouse, Linda. "Pivotal Ruling Ahead for Law on Disabilities." *The New York Times.* April 19, 1999: A1, A20.

"Hawaii, Alaska Voters Consider Bans on Same-Sex Marriage." Associated Press. March 24, 1998.

Ireland, Doug. "Maine's Gay Retreat." *The Nation.* March 9, 1998: 6.

Lacayo, Richard. "The New Gay Struggle." *Time.* October 26, 1998: 32–36.

"Laws Denying Gays Protection Stands." Associated Press. March 13, 1998.

Lopez, Steve. "To Be Young and Gay in Wyoming." *Time*. October 26, 1998: 38–40.

McCafferty, Dennis. "WWW.Hate. Comes to Your Home." *USA Weekend*. March 26–28: 6–7.

Meyers, Steven Lee. "Military Discharges for Homosexuality Double in Five Years." *The New York Times*. January 23, 1999.

"Reno Urges Broader Hate-Crime Laws." Associated Press. October 18, 1998.

Rubin, Alissa J. "Abortion Provider Numbers Fall." *The Ann Arbor News*. December 11, 1998: A4.

"Senate Leader Calls Homosexuality a Problem Like 'Kleptomaniacs.'" Associated Press. June 16, 1998.

"Suspect in Killing of Gay Man Wanted to be Skinhead." *The Ann Arbor News*. March 6, 1999: A3.

"Suspects in Student Death Could Face Death Penalty." Associated Press. October 13, 1998.

Weller, Robert. "Psychiatrists Reject 'Conversion' of Gays." *The Ann Arbor News*. December 13, 1998: A8.

Web Sites

AARP. [Online] Available http://www.aarp.org/what_is.html (last accessed on April 1, 1999).

CNN Interactive. "Beaten Gay Student Dies; Murder Charges Planned." October 12, 1998. [Online] Available http://www.cnn.com/US/9810/12/wyoming.attack.02/index.html (last accessed on March 10, 1999).

CNN Interactive. "Bias Crime Bill Rejected in State Where Gay College Student Was Killed." February 3, 1999. [Online] Available http://www.cnn.com/US/9902/03/bias.law/index.html (last accessed on February 3, 1999).

Common Cause. Employment Non-Discrimination Act. [Online] Available http://www.commoncause.org/issue_agenda/civil_rights.htm (last accessed on March 17, 1999).

Federal Bureau of Investigation. "Uniform Crime Reports: Hate Crime 1995." [Online] Available http://www.fbi.gov.ucr/hatecm.htm#bias (last accessed December 3, 1998).

The Gray Panthers. [Online] Available http://www.nonviolence.org/amhvigil/gray-pant.html (last accessed April 1, 1999).

Human Rights Campaign. The Hate Crimes Prevention Act. [Online] Available http://www.hrc.org/issues/leg/hcpa/index.html (last accessed March 31, 1999).

National Center for Policy Analysis. "Shrinking Pay Gap." [Online] Available http://www.ncpa.org/ea/eajf95/eajf95c.html (last accessed on April 3, 1999).

Planned Parenthood Federation of America. "Stop the Violence." [Online] Available http://www.plannedparenthood.org/ (last accessed on April 1, 1999).

Survivors of Stalking, Inc. [Online] Available http://www.usalaw.com (last accessed on March 31, 1999).

United States Bureau of Reclamation. Architectural Barriers Act of 1968. [Online] Available http://www.usbr.gov/laws/aba.html (last accessed on December 7, 1998).

Where To Learn More

The following list offers contact information for selected organizations and resource centers in the United States that are actively involved in civil rights issues. Please bear in mind that the focuses of the groups are wide-ranging, and that the actions the organizations take to achieve their goals are specific to their viewpoint. For books, periodicals, and web sites about the civil rights of individual groups discussed in *American Civil Rights: Almanac,* refer to the "Sources" section at the end of each chapter.

Note: the web site addresses listed below are subject to change.

American Civil Liberties Union (ACLU)
132 W. 43rd St.
New York, NY 10036
Phone: (212) 944–9800
Web: http://www.aclu.org

Amnesty International, U.S.A
322 8th Ave.
New York, NY 10001
Phone: (212) 807–8400
Web: http://www.amnesty.org/

Asian Pacific American Labor
Alliance
1101 14th St., NW
Suite 310
Washington, D.C. 20005
Phone: (202) 842–1263
Fax: (202) 842–1462
Web: http://www.apalanet.
org

Birmingham Civil Rights Institute
520 Sixteenth St.
North Birmingham, AL 35203
Phone: (205) 328–9696
Web: http://bcri.bham.al.us/
bcri/

Center for Independent Living
2539 Telegraph Ave.
Berkeley, CA 94704
Phone: (510) 841–4776
Fax: (510) 841–6168
Web: http://www.cilberkeley.
org/

Citizens' Commission on Civil
Rights
2000 M St., NW
Suite 400
Washington, D.C. 20036
Phone: (202) 659–5565
Fax: (202) 223–5302
Web: http://www.cccr.org

The Civil Rights Project
Harvard University
444 Gutman Library
Cambridge, MA
Phone: (617) 496–6367
Fax: (617) 496–3095
Web: http://www.law.harvard.
edu/groups/civilrights/

Highlander Research and Educa-
tion Center
(formerly the Highlander Folk
School)
1959 Highlander Way
New Market, TN 37820
Phone: (423) 933–3443
Fax: (423) 933–3424
Web: http://www.hrec@igc.
apc.org

Leadership Conference on Civil
Rights
1629 K St., NW
Suite 1010
Washington, D.C.
Web: http://www.lccr.org

National Association for the
Advancement of Colored
People (NAACP)
Washington Bureau
1025 Vermont Ave., NW
Suite 1120
Washington, D.C. 20005
Phone: (202) 638–2269
Web: http://naacp.org/

National Center for Youth Law
114 Sansome St.
Suite 900
San Francisco, CA 94104
Phone: (415) 543–3307
Fax: (415) 956–9024
Web: http://www.youthlaw.
org/

National Civil Rights Museum
450 Mulberry St.
Memphis, TN 38103
Phone: (901) 521–9699
Web: http://www.midsouth.
rr.com/civilrights/

National Congress of American
Indians (NCAI)
1301 Connecticut Ave., NW
Suite 200
Washington, D.C. 20036
Phone: (202) 466–7767
Fax: (202) 466–7797
Web: http://www.ncai.org

National Council of La Raza
1111 19th St., NW
Suite 1000
Washington, D.C. 20036
Web: http://www.nclr.org/
index.html

National Gay and Lesbian Task
Force
1700 Kalorama Rd. NW
Washington, D.C. 20009
Phone: (202) 332–6483
Fax: (202) 332–0207
Web: http://www.ngltf.org/

National Network for Immigrant
and Refugee Rights
310 8th St.
Suite 307
Oakland, CA 94607
Phone: (510) 465–1984
Fax: (510) 465–1885
Web: http://www.nnirr.org/

National Organization for Women
(NOW)
1401 New York Ave.
Suite 800
Washington, D.C. 20005
Phone: (202) 331–0066
Web: http://www.now.org/

National Urban League
120 Wall St.
New York, NY 10005
Phone: (212) 558–5300
Web: http://www.nul.org

U.S. Department of Education
Office for Civil Rights
Customer Service Team
Mary E. Switzer Building
330 C St., SW
Washington, D.C.
Phone: (202)   205–5413;
1–800–421–3481
Fax: (202) 205–9862
Web: http://www.ed.gov/
offices/OCR/index.html

U.S. Department of Housing and
Urban Development (HUD)
451 7th St., SW
Washington, D.C. 20410
Phone: (202) 708–1422
Web: http://www.hud.gov

U.S. Department of Justice
Justice for Kids and Youth
950 Pennsylvania Ave., NW
Washington, D.C. 20530
Phone: (202) 663–2151
Web: http://www.usdoj.gov/
kidspage/

Index

Italic indicates volume numbers
Illustrations are marked by (ill.)

Bracero Program *2:* 205–07
Brando, Marlon *2:* 288
BRC *1:* 138
Brewer, Lawrence Russell *1:* 134
Brightman, Lee *2:* 295
Bronx, New York *2:* 249
Brooke, Edward *1:* 109
Brotherhood of Sleeping Car
    Porters *1:* 30
Brown, Elaine *1:* 122
Brown, Linda *1:* 39
Brown, Oliver *1:* 39
Brown, Robert Erving *1:* 43
Brown Berets *2:* 224–25
"Brown II" *1:* 42
*Brown v. Board of Education of
    Topeka, Kansas 1:* 34, 37–40,
    42, 50, 133, 146; *2:* 208
Bryant, Roy *1:* 41
Buchanan v. Warley 1: 32
Bureau of Indian Affairs (*See* BIA)
Burke, Katherine *1:* 67
Burlingame Treaty *1:* 146
Bush, George *1:* 132–33, 134
Busing (definition) *1:* 47
Butler, Dino *2:* 301
Byrd, Harry S. *1:* 40
Byrd, James, Jr. *1:* 134

C

CAAAV *1:* 191
California Gold Rush *2:* 204
California Joint Immigration
    Committee *1:* 163
California Rural Legal Assistance
    Foundation *2:* 241
California State Personnel Board
    1: 161
Campaign for freedom in Missis-
    sippi *1:* 86–88
"Campaign to End Slums" in
    Chicago *1:* 113–15, 116
Camp Pendleton, California
    1: 185 (ill.), 186 (ill.)
Campos, Pedro Albizu *2:* 252–53
Carmichael, Stokley 1; 117–18,
    117 (ill.), 118
Castro, Fidel *2:* 255–56, 255 (ill.),
    258
Castro, Sal *2:* 226–27

Catt, Carrie Chapman *2:* 343, 343
    (ill.)
Central Pacific Railroad *1:* 143,
    144 (ill.)
Chaney, James *1:* 93–94, 95, 96
    (ill.)
*Changing America: Indicators of So-
    cial and Economic Well-Being
    by Race and Hispanic Origin 2:*
    313
Chávez, César *2:* 209, 210 (ill.),
    212, 213, 214–15
"Chicanismo," guiding principles
    2: 229
Chicano (definition) *2:* 199
Chicano Associated Students Or-
    ganization *2:* 229
Chicano Moratorium Committee
    2: 236
Chicano Youth Liberation Con-
    ference *2:* 237
Chicano youth movement *2:*
    222–29
Chief Lone Wolf *2:* 271–72
Children's Bureau *2:* 353
Chin, Vincent *1:* 190–91, 191
    (ill.), 193
Chinatowns *1:* 150, 150 (ill.)
Chinese Exclusion Act *1:* 149–50
Chinese Repealer *1:* 151, 180
Chisholm, Shirley *1:* 109
Christian Coalition *2:* 361
Christopher, Warren M. *2:* 239
Christopher Commission Report
    2: 239
"Citizenship schools" *1:* 36–37
Civil Liberties Act of 1988 *1:* 180
Civil rights, by group:
    African Americans *1:* 1
    Asian Americans *1:* 141
    Hispanic Americans *2:* 197
    Native Americans *2:* 263
    Selected immigrant groups *2:*
        315
    Selected nonethnic groups *2:*
        338
Civil Rights Act of 1875 *1:* 18
Civil Rights Act of 1866 *1:* 16
Civil Rights Act of 1964 *1:* 47,
    83–86, 100; *2:* 284, 347
Civil rights workers, murder of *1:*
    93–95, 95 (ill.), 109
Civil War amendments *1:* 12–14

E

Eagle, Jimmy *2:* 30001
Eastland, James O. *1:* 40, 69
Ebens, Ronald *1:* 190, 191
Eckford, Elizabeth *1:* 44
Edmund Pettus Bridge *1:* 105–06, 107 (ill.)
Educational Equity Act *2:* 348
EEOC *2:* 34748
Eisenhower, Dwight D. *1:* 39, 40, 44
Eisenhower, Milton *1:* 171
Elliott, Robert *1:* 72
Ellis Island *1:* 142, 156
Emancipation Proclamation *1:* 11
Emmons, Delos *1:* 167
Employment Division, Department of Human Resources of Oregon et al. v. Smith 2: 308
Employment Non-Discrimination Act *2:* 361
Endo Mitsuye *1:* 168
Equal Employment Opportunity Commission (*See* EEOC)
Equal Pay Act *2:* 346–47
Equal Rights Amendment (ERA) *2:* 344
Ethnic Studies programs *1:* 190
Evacuation Claims Act of 1948 *1:* 177–78
Evers, Medgar *1:* 87, 92–93, 92 (ill.)
Ex parte Endo 1: 168, 169, 177
Executive Order 589 *1:* 156
Executive Order 9066 *1:* 163–65
Eyes on the Prize 1: 81

F

Fair Housing Act *1:* 116, 128
Fair Housing Amendments Act *2:* 371
Fair Labor Standards Act *2:* 353
Family and Medical Leave Act *2:* 35354
Family Research Council *2:* 361
Farmer, James *1:* 64, 79
Farrakhan, Louis *1:* 137, 137 (ill.)
Faubus, Orville *1:* 43–44, 46
FBI *1:* 120, 159–60; *2:* 300–02

Federal Bureau of Investigation (*See* FBI)
Federated Alliance of Land Grants (*See* Alianza Federal de Mercedes)
Federated Women's Clubs *1:* 70
Fellowship of Reconciliation *1:* 62
Fellowship of Southern Churchmen *1:* 35
Ferré, Maurice *2:* 249
Fifteenth Amendment *1:* 14; *2:* 341
Fifth column (definition) *1:* 170
Fillmore, Millard *2:* 318
Fish-ins *2:* 288, 289–90
Foraker Act *2:* 246
Ford, Gerald *1:* 178 (ill.)
Ford, Henry 1: *2:* 331
Ford, Leland *1:* 161
Foreign miners' tax *1:* 144
Forman, James *1:* 96
Fortune, T. Thomas *1:* 22, 25
"Forty acres and a mule" *1:* 14–15
Fourteenth Amendment *1:* 13–14, 148
Frank, Leo *2:* 330
Free blacks *1:* 6
Freedmen's Bureau *1:* 17
Freedom Party *1:* 89
Freedom Rides *1:* 64–69
Freedom Singers *1:* 70
Freedom Summer *1:* 92–98
Freedom Vote *1:* 89–91
Freedpersons *1:* 14–15
Free Southern Theater *1:* 97

G

Gadsden Purchase *2:* 202
Gandhi, Mohandas *1:* 59; *2:* 214
García, Robert *2:* 249
Garrison, William Lloyd *1:* 8 (ill.), 9
Gaston Motel *1:* 78
Gay activism *2:* 359
Gay and Lesbian Civil Rights Bill *2:* 360–61
Gay marriage *2:* 362–63
Gay pride march *2:* 357 (ill.)
General Allotment Act *2:* 270–71
Gentlemen's Agreement *1:* 155
German American Alliance *2:* 324

H

I

M

N